The Dynamics of Change
in North Korea:
An Institutionalist Perspective

Explorations in Korean Studies

The Dynamics of Change in North Korea:
An Institutionalist Perspective

Edited by
Phillip H. Park

IFES

KYUNGNAM UNIVERSITY PRESS

Distributed Outside of North and South Korea by
Lynne Rienner Publishers, Inc.
1800 30th Street, Boulder, CO 80301, USA
www.rienner.com

ISBN 978-89-8421-294-7

Contents

Tables and Figures

Figures

Foreword

When we read the international headlines about North Korea, they're rarely optimistic—phrases like "failed economy," "food shortages," "nuclear weapons," "provocative behavior," and "international sanctions" do little to conjure up positive images of what might be going on in the country.

Since North Korea made its plea back in the mid-1990s for international assistance to help feed its people, the keyholes in which we look through to see what's going on inside the DPRK have widened. This comes as a result of the work of various international and non-governmental organizations who have developed relationships with the North, mainly as donors of humanitarian and development assistance; the South Korean government's engagement policy of the last ten years; the expanding body of economic data provided by countries who engage in business with the North; and the North Korean government's own increasing—though still limited—interaction with Western countries. While these keyholes are still relatively few, one can see the visible signs of economic and, most importantly, societal transformation going on within the country's borders.

This book sets out to show that dynamic, encouraging change is taking place in North Korea. While Pyongyang's behavior is at times perplexing and its intentions often difficult to discern, North Korean society itself is experiencing a post-cold war transition toward a market economy—a transition that has been described as cautious, piecemeal, and not without its limitations and challenges, but nevertheless irreversible. Looking carefully at the micro-level changes allows one to see the subtle yet dynamic transformation unfolding. The authors of this book examine these micro-level changes—from the introduction of special laws and economic adjustment measures to the emergence of farmers' markets, the growing autonomy of enterprises, and training of officials in the West—to reveal dynamics within the DPRK that hopefully will move the country toward a better future.

This book is a by-product of collective research conducted by IFES's research fellows and faculty members of the University of North Korea Studies, Seoul. I am grateful to Dr. Dae-kyu Yoon, IFES's former director, whose initiative got this English monograph project off the ground. I am also grateful to Jae-Kyu Park, President of Kyungnam University, whose continuing support of the Institute's activities gave the project its wings.

Su Hoon Lee
Director, Institute for Far Eastern Studies
Kyungnam University

Chapter 1

Introduction:
Economic Reform and Institutional
Change in the DPRK

⊣ Phillip H. PARK ⊢

In the 1990s, after the demise of the Soviet Union and its socialist bloc, an imminent collapse of the Democratic People's Republic of Korea (North Korea, or the DPRK) was predicted by many experts. This gloomy prediction of the collapse was reinforced by reports of massive starvation, caused by an acute food crisis in North Korea. Consequently, collapse of the North Korean economy was perceived to be inevitable or inescapable, and virtually no one second-guessed these opinions. It was a basket case of mismanagement under the socialist economic system, and its isolation from the rest of the world, especially from the Western world, was perceived to be a sufficient condition for North Korea's collapse.

It is no surprise to learn that in 1993, the Clinton administration's sudden change of North Korea policy, from one of considering a preemptive strike to one encouraging engagement, stemmed from the belief that the North Korean regime would soon collapse. However, despite the fact that more than one decade has gone by since the predictions of collapse came about, North Korea has neither imploded nor exploded, and still poses a threat in the eyes of those concerned about American security. Moreover, it is reported that the North Korean economy bottomed out in 1998, and has even begun to rebound since 1999.[1] Recently, North Korea has implemented large-scale economic reform, and economic cooperation with South Korea is gaining momentum, despite political tensions due to the policies of the Lee Myung-bak government, as the second-largest city in North Korea, Kaesung, is now open to South Korean investors and industrialists as a Special Economic Zone. Despite North Korea's recent efforts to improve its economic situation and the internal resilience of the North Korean economy, for North Korea experts in the United States, especially those who study North Korea's economy, North Korea's future still seems bleak. They either persist with the view that North Korea's collapse is imminent[2] or argue for regime change in order to have genuine reform in North Korea.[3] Nonetheless, a careful study of North Korea's institutional transformations shows that North Korea is increasingly moving toward a market-guided economy.

I. North Korea's Economy According to the American Experts

The North Korean economic system is described as a rigid, Stalinist, centrally planned economy. This is a commonly held view that is shared by many North Korea experts in the United States, and hence they start their analysis of the North Korean economy from this point. According to their view, North Korea's eco-

---

[1] *Korea Herald*, "N.K. economy grows for fifth year in a row" June 9, 2004, (Internet version: http://news.naver.com/main/read.nhn?mode=LSD&mid =sec&sid1=108&oid=044&aid=0000044369).

[2] Nicholas Eberstadt is a representative scholar in this category.

[3] Marcus Noland is a representative scholar who argues for regime change in North Korea.

nomic system and its institutions are based on a rigid form of Stalinist socialist planning that has not undergone change since the inception of the DPRK in 1948. Consequently, most works of the North Korean experts are attempts to find inherent problems and contradictions in the socialist planned economy. Moreover, these experts on North Korea see that the sole aim of economic development in North Korea is to maintain its regime survival, and since they view the North Korean regime as evil and totalitarian, North Korea's economic failure and inevitable regime collapse is viewed to be a welcome outcome. Such a view is well expressed by two of the most influential experts on the North Korean economy in the United States, Nicholas Eberstadt and Marcus Noland.

Nicholas Eberstadt has published hundreds of articles and four books on North Korea since his first major publication, *The Population of North Korea*, in 1992. Although more than a decade has gone by, the underlining emphasis in the content of his work has not changed since his first publication. There are three important points he repeatedly brings out in his work on North Korea. They can be summarized as follows: First, the DPRK is an inherently wicked or evil state, like Nazi Germany. The sole aim of the North Korean regime is to take over South Korea by force, and the regime is willing to sacrifice anything for this. Second, the North Korean economy is fundamentally based on military needs. A substantial portion (over 120 million) of its working-age male population (aged between 16 and 55) is in the military, and the DPRK's major objective of development of heavy industries is to make weapons of mass destruction and for preparation of war against South Korea and the United States. Third, North Korea's self-reliant strategy, known as *Juche*, is simply a sham. North Korea has never been self-sufficient. Its survival so far has been maintained by "aid-maximizing," "gambits" and "mendicant" methods of dealing with its economic crises.

Based on his analysis of the North Korean economy, Eberstadt gives policy recommendations for the United States government; basically, there are four points in his recommendations. First, the cherished vision of a gradual and orderly drawing together of the two Koreas is today nothing more than a fantasy. Second, as time goes on, North Korea will only grow poorer and more dangerous. Third, the North Korean nuclear "problem," for its part, does not derive from anything other than the inherent character and intentions of the North Korean state. The North Korean regime is the North Korean nuclear problem, and unless its intentions change, which is unlikely, that problem will continue as long as the regime is in place. Lastly, the United States and its allies should cooperate to make Korean reunification successful by facilitating the demise of North Korea (Eberstadt 1992, 1995, 1997a, 1997b, 1999, 2002, 2004, 2005a, 2005b, 2006).

While Nicholas Eberstadt took an interest in the DPRK economy at an early point in his academic career, Marcus Noland did not produce anything related to the North Korean economy until 1996.[4] Nevertheless, his article, "The North Korean Economy," received a fair amount of attention because it was probably the first article on the DPRK's economy by an American economist[5] since Joseph Sang-hoon Chung, who published *The North Korean Economy: Structure and Development* in 1976. Since his first article, Noland has produced numerous articles and three books on topics

---

[4] His first major book, *Reconcilable Differences? United States-Japan Economic Conflict*, was written with Fred Bergstein in 1993, and his first academic article on the North Korean economy, "The North Korean Economy," was presented to Joint U.S-Korea Academic Studies in 1996.

[5] Nicholas Eberstadt is not an economist by training; he is a political economist who is trained in demography.

related to the North Korean economy. These topics cover a wide range of economic issues such as external relations of the DPRK's economy, cost-and-benefit analysis of Korean unification, and North Korea's economic reform. When the prediction of the DPRK's imminent collapse was well shared by most other North Korean experts, he wrote an article to *Foreign Affairs* in 1997 arguing that North Korea would not collapse immediately, but rather, would muddle through for a considerable time. "Muddling Through" became a sort of leitmotif for Noland's work on the North Korean economy.

According to Noland, the North Korean regime cannot implement genuine economic reform because such reform would involve hundreds of thousands of people moving from the countryside to the cities, and literally millions of people changing jobs. Reform, therefore, would be a high-risk, big-payoff strategy for the regime. However, since the North Korean regime is weak and risk adverse, it prefers to maintain the status quo. Moreover, according to Noland, the experiences of China and Vietnam may be inapplicable to the DPRK because at the time of their reforms, these economies were far more agrarian than North Korea, and their ability to shift extremely low-productivity labor out of agriculture and into the emerging non-state-owned light industrial sector has been a key to their success thus far. Successful reform of a more industrialized economy such as North Korea is likely to be far more difficult for purely technical reasons, and would imply tremendous change for the North Korean economy (Noland 1998, 2000, 2004).

Noland argues that if the North Korean regime pursues a strategy of maintaining the status quo, it will survive in the short run, though economic crisis persists. In the long run, the status quo would bring about a collapse of North Korea due to regime instability, exhaustion of coping mechanisms, and irreparable economic structural problems. Noland predicts that the North Korean regime would choose a "muddling through" strategy that lies between the two polar extremes of reform and collapse. According to Noland, the DPRK is following a Romanian model of muddling through since the DPRK and Romania are similar in population, income, social indicators, composition of output, and shared central planning and its attendant maladies, and the Romanian regime (the former Communist Party embodied in Ion Iliescu's Party of Social Democracy (PDSR)) appears to have had some success with its muddling through strategy. Although Noland cautions that one should not push such analogies too far, the experience of Romania suggests that muddling through could last for years, until a more concrete and permanent change toward reform takes place. Noland doubts that the current North Korean regime can launch permanent and genuine reform. He suggests that muddling through is the North Korean regime's survival strategy and only regime change would bring about genuine reform and help to solve the chronic food crisis in the DPRK (Noland 1997, 1998, 2004, 2007).

As Geoffrey Hodgson argues, in order to understand any particular socio-political or economic system of a country, investigation and analysis of the internal and external dynamics that comprise the evolution of the country's economic system should be considered essential prerequisites.[6] However, it is very difficult to see any attempt to analyze internal and external dynamics in North Korean economic development in the work of leading American experts. What is ostentatiously missing in their works is a historical assessment of North Korean economic development.

---

[6] Geoffrey Hodgson, *Economic and Utopia* (London: Routledge, 1999), 140-146.

As Douglass North observes, the actual institutions at any given moment represent adaptation to past as well as present difficulties.[7] Hence, history matters. Like any other economy, North Korea's economic system has evolved over time, albeit slowly, in order to meet the challenges it has faced.

Perhaps one of the important factors that contribute to the American scholars' preference for static and ideological approaches in their investigation of the North Korean economy is a language barrier. North Koreanology, as B.C. Koh aptly points out, typically necessitates the practice of "Kremlinology"—the excruciatingly tedious task of sifting through official publications, including the strictly-controlled print media, with the aim of penetrating the veil of secrecy surrounding North Korean policy and, especially, the motives and goals that undergird its externally visible behavior. Such an exercise demands not only a high degree of patience and perseverance but also an ability to read between the lines, an ability that can only be acquired through prolonged immersion in North Korean publications, most of which are written in Korean.[8] This requires, at a minimum, a high degree of proficiency in the Korean language. As most North Korean economy experts in the United States face a language barrier that limits their ability to conduct deeper research on the North Korean economy, their work contains very few if any primary sources from the DPRK. As a consequence, it is highly difficult for them to understand internal and external dynamics in policy changes that lead to institutional change in the North.

---

[7] Douglass C. North, "Structure and Performance: The Task of Economic History," *Journal of Economic Literature*, 16(3), (September, 1978), 963-978.

[8] Chung-in Moon, ed., *Understanding Regime Dynamics in North Korea* (Seoul: Yeonsei Univ. Press, 1998), 85.

The following collection of articles, in seeking to map the shifting North Korean economic atmosphere, examines a range of factors, from marketization to decentralization, from grassroots movements to international assistance, and from legal transformations to the growth of illegal economies. All of the articles in this volume fully utilize materials from North Korea and furthermore, several chapters in this book employ interviews with defectors from North Korea now living in the South; North Korean transformation through the eyes of those who have personal experience gives us a much-clearer picture than merely comparing statistics or relying on official propaganda. That said, one must be careful in analysis of defector interviews, in order to ensure the integrity of the data on which research is based. The authors here have done that by employing varying interview techniques, interviewing defectors on numerous occasions and verifying as much as possible that the information provided is accurate and consistent. This is done by engaging the defectors regarding only their specific personal experiences, avoiding speculation or second hand information, and comparing the information with existing research as well as with that information provided by other interviewees.

These personal accounts of the changing nature of the North Korean economy and society, when combined with what we know of legislative changes in the North and experiences in other transitioning post-socialist states, shed a unique new light on not only what path the North is on, but where the impetus for transformation lies, and how that transformation is impacting those who are experiencing the changes. With this insight applied to the question of international cooperation for encouraging transformation of the North Korean regime, combined with lessons learned by agencies currently working with the North and input from those countries that have already undergone similar changes, a new model for

North Korean transition can more effectively encourage and support the kind of change that can improve stability in the North, on the Korean Peninsula, and throughout the region. As an introduction, first, let us examine and assess changes in North Korea's industrial sector in the context of institutional changes in North Korea.

II. Institutional Changes in North Korea (1961-2002)

As the first socialist country, the Soviet Union provided a model for most other socialist countries. During the Depression Era (1930-1940), the apparent failure of capitalism gave developing countries more reason to emulate and learn from the Soviet Union. The communists in Korea were no exception. Following the division of the Korean Peninsula, communists in North Korea, lacking knowledge and experience in building a socialist country, were eager to learn much from the Soviet Union and "learn from the Soviets" became a popular slogan during the 1940s and 1950s in North Korea. In the beginning, North Korea adopted the Soviet model of economic development, which was a strategy of industrialization with a large agricultural sector.[9]

The Soviet model had three distinctive features: First, strong emphasis on rapid industrialization—the leaders of the Soviet Union believed rapid and centrally planned growth coupled with state ownership of the means of production would provide the

---

[9] Gordon White, "North Korean Juche: The Political Economy of Self-Reliance," in Manfred Bienefeld and Martin Godgrey eds., *The Struggle for Development: National Strategies in a International Context* (New York: John Wiley and Sons, 1982), 324.

basis for massive increases in consumption in the future. Second, strategic emphasis on squeezing the surplus from the agricultural sector; agricultural investment was held to the minimum necessary to provide industry with a growing marketed surplus of agricultural products and expanding sources of labor supply. Third, emphasis on a high rate of capital formation, with the majority of investment allocated to the industrial sector. Following Feldman's model, industrial investment was allocated on an unbalanced growth pattern, and Soviet planning concentrated on certain key sectors in each plan period to avoid and overcome particular bottlenecks.[10]

However, there are two outstanding problems with such a system, namely the problem pertaining to bureaucratization of economic management and the problem of incentives. In such a system, if a machine breaks down, then an enterprise cannot simply go out and order spare parts or a replacement. It must seek the approval of its administrative superior, which then must deal with the agency that is superior to the producer of replacement machinery or spare parts. Since enterprises were evaluated above all in terms of quota fulfillment or gross output, they naturally resist special orders, or give them low priority; the problem is compounded because the potential producer of replacement parts will already have its output for the year allocated according to plan. The replacement is apt to take a long time to arrive, and if it is defective in any respect, the problem becomes a vicious cycle of delay and waste. Furthermore, defective or low-quality products are endemic in the system; since the prime measure of success is in meeting or surpassing the quota in quantitative terms, often quali-

---

10 Phillip Park, *Self-Reliance or Self-Destruction* (New York: Routledge, 2002), 14.

ty must be sacrificed to meet the quantitative targets.

The second category of problems has to do with incentives. As far as enterprise management in a Soviet-type economy is concerned, the state receives all profits and absorbs all losses, limiting incentives in this area as well.[11] Moreover, since managers are given their production plans and have their supplies, suppliers, and product recipients designated, they have very little room for initiative or innovation. These inherent problems of the planned economy were visible since the early period of economic development in North Korea.[12] The (former) Soviet Union and the Eastern Bloc socialist countries started to relax the rigid planning system by adopting partial decentralization and giving more autonomy to local enterprises in decision-making processes based on the Liberman model during the 1960s. Although North Korea criticized other socialist countries, including the (former) Soviet Union, as revisionists, North Korea also introduced a new industrial management system in 1961. The new industrial management system that was introduced in North Korea was not an exact replica of the (former) Soviet Union or other socialist countries. North Korea introduced a new industrial management system in which incentives were strengthened while keeping the Korean Workers' Party (KWP, the Party) leadership intact.

In December 1961, Kim Il Sung visited the *Daean* electric machine plant, where he gave on-the-spot guidance to industrial workers and party functionaries in charge of management.[13]

---

[11] Victor Lippit, *The Economic Development of China* (New York: M.E. Sharpe, 1987), 203.

[12] Office of Intelligence Research, "North Korea: A Case Study of Soviet Satellite," Report of the Department of State Research Mission to Korea, Dept. of State, Report No. 5600, May 20, 1951, 80-84.

[13] Kim Il Sung, "*Daeanui Saup Chekhwereul Duook Palchunsikil dae dahayeo* (On

Kim's discussions with the workers and his recommendations to them, known as the *Daean* System, became the standard working procedure for all North Korean industries. The *Daean* System was a departure from the previous "one-man management system" inherited from the Soviet Union. Under the *Daean* System, the highest managerial authority was Party committees. Each committee consisted of approximately twenty-five to thirty-five members elected from the ranks of managers, workers, engineers, and leaders of the working people's organization. A smaller executive committee, made up of the committee secretary, the factory manager, and the chief engineer, was responsible for daily plant operations and major factory decisions.[14]

Methods of resolving issues affecting production and worker activities, as well as the implementation of resolutions, were decided through collective discussions within the committee. Each factory had two major lines of administration, one headed by the manager and one headed by the party committee secretary. A chief engineer and his or her assistants directed the general staff in charge of all aspects of production, planning, and technical guidance. The manager established various supporting departments such as material supply, labor administration, and financial affairs, as well as welfare work departments to ensure smooth operation of the factories and to attend to the workers' welfare. For instance, the deputies in charge of the supply department were responsible for securing, storing, and distributing all materials for factory use,

---

Improving the Daean System of Industrial Management)," in *Kim Il Sung Works*, Vol. 3 (Pyongyang: Chosun Rodongdan Chulpansa, 1996), 433.

[14] Kim Ku Sik, "*Kiup Kwanriesu Gongjangdangwewonhoereul Choko kiwhauiro hanun Dangjuk Jido Chekhwe* (The Party System that Puts Factory Party Committee as a Chief Office in the Management of Industrial Operation)," *Kyungjae Yeonkoo*, Vol. 1 (1966), 6.

as well as for storing and shipping finished products out of the factory.

The deputies in charge of labor administration assigned workers to their units and handled the factory accounts and payroll. The deputies in charge of the workers' welfare were responsible for directing all farming on factory lands, stocking factory retail shops, and taking care of all the amenities for the staff. In the case of very large enterprises, the factory deputy manager, the heads of the schools, kindergartens, and nurseries, and the director of the local hospital, etc. formed a district committee. This committee was responsible for all aspects of the lives of the workers and their families, including housing, fuel, and deliveries of consumer goods, education, health, cinemas, and other leisure activities. On the other hand, the party committee secretary was responsible for all political activities in each of the factory party cells and attempted to ensure loyalty to the party's production targets and management goals.[15]

The *Daean* industrial management system was a direct product of the *Chollima* movement. As the North Korean development strategy shifted from the Soviet model to the self-reliant model based on mass mobilization, worker participation in management was perceived to be essential. The *Daean* System, however, encouraged a more rational approach than that practiced previously. Although party functionaries and workers became more important to management under the new system, the engineers and the technical staff also received more responsibility in their areas. Furthermore, under the system, the importance of material incentives as well as politico-moral incentives was recognized. The Independent Accounting System (IAS) was beginning to be applied to

---

[15] Kim Ku Sik, op. cit., 8-9.

various small production units within the enterprise. Each enterprise was allowed to keep surplus revenue and to distribute the profits among workers. The IAS, in which profits were distributed according to each worker's contribution, was also introduced as an intra-enterprise incentive system. By checking the input-output record of each work team and group, bonuses were granted to those work units showing the most efficient use of raw materials and equipment.[16] This was a clear measure to increase material incentive, but since the bonuses were given to the work team instead of to each individual member, it was also designed to prevent the rise of rampant individualism.

The *Daean* System was North Korea's industrial management system, and was designed to alleviate the problems of bureaucratization of the economic system and incentives. However, when North Korea became embroiled in intense ideological debate in the mid-1960s, North Korea reversed much of its reform policy and went back to the rigid planning model.[17] In 1964, a measure to reinforce the planning method was introduced, known as the Unified and Detailed Planning System. Clearly, this was a policy that put more weight on ideology and politics, rather than on advocating policy that emphasized the importance of rationalizing the economy. As such, the state tried to get a firm grip on economic planning by implementing closer and more intensive supervision over local industries, and regional administrative planning commissions were established in the country's provinces under the direct supervision of the state planning commission. Similar state

---

[16] Phillip Park, op. cit., 36.

[17] Chosunrodongdnag Chulpansa, *Wedahan Suryong Kim Il Sung Dongjiui Bulmyului Hyuckmyung Upjuk 15* (Great Leader Kim Il Sung's Revolutionary Achievement 15), Vol. 15 (Pyongyang: Chosun Rodongdan Chulpansa, 1999), 157.

planning organs were set up in cities and counties, with corresponding sections at factories and enterprises.[18] By establishing local branches of the State Planning Commission, the state commissioners were to go into the factories and enterprises to supervise the execution of the plan.

In 1965, there were also changes in plan formulation procedures. This change was implemented in order to resolve the conflict between central planners who asked for maximum output from production units without guaranteeing more than the minimum supplies of materials, and producers who requested maximum supplies without guaranteeing maximum effort and output. According to Kim Il Sung, the new procedures were introduced to reduce subjectivism in planning by inducing more worker participation in the planning process.[19] The stages of plan formulation in the DPRK were as follows: Each factory, enterprise, and cooperative farm formulated its own plan. This preliminary plan was submitted to the State Planning Commission. The Commission then compared the drafts received and arrived at a set of control figures. After these figures were examined and discussed by the Administrative Council, they were submitted to the economic branches of the relevant administrations. Based on the control estimates set up by the State Planning Commission, all administrative branches, factories, and enterprises formulated their respective plans and resubmitted them to the State Planning Commission. The State Planning Commission then finalized the overall draft plans. The draft was submitted to the Supreme People's Assembly

---

[18] Phillip Park, op. cit., 36.

[19] Kim Il Sung, "To Give Full Play to the Great Vitality of the Unified and Detailed Planning of the National Economy," in *Kim Il Sung on the Management of the Socialist Economy* (Pyongyang: Foreign Language Publishing House, 1992), 200-211.

for final approval.[20]

In the mid-1960s, the (former) Soviet Union implemented an important reform measure. This reform was designed to increase managerial power at the local level, reducing considerably the number of compulsory indicators "passed down" from central authorities. Prices were recalculated on the basis of cost plus a percentage of the value of capital assets. Moreover, under this reform scheme, managers were to have greater freedom to decide how to use their profits, including as incentive payments to workers, for reinvestment, or for payment into amenities funds. This reform, overall, moved away from rapid industrialization and toward more balanced growth—relaxation of central planning and greater embracement of market measures spread to other socialist countries.[21] In North Korea, the *Kapsan* group, who were inspired by the reform in the Soviet Union, challenged Kim Il Sung's rapid industrialization strategy by pointing out the accumulation crisis during this period.[22] Nevertheless, the Kim Il Sung group prevailed in this power struggle and consolidated its monolithic polit-

---

[20] Kim Il Sung, op. cit., 214-220.

[21] Alec Nove, *An Economic History of the U.S.S.R.* (London: Penguin Books, 1989), 367-368.

[22] As the external environment became hostile to North Korea, North Korea adopted the strategy of simultaneous development of defense and economy. Combined with the accumulation (investment) problem, North Korea's industrial growth experienced negative growth in 1966 and 1969 during this period.

Year	1961	1962	1963	1964	1965	1966	1967	1968	1969
Growth rate	14%	20	8	17	14	-3	17	15	-.25

Source: Lee Tae Sup, *Bukhanui Jipdanjuuichuk Balchun Chulyakhwa Suryong Chekyeui Hwakrip* (The Collectivist Development Strategy and the Establishment of the Suryong System in North Korea, 1956-1967), Ph.D. dissertation, Dept of Political Science, Seoul National University (2001).

ical system of *Suryong* (Supreme Leader). The reversion of more rigid planning, such as unified and detailed planning, should be understood in this context.

North Korea's rigid planning continued until the end of the 1960s. However, when Kim Il Sung had firmly consolidated his leadership position internally and the U.S.-Soviet Union détente eased tensions and improved its external environment, North Korea relaxed its rigid planning system once again. During the fallback on rigid planning, the IAS was not properly practiced and most measures that were designed to stimulate material incentives were also de facto abolished. In 1973, Kim Il Sung criticized Party officials' tendency to ignore material incentives and the principle of socialist distribution (each according to his/her contribution), and urged them to observe the independent accounting system and piece-rate measures within the *Daean* system.[23]

Despite Kim Il Sung's criticism, the *Daean* system did not function properly. Under the existing system, the highest managerial authority was the Party committee; since the Party committee was organized locally, in order to ensure proper working of the *Daean* system, delegating authority to the local level was essential. Nonetheless, during the fallback on rigid planning, administrative recentralization had occurred. During this period, state enterprises were no longer permitted to retain a portion of their profit, and most were reassigned administratively to the central government. The problems to which it had given rise were overcome, but the problems that had generated the decentralization naturally reemerged.

During the 1970s, the DPRK attempted to make the changeover from an extensive to an intensive growth strategy. However, there were basically three major impediments that made the transition

---

[23] Chosunrodongdnag Chulpansa, op. cit., 249.

difficult. First, starting in the late 1960s, there was a sharp rise in national defense expenditure as the international political environment became hostile to the DPRK. The deterioration of the DPRK-Soviet and the DPRK-China relations compounded the DPRK's defense burden as both the Soviet Union and China abruptly reduced their economic and military aid to the DPRK because the DPRK refused to side with either country in the Sino-Soviet confrontation.[24] Second, the DPRK's efforts to achieve the technological modernization necessary for increasing productivity through large-scale imports of capital equipment from Japan and Western Europe were frustrated when the DPRK's exports failed to keep pace with imports. This was primarily due to a softening of the world markets for magnetite, lead, zinc, tungsten, and other metals on which the DPRK's hard currency earnings depended. Third, the DPRK regime's disposition toward a paternalistic management style and its rigid adherence to central planning for managing the economy were incompatible with the measures that were introduced to encourage intensive growth.

North Korea did not take any dramatic measures until the early 1980s. During the 1970s, North Korea consolidated the political system of monolithic *Suryong* and its self-reliant development strategy, *Juche*. *Juche* was officially elevated to the guiding principle of the state in North Korea's 1972 Constitution. However, when political stability was ensured as Kim Jong Il was designated to be the heir of Kim Il Sung in 1980,[25] North Korea resumed its eco-

---

24 Kim Il Pyung, *Communist Politics in North Korea* (in Korean) (Seoul: Hanwool, 1986), 134-135.
25 Kim Il Sung, *"Chosunrodongdang Je6chadahoe Joongangwewonhoe Saupchonghwa Boko* (Report of 6th DPRK's Labor Party's General Meeting),"* in Ministry of Unification, *Chosun Rodongdang Daehoe Jaryozip* (Collection of the DPRK Labor Party's General Meetings (Seoul: Ministry of Unification, 1988), 155.

nomic reform process, which had halted nearly a decade earlier, and from 1981, some administrative authority was transferred back to the localities. In 1985, the "enterprises complex initiative" was introduced.[26] The enterprise complex was an important stepping-stone for subsequent decentralization, and had three significant features.

First, the initiative allowed local party committees to be managed under the enterprise complexes. Before the initiative, a local party committee functioned under a regional party committee, and accordingly, enterprises under the management of each different local party committee were not allowed to cooperate interregionally. However, since national horizontal integration was possible under the new initiative, and each local party committee was under the leadership of the enterprise complex, an enterprise complex could make decisions without the interference of local or regional party committees.[27] Second, in order to increase the autonomy of a manager within an enterprise complex, the role of the Party had been reduced in decision-making processes within the complex.[28] Third, the new initiative required the IAS to be

---

[26] Lee Sang Sul, "*Daeanui Saupchekwe Kwanchul kwa Ruynhapkiupso* (On Completion of Daean Industrial Management and Industrial Complexes)," *Kunlloja*, No. 7 (Pyongyang: Kunrojasa, 1986), 49.

[27] Kim Il Sung, "*Yeophyupkiupsoeryul Chozikhamyue Chungmoowonui Saupchejewha Banbupryel Kasunhal dae Dahayeo* (On the Improvement of Method and Work System of State Affair Office in Organizing Enterprise Complex)" *Sahoejuui Kyongjaekwanrimoonjae Dahayeo 7* (On the Problems of Socialist Economic Management, vol. 7) (Pyongyang: Chosun Rodongdang Publishing Company, 1985), 247.

[28] As the rank of party secretary was lowered, a manager of an enterprise would be higher in rank than the local party secretary. Kim Jong Il, "*Dang hwa Hyukmyungdaeo ui Kangwhabalchun hwa Sahoejuui Kyungjae Kunsul ui Saroun Yangyang ul uwhehae su* (For the Strengthening Party's Revolutionary Spirit and New Enhancement of Socialist Economic Development),"

strengthened and strictly reinforced in the enterprise complex. These reform measures of decentralizing authority to local levels and of reinforcing the independent accounting system, in actuality, paved the way for transferring North Korea's economic relationship from one of bureaucratic command to one based on contractual relationships.[29]

Of course, the contract system that was stressed during this period was not the free contract system of a market economy. The contract system should be understood in the general context of planning; accordingly, the contract system that was emphasized during this period was enacted to remedy defects in the planning system by finding shortcomings of supply-demand contracts and correcting them. In the implementation process, however, significant changes had occurred. Since the enterprise complex became the basic unit of planning, it now had the authority to make contracts with other complexes, and was allowed to keep any profit that was generated from these transactions. Moreover, planning could become much more flexible, as the complexes could cancel supply contracts if they did not need pre-contracted materials, or readjust contracts if there were needs for change. On the other hand, the regulations that enforced contracts became stricter, as there were penalties for violating contracts, and heavy penalties could be imposed if a supplier did not ensure the quality of sup-

---

in *Selected Works of Kim Jong Il*, Vol. 8 (Chosun Rodong Publishing Company, Pyongyang, 1986), 354.

[29] Kim Il Sung, "*Yeonhapkiupsoe rul Chozikhamyo Chungmoowon ui Saupcheje wha Bangbub ul Kasunhal dae Dahayeo* (On Improving Working Method and System of Chungmoowon by Organizing Enterprise Complex)," *Sahoe kyungje kwanrimunjae e Dahasu* (On the Problems Related to Management of a Socialist Economy), Vol. 7 (Pyongyang: Chosun Rodong Publishing Company, 1985), 431.

plies.[30] As the contract measures were implemented, they became an important tool in utilizing the means of production in commercial form, and the IAS was further strengthened, despite the fact that the measures were implemented within the planning scheme.

In 1990, Kim Jong Il delivered a speech titled "On Improvement of Banking and Finance" to high-ranking state officers. In the speech, Kim Jong Il emphasized the importance of observing the independent accounting system, wholesale prices, and profits when conducting economic activities.[31] After the speech, several reform measures were implemented. The new measures allowed an enterprise complex to determine prices of certain items and encouraged active utilization of a "negotiated price." Although the measures were applied to only a few select items, they could be considered as one of North Korea's first experiments with market mechanisms, because negotiated prices were determined by supply and demand in a market environment. Moreover, the new measures included "Due Diligence of Socialist Asset Evaluation." As this measure was implemented in the same year, a total of 3.2 percent of previously omitted assets could be recovered.[32] As all the assets in North Korea now had been appraised in cash terms, this measure also provided a strong basis for the proper function-

---

[30] An Yoon Ok, "*Kiupkwanri ui Haprihwa asu Kyeakwankye ka Nonun Yeokwal* (The Role of Contract in Rationalization of Industrial Management)," *Kyungje Yeonkoo* (Study on Economy), Vol. 1 (Pyongyang: Pakhwasachunjongha Chulpansa, 1993), 38.

[31] Kim Jung Il, "*Jajungeunhangsaup ul Kasunhaldae Daehayeo* (On Improving Banking and Finance)," *Selected Works of Kim Jong Il*, Vol. 10 (Pyongyang: Chosunrodongdang Chulpansa, 1990), 161-185.

[32] Chosunrodong Chulpansa, *Uwedahan Suryong Kim Il Sung Tongie ui Pulmyul ui Hyukmuyng Upjuk 15* (Immortal Revolutionary Achievement of Great Leader Kim Il Sung Vol. 15), (Pyongyang: Chosunrodongdang Chulpansa), 305.

ing of the IAS.

Strengthening of the IAS within enterprises was, on the other hand, an effort to improve an individual worker's incentive. It was a basic scheme of rewarding greater productivity with higher pay and bonuses, and penalizing lower productivity with lower pay and no bonuses. The new measures allowed each enterprise to keep up to 5 percent of their profits as a reserve fund, and an enterprise could award an individual worker with higher productivity even if the enterprise as a whole did not make a profit.[33] Since, in the past, the funds available for bonus payments depended on the enterprise's meeting basic state planning quotas for output, the new measure for rewarding individual workers for higher productivity was unprecedented, and a significant departure from the past.

The extension of the IAS system could be viewed as strengthening professionalism in management. The highest authority still resided with the party committee, but the director's rank was half a step higher than that of the party secretaries. The guidelines for evaluating management performance were also provided, and party committees had been ordered to refrain from involving themselves in the management of the complexes and to restrict their roles to assuring compliance with Party and state directives. Responsibility for the economic performance of the enterprise had been restored to the director, working together with the chief engineer and accountant.[34]

Beginning in the early 1990s, however, North Korea under-

---

[33] Lee Jeong Chul, *The Economic Dynamics and Political System of Socialist North Korea*, Ph.D. dissertation, Dept. of Political Science, Seoul National University (2002), 165.

[34] Kim Jung Il, op. cit., 354.

went a severe economic crisis, and consequently, its economic reform process had to be halted until the end of an adjustment period (1993-1996). It appears that since this time, there has been an intense debate on the development strategy between two different groups in the government; one that favors reform based on a balanced growth strategy, and the other that insists on the traditional socialist strategy of unbalanced growth. One of the most influential economic journals in North Korea, *Kyungjae Yeongu* (Research on the Economy), features two contrasting views on the development strategy of the latter half of the 1990s and onward. The first group argues that when a country has passed a certain developmental stage, the country should adjust the speed of development of heavy industry by reducing investment to it, and concentrating its efforts on the development of light industry and agriculture. In this way, the paper points out, as the growth rate of consumption should be set according to the growth rate of accumulation, people's living standards can be raised decisively. The paper further argues that since light industry's return on investment and cash flow are faster than those of heavy industry, a greater portion of investment should be given to light industry than to heavy industry.[35]

On the other hand, the second group insists that only adequate development of productive means (heavy industry) would ensure proper restoration of normal production.[36] Since North

---

[35] Kim Sang Hak, "*Uri Tangui Hyukmyongchuk Kyongjaechulyakhwa Chookchukhwa Sobisaiui Kyunhyung* (Equilibrium between Accumulation (Investment) and Consumption and Our Party's Revolutionary Economic Strategy)," *Kyongjae Yeongu*, Vol. 2 (Pyongyang: Pakhwasachunjongha Chulpansa, 1996), 9-10.

[36] Lee Joon Hyuk, "*Hyukmyongchuk Kyongjaeui Kwanchulhwa Sahoejuui Kyongjaechuk Jinziui Kongkowha* (Fulfillment of Revolutionary Economic Strategy

Korea rarely showed differences in opinion regarding the direction
of the country, this exchange demonstrated how intense debate
was in the middle of the 1990s. However, it has been observed that
although North Korea acknowledged the importance of development of light industry and agriculture[37] by creating Light Industry
First, Agriculture First, and Trade First policies (giving priority to
development of light industry, agriculture, and trade) as the state's
official economic agenda, in actuality more investment was allocated to heavy industry.[38]

As North Korea's economic situation in the 1990s became
even more dire, and its economic isolation was accentuated due to
the collapse of the (former) Soviet Union and the CMEA (Council
for Mutual Economic Assistance), North Korea fell back on the traditional strategy of giving priority to the development of heavy
industry and a reliance on extensive sources of growth such as
increasing labor (i.e., mass mobilization such as the second *Chollima* movement) without technological improvement. Nonetheless,
North Korea did not completely abandon its economic reform programs. As soon as its situation improved, North Korea first ratio-
nalized its economic system, and then launched even more drastic
reform measures later on.

Starting in 1999, North Korea began to move away from the
enterprise complex.[39] There were, basically, two reasons for this.

---

and Solidifying Socialist Economic Position)," *Kyongjae Yeongu*, Vol. 3
(Pyongyang: Pakhwasachunjongha chulpansa, 1996), 14-15.

[37] Lee Jung Chul, op. cit., 213.

[38] According to *Chosunjoonangtongshin* (North Korea Central News) on April
7, 1999, the share of the people's economy that included light industry
increased 2 percent compared to the previous year, while electric, metal,
transportation increased 15 percent, 10 percent and 10 percent, respectively, in the 1999 budget.

[39] Ham Jin Soo, "*Kyungjae kwanriui Jungkyuhwanun Sahoejuisahoeui Bonsungkwa*

First, it was an effort to shed the unprofitable sectors within the enterprises during economic downturns. Second, since one of the reasons to establish the enterprise complex was to solve or at least to improve supply management problems, the enterprise complex absorbed factories and enterprises that originally belonged to other types of industry, but were vital to the complex's supply chain. However, each different state entity that originally had authority over management of the factories and enterprises continued to extend its influence over to the enterprises and the factories even after the establishment of the complex. Hence, it was extremely difficult for the complex to manage absorbed factories and enterprises, and as a result, the enterprise complex could not enjoy the much-expected synergy.[40]

North Korea's national economic management was carried out by two organizations: *Joonang Inmin Wewanhoe* (Central People's Committee) and *Chungmoowon* (Office of State Affairs), and this overlap of leadership caused confusion in management. Therefore, in 1998, North Korea made the Cabinet solely responsible for economic management through a constitutional amendment. This change entailed two significant developments in the management of enterprises. First, as the Cabinet was solely responsible for the economy, it was possible to separate the Party from enterprise management, and consequently, politics from economics. Second, ministries and departments under the Cabinet were allowed to establish divisional ownership in industries. Let us examine each in turn.

Daekyumo Sahoejuikyungjaeui tuksuneul chunmyunjukuro Kuhyunhakoinun Tokchangjukin Kwanriunyungbangsik (Giving Regularity in Economic Management is a Unique Management Method that Embodies Characteristics of Socialist Economy)," *Kyongjae Yeongu*, Vol. 3 (1999), 12.

[40] Lee Jung Chul, op. cit., 233.

The constitutional revision in 1998 restricts the Party's involvement in economic management. Although in the past North Korea put some effort into preventing Party bureaucracies from intervening in economic affairs, they were not successful. For instance, starting in 1989, the Korean Workers' Party's Political Office supposedly should not involve itself in the process of economic policy making, but in reality, it did intervene, as the Central Party of KWP is directly under the Joosuk (President Kim Il Sung) and the Political Office of KWP allegedly possessed enormous power and could exert significant influence within the KWP. Hence the Political Office, if they wished to, would not hesitate to intervene in issues important to the entire country, including issues related to the economy. However, this intervention by the Political Office was minimized in 1998 by a constitutional amendment that allowed for such a practice to be punished. Moreover, the responsibility of managing the economy was given to the Office of State Affairs in 1994, but politics were not absent in the realm of economic management. Because a local-level party secretary held the concurrent position of chair of the local People's Committee, the Office of State Affairs needed to deal with the local party secretary in getting local cooperation and participation in the management of the national economy. Since these concurrent posts were abolished by the 1998 constitutional amendment, and as the previous Administrative Economy Committee chair now also assumed the local People's Committee chair position, technically, the Party was not allowed to intervene in economic affairs at a local level.[41]

The other important change that was initiated by the constitutional amendment of 1998 was the Cabinet ministries' and depart-

---

[41] Pak Hak-soon, *Kim Jong Il Sidaeui Kukakikoo* (National Organs in Kim Jong Il's Era) (Seoul: Sejoing Yeonguso, 2000), 59-60.

ments' assumption of de facto ownership of industries. Before the amendment, a local enterprise received quotas from the ministries or departments, and the central government was directly in charge of all local enterprises, so rational and proper management was difficult. After the amendment, the local enterprises were under the direct control of the relevant ministry or department of the Cabinet. More important, ministries and departments now had their own funds to guide local enterprises.[42] As a result, ownership of local enterprises transferred from the central government to ministries or departments under Cabinet control, and they became the basic unit of ownership in North Korea.

The latest reform measure was the Economic Management Reform Measure (the 7/1 Measures) implemented on July 1, 2002. There were three important aspects of the reform. First, as the 7/1 Measures allow local enterprises to have the authority to plan their own production, it is the transfer of decision-making authority from supervisory-administrative organs to production levels, the local enterprises. The direction of the reform is toward allowing more decision-making power at the level of the producing units, while reserving for state planning for the central role in determining such macroeconomic parameters as the level and direction of investment, sectoral balances, economic growth, and structural design, and the overall direction of the economy. North Korea seemed to be moving toward a mixture of planning and market guidance for enterprises, with planning taking precedence. The priority of planning was reflected in the fact that in key areas,

---

[42] Lee Dong Koo, "*Nakakchungsimjaenuen Kyongjaesaupue daehan Kukaui Tongilchukkwanrigyungtae* (The Cabinet Is North Korea's Unified Form of Management in Economy)," *Kim Il Sung Jonghap daehak hakboe* (summer 2001), 46.

enterprises must first fulfill plan requirements with a certain proportion of their output before they could seek out their own suppliers, markets, and so forth with their remaining capacity.[43]

Second, the 7/1 Measures enabled price reform according to market signals. The procurement price of rice was now lower than the retail price, i.e., the state stopped subsidizing this basic grain.[44] It was presumed that the price of rice in the black market was reflected in the state's selling price.[45] The wages of workers also increased dramatically; for an industrial worker, the wage increased from 110 won to 2000 won, so the workers now had a realistic degree of purchasing power to sustain their livelihood. These changes indicated the abandonment of rationing and reliance on market mechanisms for the distribution of goods. Third, the 7/1 Measures allowed for the acceleration of replacement of direct administrative control over the economy for indirect economic measures to assure that enterprise behavior would be consistent with national economic goals. As a result, money became an important tool in the North Korean economy. State subsidies were abolished, and at the same time, cost and scarcity were reflected in the prices of consumption and intermediary goods.

Although many experts on the North Korean economy cast strong doubts on the veracity and intention of North Korea's economic reform,[46] North Korea is gradually moving away from the

---

[43] Kim Yeon Chul, *Bukhan Kyongjaekwanriui Sungkyukhwa Chunmang* (Characteristics of North Korea's Economic Reform and its Prospect) (Seoul: Humanitas, 2002), 14-15.

[44] In the past, the state bought rice from the peasants at 80 chun per kilo and distributed it to urban workers at 8 chun per kilo. After the reform, the state bought at 40 won per kilo and distributed at 44 won per kilo.

[45] Kim Yeon Chul, op. cit., 15.

[46] The most notable examples are as follows: Marcus Noland, *North Korea After Kim Jong Il* (Washington DC: IIE, 2004); Nicholas Eberstadt, "Persis-

rigid Stalinist planned economy to an economy where market measures increasingly play significant roles in the overall economic structure. The extent of reform, however, is dependent on the North Korean leadership's perception and understanding of its external environment. North Korea's most important objective of economic development is to achieve and maintain national sovereignty. So, after the Korean War, North Korea decided to develop an independent economy, but this decision is not absolute, nor has it ever been. In large part, as John Merrill argues, the history of North Korea has been a history of choices and consequences of the conflict between its desire for maximum independence and its acknowledgment that it could not isolate itself totally from the political and economic currents sweeping the world.[47] Whether North Korea successfully completes its reform and rescues itself from economic crisis is not only dependent on its own efforts, but also heavily depends on its external environment. Without favorable environmental factors such as infusion of capital and technology from abroad, access to foreign markets, and an international environment generally friendly to smooth economic relations, one country's economic reform can only go so far.

In this respect, North Korea's diplomatic and military confrontation with the United States can be considered to be one of the biggest obstacles in North Korea's economic reform. As of now, the United States perceives North Korea's nuclear development program to be a threat to its security, but North Korea, on the other hand, perceives it to be the only deterrence to outside aggres-

---

tence of North Korea," *Policy Review* (October 2004).

[47] John Merrill, "North Korea's Halting Efforts at Economic Reform," in Lee Chong-sik and Yoo Se-Hee, *North Korea in Transition* (Berkeley: Institute of East Asian Studies, 1991), 142.

sion. The development of nuclear weapons should be discouraged and prevented; nevertheless, like the reform programs in North Korea, its nuclear program has a long history and should be understood in terms of North Korea's self-rescue measures instead of as offensive or aggressive measures, in order to keep its national sovereignty. Let us investigate this issue further.

III. North Korea's Nuclear Development Program and Economic Reform

As we have seen in its earlier development period, North Korea pursued a development strategy of giving priority to the development of heavy industry. However, this line of North Korean development clashed with the Soviet's socialist common market and cooperation scheme, CMEA. Relations between North Korea and the Soviet Union became tense after Nikita Khrushchev came to power. The Soviets, irked at not being sufficiently consulted in the process of designing a new economic plan (the Post-War Economic Construction Plan), expressed their reservations and urged North Korea to give more attention to consumer goods and agricultural sectors instead of giving priority to the development of heavy industry.[48]

The Soviets' opposition to North Korea's self-reliant strategy had direct consequences. Soviet aid to the DPRK was significantly reduced after the completion of the Three-Year Plan (1954-1956); Soviet aid to North Korea was reduced from $367.5 million during the 1954-1956 period to $156 million during 1957-1960 period. North Korea did not receive any aid from the Soviet Union until 1967,

---

[48] Gordon White, op. cit., 331.

when the Soviet foreign minister Aleksey Kosygin visited North Korea and realigned the relationship between two countries.[49] Moreover, the Soviet military guarantee embodied in the 1961 Korea-Soviet treaty diminished and military aid was shut off for several years when North Korea refused to side with the Soviet Union during the Sino-Soviet dispute. On top of this, a military coup d'etat in South Korea in 1961, the Cuban Missile Crisis in 1962, and heightened involvement of the United States in Vietnam in 1965 accentuated increased tension on the Korean Peninsula during the 1960s. North Korea did not even get along with China during the Chinese Cultural Revolution (1966-1976). The DPRK criticized China for its hard-line policies during the Cultural Revolution, and the Red Guard in China reportedly attacked Kim Il Sung as a "fat revisionist" which almost ignited a military confrontation along the border between the two countries. In this situation, North Korea figured that it could not rely on any other country for its national defense, but to have its own national defense through the development of heavy industry. Kim Il Sung made this point clear when he said:

> Heavy industry is the foundation of development of the national economy. Without developing heavy industry, light industry and agriculture cannot be developed, and modernizing the national economy would not be possible. Heavy industry is a basis for national independence and enables us to pursue self-reliant development of national economy and to defend ourselves.[50]

---

[49] For more detailed discussion of this issue, please read Phillip Park, *Self-Reliance or Self-Destruction?* (New York: Routledge, 2002).

[50] Kim Il Sung, *Kim Il Sung Works* 19 (Pyongyang: Chosun Rodongdan Chulpansa, 1996), 295.

The intensification of Cold War tensions on the Korean Peninsula and in other parts of the world, combined with the weakening solidarity among the communist bloc nations, compelled the DPRK to divert a greater amount of resources to defense. In the beginning of 1965, the DPRK adopted a series of policy measures to pursue a parallel development of the defense and economic sectors,[51] and the policy of parallel development continued since.

Table 1. Estimation of North Korea's Defense Expense (1960-1990)

Year	1960-1966	1967	1970	1975	1980	1985	1990
Defense/ budget	19.0%	30.4%	29.2%	16.4~ 24.6%	14.6~ 21.9%	14.4~ 21.6%	12.0~ 18.0%

Source: Ham Taik-young (1995), *"Bukhan Kyungjaeui Chimchewha Daehoekwankye"* (North Korea's Economic Downturns and Its External Relations), in *Bukhan Sahoejuuikyungjaeui Chimchewha Daeung* (North Korean Socialist Economic Downturns and Its Response), Kyungnam Univ. Press., Seoul, 122-123.

North Korea's heavy burden of defense expenditure became an enormous barrier to economic development and the country's development as a whole. Trying to achieve economic development in a relatively small and mountainous country where only 20 percent of the land is arable was an extremely tall order. On top of this physical constraint, North Korea had to channel a large portion (approximately around 20 percent of the total national budget) of the budget into defense (see Table 1). This huge expenditure on defense had direct consequences to economic development. Nonetheless, in a situation where capital necessary for growth could only come from within the country's self-contained and self-

---

[51] The parallel development of defense and non-defense sectors was chosen as the official Party policy in the Fifth Plenary Meeting of Central Committee of KWP (Korean Workers' Party) in December 1962.

reliant economic structure, North Korea's huge defense burden became an absolute barrier to economic development, because as defense expenditures increased, the portion allocated to non-defense sectors such as light industry and agriculture became increasingly smaller. One of the most difficult problems that North Korea encountered pursuing this kind of development strategy was an energy problem. According to its self-reliance policy, North Korea built its energy supply structure centered on coal (see Table 2).

Table 2. North Korea's Sources of Energy Supply: unit 1000 TOE[52]

	Coal	Oil	Hydraulic	Total Supply
1972	19,885 (85%)	749 (4%)	2,681 (11%)	23,315 (100%)
1977	24,690 (83%)	1,247 (4%)	3,909 (13%)	29,846 (100%)
1983	29,384 (77%)	2,779 (7%)	5,808 (16%)	37,971 (100%)
1987	31,244 (72%)	3,355 (8%)	8,523 (20%)	43,122 (100%)
1992[53]	32,520 (75%)	3,555 (8%)	7,332 (17%)	43,407 (100%)

Source: IEA (International Energy Agency) (1992), Energy Statistics and Balances.

As Table 2 indicates, coal is the most important source of energy in North Korea. When North Korea started to launch economic development programs after the Korean War, many other nations had a similar energy supply and consumption structure based on coal. Moreover, since North Korea had abundant deposits of coal, utilizing its own natural resources went well with its development strategy of self-reliance. However, the energy source of the world economy shifted from coal to oil in the 1950s, as oil was more efficient and had a far wider range of application than coal. North Korea could not shift its energy source because it feared that it

---

[52] Ton of Oil Equivalent
[53] IEA (1993) Balances of non-OECD countries 1991-1992, 379.

would lose its economic sovereignty by integrating into the socialist economic bloc, CMEA. The U.S. economic embargo, which was
imposed on North Korea in 1948, accentuated North Korea's economic isolation. In the 1990s, North Korea had undergone severe
economic crisis. During the entire decade, North Korea experienced
negative growth, and according to North Korea's own report, the
1999 government budget was half that of 1989.[54] At the heart of
the North Korean economic crisis is its energy shortage.

As the Soviet Union rapidly abandoned socialism after the
failed coup of August 1991, diplomatic relations between the newly
created CIS (Commonwealth of Independent States) and the
DPRK worsened. After the coup, the Yeltsin government cut off its
economic support and asked the DPRK to trade in hard currency
at world prices. As a result, trade between the CIS and the DPRK
fell dramatically (see Table 3). Since the DPRK had relied on the
former Soviet Union for approximately a third of its crude oil
supply, petroleum products, coking coal, and parts for machinery
and equipment, this reduction in the supply of energy and tech-

Table 3. The DPRK's Crude Oil and Coking Coal Imports from the USSR/
Russia: 1988-92

(Unit: 1000 tons)

	1988	1989	1990	1991	1992
Crude Oil	640	506	410	42	190
Coking Coal	1,037	939	827	184	0

Source: Japanese External Trade Organization, Kita Chosen n Keizai to Boeki no Tenbo
    (Prospect for the North Korean Economy and Trade) 1991. p. 73 for 1988 and
    1993. p. 52 for 1989-92. Reprinted from Lim Kang-taeg's Ph.D. dissertation,
    North Korea's Foreign Trade (1962-1992), State Univ. of New York at Albany.
    Dept. of Economics, 1996.

---

[54] Chung Young Chul, *Bukhan ui Kaehyuk, Kaebang* (North Korea's Reform and
    Opening) (Seoul: Sunin, 2004), 132.

nology was felt throughout the entire DPRK economy. As we can see, and as North Korea continually brings up the energy issue as its most critical economic problem, solving the energy problem is the one of the most critical issues in the North Korean economy.

Looking from this angle, it is not too difficult to imagine that North Korea, which is facing economic isolation and endeavoring under the self-reliant development strategy, has put much effort into solving its energy problem by itself. North Korea also has to resolve the huge burden of its defense expenditure. In this respect, nuclear energy is likely to be considered as a solution for solving two outstanding problems (energy and defense) in North Korean economic development. In fact, developing nuclear power is perceived to be "killing two birds with one stone" for North Korea because it has considerable deposits of uranium, a fundamental and basic resource for nuclear development, and using its own natural resources is well in line with its self-reliant development strategy. On the other hand, nuclear weapons, a by-product of its nuclear program, are potent strategic weapons that could help North Korea to reduce the cost of defense significantly.

Considering these possible motivations for nuclear development, North Korea's penchant for nuclear energy is obvious. North Korea's nuclear program began as early as 1955, and the program was accelerated in the mid-1960s and the late 1980s.[55] As we can see from the above argument, North Korea's nuclear program was launched neither because of its hostility toward the United States nor any aggressive intention directed at neighboring

---

[55] In January 1962, North Korea built a civilian-use IRT-2000 research reactor at Yongbyon. A nuclear research lab was established in February 1964. Please refer to "North Korean Nuclear Developments: An Updated Chronology" (http://cns.miis.edu/research/korea/nuc/chr4789.htm) for a complete chronology of North Korean nuclear development.

countries such as South Korea or Japan. North Korea's nuclear development should be understood in the context of North Korea's self-reliant development strategy and its stubborn adherence to maintaining national sovereignty. In this perspective, North Korea's nuclear program should be interpreted as North Korea's defensive and self-rescue measure rather than its inherent wicked- ness or evilness. Hence, attempting to force North Korea to give up its nuclear program by pushing regime demise or regime change policies, as some North Korea experts recommend, would only succeed in causing North Korea to abandon its reform pro- gram and concentrate its efforts on utilizing its nuclear capability, because North Korea would likely prefer to choose a strategy that maintains its national sovereignty rather than giving itself up to a greater power.

The confrontation on the Korean Peninsula must be resolved in a peaceful manner, because the alternative would not only lead to devastating destruction for North and South Korea, but it is also likely to extend to other neighboring countries. However, as an alternative to military and diplomatic confrontation, the peaceful resolution of the Korean War, a peace treaty between the DPRK and the United States, normalization of diplomatic relations between the two countries, and lifting of sanctions would indu- bitably not only reduce tensions on the peninsula, but also facili- tate North Korea's economic reform process and ultimately turn the enemy into an economic and security partner.

Bibliography

English-language Publications

Eberstadt, Nicholas and Judith Banister, *The Population of North Korea*. Institute of East Asia Studies (Berkeley: University of California, 1992).

Eberstadt, Nicholas, *Korea Approaches Unification* (New York: M.E. Sharpe, 1995).

_____. "The DPRK as an Economy Under Multiple Severe Stresses: Analogies and Lessons from Past and Recent Historical Experience," *Korean Journal of National Unification*, December 1, 1997a.

_____. "Hastening Korean Reunification: The Writing on the 38th Parallel," *Foreign Affairs*, March/April, 1997b.

_____. *The End of North Korea* (Washington, DC: AEI Press, 1999).

_____. "Economic Recovery in the DPRK: Status and Prospect," *International Journal of Korean Studies*, vol. IV, no. 1 (Fall/Winter 2000), 15-35.

Eberstadt, Nicholas and Richard J. Ellings, *Korea's Future and the Great Powers* (Seattle: University of Washington Press, 2002).

Eberstadt, Nicholas, The Persistence of North Korea, *Policy Review*, October 1, 2004.

_____. "Pyongyang's Option: 'Ordinary' Stalinism, *Far Eastern Economic Review*, March 21, 2005a.

_____. "Economic Implications of a 'Bold Switchover' in DPRK Security Policy," *The Korean Journal of Defense Analysis*, April 20, 2005b.

_____. "Economic Implications of a Fundamental Shift in North Korean Security Policy," *Asia Policy*, No. 2, (July 2006).

Hodgson, Geoffrey M., *Economic and Utopia* (London: Routledge, 1999).

Lippit, Victor, *The Economic Development of China* (New York: M.E. Sharpe, 1987).

Merrill, John, "North Korea's Halting Efforts at Economic Reform," in Chong-sik Lee and Se-Hee Yoo, *North Korea in Transition* (Berkeley:

Institute of East Asian Studies, 1991).

Moon, Chung-in, ed., *Understanding Regime Dynamics in North Korea* (Seoul: Yeonsei University Press, 1998).

Noland, Marcus, "The North Korean Economy," US-Korea Academic Symposium, 1996.

_____. "Why North Korea Will Muddle Through," *Foreign Affairs*, July / August 1997.

_____. *Economic Integration of the Korean Peninsula* (Washington, DC: IIE Press, 1998).

_____. *Avoiding the Apocalypse: The Future of the Two Koreas* (Washington, DC: IIE Press, 2000).

_____. *North Korea After Kim Jong Il* (Washington, DC: IIE Press, 2004).

Noland, Marcus and Stephan Haggard, *Famine in North Korea: Markets, Aid, and Reform* (Washington, DC: IIE Press, 2007).

North Douglass C., "Structure and Performance: The Task of Economic History," *Journal of Economic Literature*, 16(3) (September, 1978).

Park, Phillip, *Self-Reliance or Self-Destruction?* (New York: Routledge, 2002).

Wilber, James, ed., *The Political Economy of Development and Underdevelopment* (New York: McGraw-Hill, 1989).

White, Gordon, "North Korean *Juche*: The Political Economy of Self-Reliance," in Bienefeld, Manfred, and Godgrey, Martin, eds., *The Struggle for Development: National Strategies in an International Context* (New York: John Wiley and Sons, 1982).

Korean-language Publications

Chosunrodongdnag Chulpansa, *Wedahan Suryong Kim Il Sung Dongjiui Bulmyului Hyuckmyung Upjuk 15* (Great Leader Kim Il Sung's Revolutionary Achievement), Vol. 15 (Pyongyang: Chosun Rodongdan Chulpansa, 1999).

Kim, Il Pyung, *Communist Politics in North Korea* (in Korean) (Seoul: Hanwool, 1986).

Kim Il Sung, *Kim Il Sung Jusak Sunzip* (Kim Il Sung Works 1-42) (Pyongyang:

Chosun Rodongdan Chulpansa, 1996).

Kim Jong Il, *Kim Jong Il Jusak Sunzip* (Selected Works of Kim Jong Il 1-14) (Pyongyang: Chosunrodongdang Chulpansa, 1995-2000).

Kim, Yeon Chul, *Bukhan Kyongjaekwanriui Sungkyukhwa Chunmang* (Characteristics of North Korea's Economic Reform and its Prospect) (Seoul: Humanitas, 2002).

Kyungje Yeonkoo (Study on Economy), (Pyongyang: Pakhwasachunjongha Chulpansa, 1961-2004).

Lee, Dong Koo, *"Nakakchungsimjaenuen Kyongjaesaupue daehan Kukaui Tongilchukkwanrigyungtae* (The Cabinet is North Korea's Unified Form of Management in Economy)," *Kim Il Sung Jonghap daehak hakboe* (summer 2001).

Lee, Jeong Chul, *Sahoejui Bukhanui Kyungjaedonghak kwa Chungchicheje* (The Economic Dynamics and Political System of Socialist North Korea), Ph.D. dissertation, Dept. of Political Science, Seoul National University (2002).

Lee, Tae Sup, *Bukhanui Jipdanjuuichuk Balchun Chulyakhwa Suryeong Chekyeui Hwakrip 1956-1967* (The Collectivist Development Strategy and the Establishment of the Suryong System in North Korea, 1956-1967), Ph.D. dissertation, Dept. of Political Science, Seoul National University (2001).

Pak, Hak-soon, *Kim Jong Il Sidaeui Kukakikoo* (National Organs in Kim Jong Il's Era) (Seoul: Sejoing Yeonguso, 2000).

Chapter 2

Economic Reform and Institutional Transformation: A Legal Perspective

⊣ Dae-Kyu YOON ⊢

I. Introduction

The Democratic People's Republic of Korea (DPRK, or North Korea) has undergone significant change since the collapse of the former Soviet Union and the Socialist Bloc in Eastern Europe at the end of the 1980s. Transformation of those socialist states into more market-oriented economies and democratic political systems made their relations with North Korea, formerly based on socialist brethren camaraderie, impossible to maintain, leading them to cease providing economic aid to Pyongyang. The death of Kim Il Sung in 1994, the ruler of North Korea for 50 years and the only leader the country had ever known, combined with natural disasters in the mid-1990s, aggravated the North's economic situation, bringing about widespread famine and large-scale starvation. Deterioration of its relationships with the United States and South Korea dampened these governments' enthusiasm to provide the North with aid, while at the same time, former socialist allies were either not inclined or not able to help the DPRK avoid food shortages. Since then, the North's economic difficulties have continued without prospective hope for recovery, despite desperate efforts to pull itself out of its economic quagmire.

This situation seriously undermined North Korea's cherished system of a centrally planned economy and public distribution system, which has been driven to the verge of collapse in the post–Cold War era. The ongoing one-man rule by Kim Il Sung's son, Kim Jong Il, has further deteriorated the situation due to the rigidity of the system implemented to maintain his dictatorship and political stability, as this system has limited the available options to renew and reform the regime in order to overcome the current hardships.

This chapter will examine how North Korea has responded to these difficult economic situations from a legal perspective. The gap between the law in print and the law in action would be tremendous in a society such as North Korea, where the rule of law is barely honored, and where a totalitarian dictatorship permeates the entire realm of residents' lives, both public and private, so that laws are not promulgated unless the state desperately feels the need for them. However, since the law is the most explicit and strongest expression of the official will of the state, a legal approach and analysis will facilitate a better understanding of, and outlook for, the current economic changes under way in the North. The law can still be an important means and mirror to help understand North Korea. Therefore, changes in laws concerning the economy since the 1990s will be the central focus of this chapter. Important legal changes, including those to the North's Constitution, will be explained and analyzed in a social context in order to understand the ongoing economic transition currently under way in North Korea.

II. Basic Legal Grounds for Economic Transition

1. Constitutional Change in 1992

The North Korean Constitution underwent two significant revisions during the 1990s, first in 1992, prior to the death of Kim Il Sung, and then again in 1998, after the leader had passed away. The primary purpose of the 1992 revision was to ensure the smooth transition of power to Kim Jong Il. It consolidated the power of the heir-apparent by upgrading the legal status of the National Defense Commission (NDC), which the younger Kim headed, to that of the highest leading organ of the state, with general jurisdiction over national defense.[1]

The 1992 revision also provided constitutional grounds for opening the country for foreign investment by creating two new provisions. Article 37 stated, "The State shall encourage institutions, enterprises or associations of the DPRK to establish and operate equity and contractual joint venture enterprises with corporations or individuals of foreign countries." Article 16 was also created to protect foreign investors, stating, "The DPRK shall guarantee the legal rights and interests of foreigners in its region." Although the DPRK enacted its Equity Joint Venture Act (*hapyeongbeop*) in 1984 using the earlier Chinese joint venture law as a model, it was not until 1992 that the constitutional grounds for such an act were explicitly provided.[2]

As the collapse of old socialist brethren countries continued

---

[1] 1992 Constitution, Article 111. The presidential authority over national defense was transferred to the Chairman of the NDC by this revision.

[2] In fact, the creation of the Rajin-Sonbong Special Economic Zone, North Korea's first Free Economic and Trade Zone, was also announced by the Cabinet in 1991, prior to the 1992 constitutional revision.

from the end of the 1980s, North Korea was forced to seek alternative sources of aid and commerce to replace the economic support
these countries had provided. Foreign investment seemed to be
the only way to invite capital inflows that could invigorate its
economy, or at least stave off its collapse. A plethora of new laws
followed, with the goal of enticing foreign investment, but these
legal attempts were of little avail without an improvement in the
investment environment rife with extremely poor infrastructure,
bureaucratic rigidity, and a lack of any practical means of dispute
resolution due to political reasons as well as the lack of the rule of
law. It was not until the North suffered serious economic hardships in the mid-1990s that more significant reforms could be seen.

2. Constitutional Change in 1998

Another constitutional revision was made in 1998, four years
after the death of President Kim Il Sung and following serious
hardships from food shortages caused by flooding and other natural disasters in the mid-1990s. The constitutional framework for
the distribution of state authority was rearranged to accommodate
the regime of Kim Jong Il after the death of his father. The 1998
Constitution repealed the office of the presidency and the Central
People's Committee and passed their authority to the Supreme
People's Assembly (SPA) and its Presidium (Standing Committee).
Since the constitutional change, implementation and management
of state policy now belongs to the Cabinet.[3] However, it goes
without saying that Kim Jong Il entertains supreme power of the
state as the Chairman of the NDC and the Chief Secretary of the
Workers' Party. As North Korea's "Military-first Politics" signifies,

---

[3] 1998 Constitution, Article 117.

his main responsibility is the military, while the economy is the responsibility of the SPA Presidium and Cabinet. That is, the failure of the economy is legally their responsibility, but not his. Although the military industry is a great burden on the state economy as a major cause of distortion of the economic structure, the leadership continues to prioritize this sector over others.

As the centrally planned economy and public distribution system has barely been functioning, the vast majority of ordinary citizens have had to survive on their own. The operation rate of manufacturing factories declined by as much as 75 percent in 1996.[4] Individuals and organizations, including enterprises, sought more leeway and discretion for their activities in order to take best advantage of their environment and opportunities and avoid starvation, while the government wanted to encourage and facilitate the increase of production.

In order to overcome economic hardships following the breakdown of the socialist economy and public distribution system, the North Korean government had no choice but to acquiesce and allow market functions to make up for state shortfalls in meeting the needs of the general population. In fact, the market has already proven indispensable for the subsistence of ordinary people. Thus, farmers' markets have been rooted permanently throughout the country since the middle of the 1990s in a variety of shapes and sizes, depending on the region and the local conditions. State enterprises and organizations also have to take advantage of market functions in order to facilitate procurement and sales.

A shortage of supply from the planned economy has inevitably

---

[4] Hyung-joong Park, *Bukhan-ui Kyeongje Kwanli Chegye: gigu-wa unyeong* (Economic Management System of North Korea: Organization and Operation) (Seoul: Haenam Publication, 2002), 29.

allowed, by default, more autonomy to enterprises, collective farms, and other organizations. Along with the structural change of government instituted to suit Kim Jong Il's leadership after the death of Kim Il Sung, another principal goal of the 1998 revision was to cope with this chronic economic predicament by providing constitutional grounds for new directions and activities.

1) Adoption of Concepts of a Market Economy

Article 33 of the revised Constitution created a new section of the North's economy, stating, "The State shall introduce a cost accounting system in economic management according to the demand of the *Daean* work system,[5] and utilize such economic levers as prime costs, prices and profits."

Although a self-supporting accounting system was introduced in the early 1960s to strengthen the responsibility of respective state enterprises, and was subsequently extended to other areas, such as agriculture and service, in the 1970s, its explicit inclusion in the Constitution was made to contribute to the further expansion of autonomy and responsibility to individual entities.

The constitutional introduction of concepts such as prime cost, price, and profit, which make up the central core of a market economy, reflects the future direction of the North's economy toward a positive attitude regarding the role of the market. Although the Constitution does not accept market economics per se, North

---

[5] The *Daean* work system is explained in the first section of the same constitutional article. The first section provides, "The State shall guide and manage the national economy according to the Daean Work System, which is a socialist economic management form whereby the economy is operated and managed in a scientific and rational way depending on the collective power of the producing masses, and according to the agricultural guidance system whereby agricultural management is conducted by industrial methods."

Korea wants to utilize markets by incorporating some aspects of a market economy within its existing socialist system in order to vitalize its dampened economy.[6] It is an expression of, and compromise with, reality, in consideration of the malfunction of its socialist economic system and the improbability of economic recovery through the existing system in the near future.

2) Commercial Activity Legitimized

Under the socialist economy, the scope of private ownership is very limited to consumable goods and household effects. Therefore, private property consists of socialist distribution of the results of labor and additional benefits of the state and society. The products of individual sideline activities, including those from the kitchen gardens of cooperative farmers, also fall under the category of private property. With the 1998 constitutional revision, a new source of private property was recognized: income from other legal economic activities would now be considered private property.[7]

This new addition in the Constitution has significant meaning and impact, as it legitimizes private trading in the farmers' markets and other local exchanges that have been prevalent throughout the country for some time, tacitly permitted and tolerated by authorities despite their unlawfulness. Commercial transactions fall under the guise of "other legal economic activities." Unless specifically prohibited, commercial activity for profit is now legally allowed on constitutional grounds. Insertion of this section foreshadowed the increase of commercial activities.

---

[6] North Korea enacted the Price Act (*Kagyeok-Beop*) in 1997, which was prepared to provide principle, procedure, and means for price setting.

[7] 1998 Constitution, Article 24.

3) Change in Ownership for the Means of Production

Under the North's previous constitutions, the means of production were owned only by the state and cooperative organizations. Article 20 of the 1998 revision included "social" organizations as eligible subjects for ownership of the means of production. A social organization can be established as a legal entity by the recognition of the relevant authority. The vocation association, the journalists' association, and the Red Cross are some examples of social organizations that became legally recognized by the North Korean government. As a result, these social organizations' scope of economic activities would be expanded.

Assets critical to the government or national interests still can be owned only by the state. Designated in the 1992 Constitution were natural resources, transportation organs, communication organs, major factories, enterprises, ports, and banks.[8] Article 21 of the 1998 revision replaced "transportation organs" with "railways [and] aviation transportation organs." This can be interpreted to mean that social or cooperative organizations can own transportation means other than railways and aviation facilities, which are still monopolized by the state.

In a similar vein, the scope of ownership by cooperative organizations was also amended. Article 22 of the 1992 Constitution provided that "Cooperative organizations can possess such property as land, draught animals, farm implements, fishing boats, and buildings as well as medium-small factories and enterprises." The same article in the 1998 Constitution replaced "farm implements" and "fishing boats" with "agricultural machinery" and "ships," while removing "draught animals" and "buildings" from the list. This means that social or cooperative organizations can own not

---

[8] 1992 Constitution, Article 21.

only fishing boats, but also cargo or passenger ships. Furthermore, an individual can now own draught animals, buildings, and farm implements other than agricultural machinery.

Through the 1998 revision, the scope of state ownership was reduced, while that of social and cooperative organizations was broadened in some realms, and at the same time, the social and cooperative organizations' ownership was curtailed while that of individuals was expanded in others. The change reflects the transformation of society, and in particular, shifts concerning economic activity. At the same time, it foreshadows a future that is shaped by economic power.

Accordingly, the Civil Code was revised in 1999 to accommodate this constitutional change. North Korea first publicly promulgated the Civil Code in 1990. Although it had a similar code on the books prior to 1990, it was not open to the public as a law. It was revised in 1993 and 1999. As a citizen could partake in more transactions and own more property, the civil law dealing with private matters would need to play a more significant role than previously.

4) Authority for Foreign Trade Diversified

The authority for foreign trade was monopolized by the state under Article 36 of the 1992 Constitution. However, the same article in the 1998 Constitution allows social and cooperative organizations to engage in foreign trade. This change was implemented in order to facilitate the expansion of overseas trade. The decentralized authority to conduct foreign trade has been proven to be very effective in vitalizing overseas economic relations. Many social entities have engaged in foreign trade in order to gain access to foreign currencies. The Trade Act (*muyeok-beop*) was also enacted in 1998 to facilitate and increase foreign trade.

5) Grounds for Establishment of Special Economic Zones

The constitutional grounds for establishing special economic zones were added in Article 37 of the 1998 revision. Although Article 37 of the 1992 revision was newly created to provide a constitutional basis to invite foreign investment, no special economic zone was prescribed in the document. As a matter of fact, despite the absence of constitutional grounds, North Korea had already created a Free Economic and Trade Zone at Rajin-Sonbong, in the northeastern coastal region, in the early 1990s.[9] It was an effort to invite foreign capital and technology following the model the Chinese had so successfully employed. In this regard, this new addition of constitutional grounds for special economic zones was belated.

If the lack of constitutional grounds for a special economic zone was not an obstacle for establishing the Rajin-Sonbong special zone, why does Article 37 now carry such explicit constitutional grounds for a special economic zone? This revision seemed to signify a more positive attitude in Pyongyang regarding special economic zones. It is an expression of strong will by Pyongyang for further economic opening in order to attract foreign investors. Indeed, North Korea created three special zones in 2002; the Sinuiju Special Administrative Region, adjacent to the Chinese border at the northwest tip of the Korean Peninsula,[10] Mount Kumgang Tourist Resort Zone, and the Kaesong Industrial Complex,[11] on the

---

[9] The governing law for this special economic zone was the Law on Free Economic and Trade Zones, which was adopted by the Standing Committee of the Supreme People's Assembly in January 1993. A series of laws followed to deal with labor, taxation, accounting, registration, foreign investment enterprises, and other details.

[10] The Basic Law of the Sinuiju Special Administrative Region was promulgated by the Standing Committee of the Supreme People's Assembly in September 2002.

[11] The Mount Kumgang Tourist Zone Law and the Kaesong Industrial Com-

border shared with South Korea. Pyongyang, concerned about the infiltration of foreign influence, seems to have a preference for special zones that are separated and isolated from ordinary administrative districts.

6) Freedom to Travel Granted

Travel has been very tightly restricted in the North. However, the unprecedented shortage of food in the mid-1990s forced residents to move around the country simply to find food for survival. Otherwise, they would have had to wait idly as starvation set in due to the state's failure to provide centrally controlled rations. Under these dire circumstances with no food distribution, it was not easy for the authorities to maintain their tight control over travel within the country. Therefore, the authorities assumed an acquiescent attitude toward unauthorized travel. As a reflection of this new phenomenon, the 1998 constitutional revision included the addition of Article 75, which provided the freedom of travel.[12] Of course, this inclusion of the freedom in the Constitution does not mean that citizens in the North actually enjoy the full freedom to move around the country. They still need several certificates of permission for multiple checks to travel. However, the authorities controlling citizens' travel take into consideration the food shortage situation, and often recognize illegal travel by default.

---

plex Law were adopted by the Standing Committee of the SPA in November 2002.

[12] Article 75 states, "The citizens shall have freedom to reside in and travel to any place."

3. The Rule of Law not Honored

In many cases in North Korea, new practices take place and new policies are implemented before legal grounds are provided. In fact, the state commands an unlimited scope of authority in the North, where the Western concept of the rule of law is not entertained. This is not limited to North Korea. According to the theory of socialism, the law is a tool to realize the dictatorship of the proletariat. Since the law under socialism is no more than a mere means, it does not hold any intrinsic value or spirit, and nor is it autonomous. The theme of law is designed to protect the socialist system and criticize bourgeois law. All law is, by nature, public, with an emphasis on its repressive aspect. This character is reinforced in the North, where one-man rule is maintained over generations through familial succession.

The state has been run by instructions or directives from the higher authority. As the Constitution provides, the highest organ in the North is the Workers' Party, which is not an official government body, but rather, leads the state from above the government.[13] Therefore, the impact of the party constitution is far greater than that of the state, while the impact of party directives is much stronger than that of laws enacted by a government body, regardless of its status. This is true even for the highest levels of government, such as the Supreme People's Assembly and the Cabinet. In fact, the most powerful authority, rising above all norms, is the authority granted to the words, teachings, and instructions of Kim Il Sung and Kim Jong Il. All laws and party orders are simply means to realize the thoughts and directives of these two men. As

---

[13] The 1998 Constitution, Article 11, states, "The DPRK shall conduct all activities under the leadership of the Workers' Party of Korea."

long as this structure is maintained, it is impossible to enforce the rule of law, de jure as well as de facto.

Therefore, the lack of legal grounds for certain acts by public agencies does not raise any issue. Law is often enacted to recognize or legitimize existing practices, rather than to create the legal justification for new ones. In particular, when a practice is not consistent with the North's ideology or principle in theory, but appears spontaneously out of necessity, the state cannot but recognize it if the authorities are not able to abolish it. Markets and the freedom to travel are but two examples.

III. Transformation of Economic System and Law

1. Markets Legitimized

Although markets have long existed under the socialist economy, along with central planning and the public distribution system, their role was very limited and complementary when the planned economy was functioning correctly. However, when the socialist economic system was not working well and public distribution was not carried out, the role of the market grew proportionally. As the state economy neared breakdown, with the exception of important military industries, and the accompanying collapse of the public distribution system loomed imminent, ordinary citizens had to rely on markets for their daily subsistence. As economic difficulties continued with no prospects for recovery, and the socialist economy was on the verge of a collapse that would imminently lead to large-scale starvation, the market became indispensable for the very survival of ordinary people. North Korean authorities could not but recognize the important role of the markets under these dire conditions.

Indeed, farmers' markets were transformed into general markets in 2003 by the implementation of an official government ordinance.[14] While the former had not been established on legal grounds, despite having been tolerated by the authorities, the latter were created based on legal statutes, and thus considered legitimate. The former came into being spontaneously, out of necessity, and thus always had a precarious status. The authorities could crack down on them at any time. Traders in the farmers' markets were vulnerable to exploitation by local government officials. In addition, the scope of items allowed for trade in the farmers' markets was also very limited. For example, only non-grain farm produce was tradable, while grain and industrial products were not allowed. On the other hand, most consumer products, including grain and electronics, are available in the general markets, unless they are strategic materials or materials needed to supply production facilities. Even imported goods are allowed.

The establishment of a legal basis for general markets by North Korean authorities has rectified the precarious status of previous farmers' markets. That is, the market is now institutionalized for commercial transactions, and so is open every day. On the other hand, such legalization allowed authorities to restrict commercial trade to the market and thereby control it more effectively. Black-market transactions were reduced. At the same time, the state could claim the legal authority to collect rents and taxes from traders conducting business in the general market. These traders and these markets became a new source of state income.

With the 1998 constitutional revision, the scope of private

---

[14] Cabinet Order (Naegak Jisi) No. 24, and Cabinet Decision (Naegak Gyeoljeong) No. 27.

ownership was extended and an individual could engage in commercial activity. Individuals or organizations could legally sell consumer goods and agricultural produce from their garden plots or patches of land distributed by the state. Cottage industries were rapidly expanded. People began to make many consumer products at home or at their factories for sale in the markets. A variety of self-employed businesses such as restaurants and photo studios cropped up. Furthermore, some individuals went so far as to hire laborers under the name of cooperatives with the permission of the authorities.

The problem is the limited institutionalization of the markets without allowing private ownership of the means of production. This is a fundamental hindrance to maximizing the positive role of markets and the development of industry. On the contrary, this is conducive to an increase in illegal activity and black-marketeering. Although the authorities are well aware of the role of markets in mitigating the economic difficulties of North Korean residents, they are also concerned about the negative impact of marketization and its potential to undermine political stability. Therefore, authorities were driven by circumstance to legitimize markets, but have not done so on their own initiative, and do not welcome all of the effects such a move may bring about.

2. Protection of Commercial Activity and Private Property

As commercial activity was legitimized and an individual could accumulate personal wealth, illegal commercial activity was to be penalized and personal property was to be protected. The new criminal code introduced in 2004[15] was a departure from pre-

---

[15] Revised by the Standing Committee of SPA on April 29, 2004. It was

vious codes, reflecting these changes in economic practices and incorporating many new provisions to cope with these aspects of marketization.

Many new types of crime related to these newly allowed economic activities also began to surface, requiring a drastic increase of new articles in the criminal law code.[16] This expansion of criminal law in order to protect market activities was an expression of the strong will of the state to punish illegal commercial activity while encouraging legitimate actions. One thing that deserves notice in this new revision is the adoption of the principle of *nulla poena* for the first time in North Korea.[17] This means that what is not prescribed as a crime will not be punished, at least, on paper. The adoption of this principle was also one of the government's efforts to respond to international pressure against the abuse of human rights in the North, as well.

Under extraordinary pressure due to the difficulties caused by the North's economic situation, residents were forced to do whatever they could to provide for their subsistence. The collapse of the public distribution system resulted in widespread criminal activity and deviance from regulations defining social activities as people from all social standings and walks of life fought for survival. New forms of deviance that had not previously existed in the North and were previously unimaginable were now prevalent throughout the country. One of the measures employed to tackle this matter was to clearly prescribe what is allowed and what is not. The

---

revised twice in 2005.

16 The Criminal Code of 2004 has 305 articles, while the previous one had only 161.

17 Criminal Code (2004), Article 6. Article 10 of the previous criminal code allowed analogical interpretation and thus was criticized by the international community for failing to protect human rights.

new criminal code is one of the most important works drafted by North Korean authorities in order to deter people from committing illegal activities by criminalizing specific modes of illegal activity. In addition, the Administrative Penalty Law (*haengjeong cheobeol-beop*) was enacted to deal with minor offenses and misdemeanors.[18] Private ownership, as well as public, or state, ownership, is better protected due to the enactment of laws, as now, infringement on private property has been criminalized and authorities have the means to inflict penalties and compensation when damage has occurred.

3. Individual Responsibility Strengthened

As citizens have been left without state provisions for subsistence since the central government lacked the material resources to supply the people through its central rationing system, the vast majority of individuals and organizations had to support themselves. It was a fait accompli. The state also accepted the new reality and tried to accommodate the needs of the population while making only a minimum impact on political stability. Legitimizing commercial and market activity and expanding the scope of private ownership were part of this effort. As the scope of individual activity was expanded, the scope of individual responsibility also needed to be strengthened accordingly.

One of the most important laws reflecting this transformation is the Damage Compensation Law (*sonhae bosang-beop*),[19] which is the North Korean version of a general torts law. This law holds an

---

[18] Enacted on July 14, 2004, by the Standing Committee of SPA.
[19] Enacted in 2001 by the Standing Committee of the SPA, and revised in 2005.

individual or any legal entity liable for its tort when damage is inflicted. Monetary compensation is the rule, while restoration is allowed when possible. Victims can resort to this law and seek compensation through the courts when suffering damage or loss.

Under the socialist system, where the state is responsible for the provision of a citizen's livelihood, tort law was of little use. For example, when a person lost a leg in a car accident, rather than bringing a civil suit against the driver or receiving workers compensation, he would be transferred to a position he could manage after receiving treatment from the state, or would recover at home or in hospital free of charge. Even in the case of death, one's family would not suffer economically since the state provided sustenance rations. Therefore, a civil case could hardly arise, although the driver at fault may be punished by the authorities, depending upon the seriousness of the accident or degree of negligence involved.

However, with the collapse of the public distribution system, the North Korean authorities could no longer maintain their socialist system. Since an individual now has to rely on his or her own devices, the loss of the employment, for example, directly inflicts a financial burden on the individual or family. Therefore, damage to property or person should be compensated for by the responsible party. The Damage Compensation Law acts as a new mechanism for the protection of private property, and strengthens individual responsibility for negligent acts that inflict damage on others.

However, what is more important than laws in books is reality on the ground. It seems premature to assume that a victim would bring a case to court, or that the court would be capable of handling such a case. Since the entire bureaucratic system, as well as the judicial system, fails to command trust, people disregard government institutions and would not utilize the judicial system unless they are imposed upon to do so.

4. The 7/1 Economic Reform Measures

The most important measure to reform the North's ailing economic system was promulgated on July 1, 2002, and was called the "7/1 Economic Management Improvement Measures." The details of this measure and those that followed were a drastic departure from previous reform measures.

Its scope was very extensive and comprehensive. For example, the dual price system of state- and market-driven prices was abolished by the measure that accommodated market-driven pricing, which led to skyrocketing prices almost 20–30 times higher than formerly state-dictated prices. In order to make up for this price increase, workers' salaries were increased accordingly. The exchange rate for foreign currency was also adjusted to reflect the extremely high rate of exchange on the black market. Free distribution from the state was abolished,[20] while an incentive system was introduced. Central planning was eased, while autonomy and independence of respective organizations was strengthened. Professional management was emphasized in order to maximize profits. The state budget underwent diversification and divestment.

As a matter of fact, many of these measures were not implemented in order to bring about new outcomes, but rather, to recognize and legitimize fait accompli in practice. The state could not endlessly ignore a reality that was in conflict with state policy and laws. Authorities needed to rectify the gap and contrast between professed official policy and reality in order to prevent instability.

Of course, this measure could not resolve all the problems the North was facing. Inflation worsened with the new measure, yet it

---

[20] Residents now have to pay for basic utilities such as electricity and water, as well as housing rent.

was necessary to legitimize the previously illegal or unlicensed practices, which were widespread. Despite its faults, the 7/1 Measures significantly facilitated commercial activities and enhanced the role of markets in North Korea.

IV. New Legal Phenomena

1. Increase in Illegal Activities

The official system in the North could not keep up with changes in society. Laws as well as directives and orders from higher authorities failed to redress deviances or prevent illegal activities. Organizational control was relaxed, as well. In its place, new criminal laws enacted in 2004 defined new types of crimes concerning anti-socialist morality as well as anti-socialist economic activities. Inclusion of these new types of crimes indicates that these illegal activities were flourishing in the North. Although it is not anomie or chaos, most of these illegal acts are dismissed by authorities as long as they do not amount to a challenge or resistance to political stability or Kim Jong Il's leadership.

The enactment of new laws has not been effective in preventing or reducing illegal activities, which are still prevalent and are becoming more sophisticated. As long as the extraordinary shortage of food continues to jeopardize the survival of North Korean residents, the situation encouraging the growth of illegal activity will not be eased. The sharp discrepancy between the state-designated prices and market-driven pricing distorts distribution order and promotes illegal transactions.

At the same time, the revised law on criminal activity falls far short of reflecting the reality of the situation. Selling goods with higher prices than that of purchase is illegal. Brokerage or money-lending for interest is illegal, as well.[21] The authorities still formally believe that seeking profit without labor is against the socialist ideology that the North professes.[22] Although these kinds of actions are the very basic activities that allow for the functioning of markets, they are restricted or banned in North Korea.

Therefore, black-marketeering and smuggling is very popular. Private loan businesses, foreign currency trade, unlicensed self-employed businesses, and even underground factories are ubiquitous. Even the trade or sale of housing occurs freely, as long as the proper local authorities are bribed, despite the fact that houses are not subjects of private ownership, in principle.

Illegal transactions or activities do not remain within the realm of the individual. The economy of shortage forces employees of state enterprises within the planned economy to engage in illegal activities, as well. Theft and embezzlement are widespread throughout most state enterprises and cooperatives. Furthermore, the state enterprise itself engages in illegal activities such as smuggling in order to provide for its employees.

It is quite natural that corruption is very pervasive. In North Korea's current situation, where the legality of an activity is obscure and illegal activity is ubiquitous, officials are quick to exploit opportunities to gain headway. Officials do not remain passive helpers or mere takers of bribes, but rather, they are often accompli or collaborators in illegal activities. In particular, corruption of law enforcement officials is most serious, since they have the authority

---

[21] See Criminal Code (2004), Articles 110, 114, and 118; Administrative Penalty Law, Article 59.

[22] This is reminiscent of the Middle Ages in the West, where loan-sharking was banned to Christians since it was against the teachings of the Bible.

to enforce laws and can exercise unlawful discretion for their personal interests.[23]

As time passed, illegal activities undertaken for subsistence developed into businesses. In particular, when undertaken in collaboration with officials with power, a primitive type of entrepreneur has now come into view. This kind of change has intensified social conflict between the haves and have-nots. Individualism has strengthened throughout the collective society in North Korea.

Illegal activities in North Korean society are so pervasive in all walks of life and every field of society, regardless of rank and location, that people do not take them seriously. They do not feel guilty about committing unlawful acts, and they go so far as to justify their illegal behavior by attributing it to the state's nonobservance of its obligation to distribute necessities such as food. This displays the conflicting values and distortion of new policies authorities are faced with in the North in the wake of the transition of its economic and social system.[24]

2. Increase of Disputes

Increased transactions inevitably result in increased disputes. In North Korea, where transactions between individuals were extremely limited in the strictly controlled totalitarian society, private disputes were very rare. When private disputes did arise, they could be resolved within organizations to which the individuals concerned belonged. Individual deviance was effectively

---

[23] Dae-Kyu Yoon, *Bukhan jumin-ui Beopuisik Yeongu* (A Study on the Legal Consciousness of Residents in North Korea) (Korea Legislation Research Institute, 2005), 95–98. This research was conducted on the basis of interviews with more than 500 defectors from North Korea.

[24] Ibid., 53–57.

restrained through rigorous organizational life and ideological indoctrination. Individual interest was protected incidentally in the course of maintenance of public order. It was very unusual to need to resort to legal means for the protection of individual interests or social order. Therefore, dispute resolution processes for private interests were much undeveloped. It goes without saying that the individual does not have the right to sue the state or public authority, other than the entitlement to petition to a higher authority in the case of an unsatisfying decision or treatment from a lower organization.[25] Although a citizen is entitled by the Constitution to submit a petition or complaint, it is handled by the grace of the state but not on the basis of a citizen's rights.

Relaxation of law and order, along with the laxity of organizational control due to economic difficulties, changed individual attitudes toward government authorities and organizations in which these individuals were members. Individuals became more independent from the state and its organizations, since both the state and more directly engaged organizations lost important means of control over individuals in society due to the lack of resources and the inability to provide basic necessities to the people.

3. Recognition of the Importance of Law

As North Korean society faced unprecedented change and its existing control system had ceased to function, voluntary observation of instructions through an internalized sense of obedience to authorities became a thing of the past, and authorities began to pay more heed to the law. As citizens who used to behave themselves in accordance with directions from above have been allowed

---

[25] 1998 Constitution, Article 69.

more autonomy and freedom, the state now needs to provide more rules governing private relations among citizens in accordance with the expansion of this autonomy and freedom. Increased trade and communication with foreigners has also enhanced the North Korean government's understanding of the importance of law.

The highlight of this attitudinal change toward law was the publication of the general legal code in 2004, which was the first time North Korean law had been made publicly available to the outside world. The government emphasized that the law is the norm for action that a citizen should observe, and so published the code to help citizens to be aware of the laws and to observe them.[26] In fact, North Korea has enacted many new laws since the 1990s.[27] These new laws display a shift toward a more pragmatic expression of the desired social order, rather than the more ideo-logical one previously touted through an abundant use of political expressions embedded in the legal code. This means that law is now turning to social norms in order to govern reality and away from employing the law as a means for political propaganda.

Active dialogue and exchange since the inter-Korean summit of 2000 has produced many inter-Korean agreements, which have provided a number of excellent opportunities for North Korea to better grasp the importance of law. The formal format of North Korean legal statutes also changed, in particular, after close contact

---

[26] Law Publication (Beopnyul Chulpansa) (Pyongyang, 2004), The Code [Beopjeon], preface.

[27] For example, Commerce Law (Sangeop-beop) (1992), Finance Law (Jae-jeong-beop) (1995), Accounting Law (Hoegyeo-beop) (2003), Trade Law (Muyeok-beop) (1997), Invention Law (Balmyeong-beop) (1998), Trademark Law (Sangpyo-beop) (1998), Industrial Design Law (Gongeop doan-beop) (1998), Copyright Law (Jeojakgwon-beop) (2001), Computer Software Pro-tection Law (Computer Software Boho-beop) (2003), Software Industry Law (Software Saneop-beop) (2004).

and exchange with South Korean business and legal experts working for the development of the Kaeseong Industrial Complex and the Mount Kumgang Resort Area. After close coordination with South Korean counterparts regarding these inter-Korean efforts, the North began to employ the South Korean format of statute not only within these special zones, but throughout its legal code, including those laws governing the activities of everyday North Korean society, many of which were made public with the publication of the Criminal Code of 2004.

However, although there have been several tort cases against North Koreans by South Koreans in the Kaeseong Industrial Complex and Mount Kumgang Resort Area, none have been resolved through legal processes, but rather, were settled after tedious and toiling negotiations. Throughout the last twenty years of inter-Korean trade, there has been no dispute between North and South Koreans that has been resolved through judicial process. The North Korean judicial system is still not capable or ready to handle disputes involving foreigners. Considering the fact that a reliable dispute resolution system is a key to enticing foreign investment, the North's enactment of relevant laws has not been sufficient to ease the concerns of those interested in investment opportunities. The operation and application of such a system in practice is necessary to protect foreign investors.

V. Prospects for Future Change

1. Enhanced Role of Law and the Judicial System

As we have seen, law will have more importance since state control over the people of North Korea through other means such as indoctrination, directives, and organizational life is no longer as effective. As the state loses direct control over the people due to its inability to provide basic necessities through public distribution, it has to rely more on the law.

For example, the most prominent role of the court in North Korea, where other types of lawsuit are very unusual, was to handle divorce settlements, since divorce through simple agreement of the two parties was not allowed. Ordinary citizens went so far as to perceive settlement of divorce to be the most important role of the court.[28] Criminal cases were also unusual. Political crime is handled through a nonjudicial process, while many deviances are resolved through unofficial processes within more local organizations. Therefore, the social status of judges is actually much lower than that of police or other law enforcement officials. Professionalism is not a quality required of judges. A judge is elected by the Standing Committee of the SPA or the local People's Committee.[29] The role of the court in resolving disputes was negligible, aside from divorce. Since the role of law enforcement agencies is to protect the state and secure the socialist system, the most important qualification for them is not legal expertise, but rather, loyalty and devotion to the North Korean ideology and system. A legal system without professional expertise could hardly command trust in a society such as North Korea, where the public has lost confidence in the authorities.

On the other hand, the Lawyer's Act of 1993 prescribes the required qualifications of a lawyer. Those who are eligible to work as lawyers are those who are certified legal professionals, those

---

[28] Yoon, op. cit., 65.

[29] Article 4 of the Court Organization Act (*Jaepanso Guseong-beop*), which was most recently revised on November 19, 1998.

who have working experience of no less than 5 years in legal affairs, or those who have a professional license in a certain area and have passed the bar examination after a short-term course in legal education.[30] This qualification for working as a lawyer signifies that the state wants to equip the judicial system with legal professionals. Although there is no explicit professional qualification for a judge or prosecutor, we may assume that legal professionals have been elected or recruited in practice. This trend is likely to be reinforced as these social changes continue to unfold.

However, the vast majority of residents have to live their lives without assistance or guidance from the state, and there is now an enlarged sphere of independent activity of individuals and social entities. This means that legal relations among individuals and social entities have drastically increased. However, neither has an existing legal mechanism in place that is capable of handling the new phenomena brought about by these changes. Nor has the new legal system developed at a pace sufficient to keep up with the rapid change. It takes time to implement new laws and systems. Therefore, a legal vacuum, or lawlessness, often exists, and the gap between the legal preparedness and reality is significant. Where effective official mechanisms to resolve disputes have not yet developed, people seek self-remedies rather than resorting to ineffective and burdensome official means.[31]

However, the growing prevalence of the resort to self-remedy can hardly be long left outside the realm of state supervision, as the government's continued failure to offer legal recourse for dispute resolution would undermine the authority of both the state and the judicial system. The reason for implementing a provision

---

[30] The Lawyer's Act (*Byeonhosa-beop*), Article 20.
[31] Yoon, op. cit., 58–59.

to prohibit self-remedy in the new criminal law is to recover state authority and to further the government's desire to enhance the judicial system.[32] Several other provisions were also introduced to reinforce the judicial system. For example, interference with a law enforcement official's performance of duties is now a punishable offense;[33] threatening a witness or exacting revenge has been criminalized;[34] and non-execution of judgment will now be punished.[35] Although the introduction of these provisions was an expression of the government's effort to bring in a more effective judicial system, it would not be an easy task under the vague status of transformation. The state is very cautious and reluctant to undertake bold or fundamental changes due to concerns about political instability. Therefore, it takes time for various coherent mechanisms to fully support a market system.

2. Rise of Illegal Activity and Corruption

Even after the socialist economic system of central planning and public distribution teetered on the brink of collapse, the leadership has made clear its intention to maintain the old system wherever possible. Adoption of a primitive stage of market economics was not sought by official initiative, but was recognized fait accompli, and this situation has contributed to the broadening of the gap between reality and law. Until a new system replaces the current one with a full panoply of more sophisticated means, illegal activity and corruption will continue. In particular, the law

---

[32] Criminal Code (2004), Article 269.
[33] Criminal Code (2004), Article 221.
[34] Criminal Code (2004), Articles 237, 238.
[35] Criminal Code (2004), Article 256.

cannot function unless the government can provide basic necessities to the people. As long as the absolute quantity of supply is far short of demand, legal bans or punishment will continue to fail to curtail illegal activity. If new laws are provided without an improvement of material supply, illegal trade and corruption will simply develop into more sophisticated transactions, staying one step ahead of the law.

Unfortunately, the prospects for the improvement in material supply are discouraging as the spread of deviant behavior will continue to grow in both volume and diversity. The discrepancy between the law on the books and the law in action will also continue to grow as more laws are enacted and the role of law increases.

VI. Conclusion

North Korea is in transition from the legal perspective, too. There has been significant change in the law, including the Constitution, in order to cope with a new economic environment. Since the law is one of the most important means to govern social relations, North Korea also has taken advantage of law to cope with new social relations that have been emerging rapidly since the 1990s. In order to overcome the impoverished economic conditions and accompanying uncontrollable volume of deviance and illegal activities, the state has responded with legitimization, criminalization and punishment. Individual responsibility for torts has also been reinforced.

While the existing system is not functioning and a new system has yet to be institutionalized, there is bound to be confusion and a lack of laws. However, it is not likely that a new system will be established in the foreseeable future, considering the nature of the North Korean regime. In particular, the status of law in North Korea is quite different from that in a democratic society. The authority and effectiveness of the law is much lower than that of the directives of the Party, as well as words or teachings of its dear leaders Kim Il Sung and Kim Jong Il. In this regard, North Korea is a society that is ruled mainly by moral instruction and organizational edicts rather than by law, similar to the feudal society of the Middle Ages in the West or Confucian society in the East.

As long as the North fails to recognize a long-term vision, and denies fundamental and structural transformation, it will take longer to normalize its economic, social, and political situation. In particular, the nature of the regime, with its long-lasting one-man rule, will be a decisive obstacle to any drastic attempts at reforming the system.

As the socialist system does not function and the existing norms governing the people through socialist morality and dictatorial indoctrination no longer suffice for social control, the law will gain more efficacy and importance. The most remarkable virtue of the law is its stability and objectivity. Although the rule of law is not honored in North Korea, the law will be utilized now more than ever as it moves toward a market-driven economy and transactional relations among individuals continue to increase. Regardless of official policy imposed on the people, the change from the bottom up will have a snowball effect in the future and enhance the necessity of law. In particular, as those in the North gain increasing exposure to foreigners and the international community, the law will entertain a more positive role and merit in the coming in North Korea.

On the other hand, however, the vicious circle of legal functionality may continue unless economic conditions improve. The weakening of social control due to the shortage of supplies will demand more laws, but the efficacy of the law will decline since the law cannot govern reality and practice in action. Citizens will ignore and despise laws while officials exploit them at the cost of residents. The role of law in governing social relations will be undermined. Therefore, the fundamental structure of politics and economics is directly related to the development of the law in North Korea.

Bibliography

Kim Il Sung, *Kim Il Sung Works 1-42* (Pyongyang: KWP Press, 1996).

Kim Jong Il, *Selected Works of Kim Jong Il 1-14* (Pyongyang: KWP Press, 2004).

Park, Hyung-joong, *Bukhan-ui Kyeongje Kwanli Chegye: gigu-wa unyeong* (Economic Management System of North Korea: Organization and Operation) (Seoul: Haenam Publication, 2002).

Yoon, Dae-Kyu, *Bukhan jumin-ui Beopuisik Yeongu* (A Study on the Legal Consciousness of Residents in North Korea) (Korea Legislation Research Institute, 2005).

_____. *Bukhana Kyungjaekaehyukuel wehan Saroun Pardigm* (New Paradigm For North Korea's Economic Reform) (Seoul: Hanwool Academy, 2006).

_____. *Bukhanui Chejechunhwan khwa Beopjedo* (North Korea's Transformation and Legal Institution) (Seoul: Hanwool Academy, 2008).

Chapter 3

The Development of Farmers' Markets in North Korean Cities

⊣ Bong Dae CHOI and Kab Woo KOO ⊢

I. Introduction

Growing attention is being given to the development and changes of farmers' markets in North Korea.[1] A shortage of foodstuffs and basic necessities resulted from the failure of the state rationing system, as the nation's planned economy experienced near collapse in the latter half of the 1990s. This, in turn, led to the reemergence of the private economy, which had long been marginalized in the daily lives of North Korean people. More importantly, the symptoms of change seem to indicate the possibility of a system transformation, preceding examples of which can be found in other socialist states. Furthermore, the introduction of "Economic Management Improvement Measures" in July 2002 (known as 7/1 Measures), followed by reorganization of farmers' markets into "general markets" in March 2003, has led to the justification by the

---

[1] According to our survey of North Korean defectors, North Koreans have used the terms "market place" and/or "fair" more frequently since the 1950s than the term, "farmers' market." Given that it is the official term used by the North Korean government, however, the authors will use the term "farmers' market" throughout this paper.

North Korean government of these economic activities within the private sector.

The government proclaims, "The state will implement more aggressive policy measures to ensure the functioning of the market as a venue for meeting the social demand."[2] These developments evolving around the farmers' markets deserve attention, as they potentially signify a transformation of the North Korean system. Farmers' markets are one form of "socialist commerce" officially recognized by the North Korean government. However socialist they may be, farmers' markets are still markets in essence, displaying characteristics similar to those found in any other market, including the possible existence of black markets. While the establishment of general markets through expansion and reorganization of farmers' markets can be understood within the broader context of economic policy implementation under the planned economy, it could also be interpreted as the North Korean government's effort to bring under control and legalize the rapidly proliferating farmers' markets and black markets.

In light of North Korea's prolonged economic difficulty, many scholars have wondered whether such an expansion of market coordination mechanisms could eventually induce North Korea's transition. For this reason, much research has been focused on the period of the "Arduous March," in the 1990s, during which the farmers' markets began to show traces of black markets, gradually moving away from their traditional role of being part of the

---

[2] Although the renaming of farmers' markets as general markets was reported to have been originally limited to Pyongyang only, it would be safe to assume that farmers' markets in other areas have also become subjected to "aggressive management" under the planned economy (*Chosun Sinbo*, April 2, 2003). North Korea also began to use the term "economic reform" around this time (*Korea Central News Agency*, June 9, 2003).

socialist commerce system.[3] In order to understand the political
and economic implications of the proliferation of farmers' markets
in the latter half of the 1990s, however, one needs to look further
back into the history of farmers' markets.[4]

For example, was the expansion of farmers' markets a reaction
to the collapse of socialist trade around 1990 and the series of natural disasters during the first half of the decade, which led to the
failure of the state rationing system? Or rather, did these external
factors merely act as a catalyst for the proliferation of farmers'
markets, as more fundamental, immanent market forces that had
been suppressed under the chronic shortage situation have erupt-
ed under special economic and political circumstances, such as the
failure of the state rationing system or the death of their great
leader Kim Il Sung?

It is important to understand the underlying mechanism of
the expansion of farmers' markets because it helps in our efforts to
compare and contrast the farmers' markets in pre- and post-1990s,
and determine whether they show any trace of similarities, or are

---

[3] On political-economic implications of North Korea's farmers' markets during the 1990s, see Seung Ryul Oh, "North Korea's Strategy for Economic
Survival: Functions and Limitations of the Informal Sector (in Korean)," *Collection of Unification Research* 5, no. 2 (1996); Soo Young Choi, *North Korea's
Second Economy* (in Korean) (Seoul: Korean Institute for National Unification, 1998); Kum Sook Lim, "Characteristics and Development of North
Korea's Proprietorship (in Korean)," *Unification Economics*, March and April
(2002); Se Jin Chung, *Planned Economy to Market Economy* (in Korean) (Seoul:
Hakwool, 2000), ch. 3.

[4] On development of farmers' markets since Korea's liberation from Japanese
occupation, see Young Yoon Kim, "Economic and Social Impact of North
Korea's Black Markets (in Korean)," *Collection of Unification Research* 6, no. 1
(1997); or Jung Kil Chung and Chang Kon Jeon, "Analysis of the Realities of
Farmers' Markets in North Korea (in Korean)," *Rural Economics* 23, no. 2
(2000).

fundamentally and qualitatively different. A thorough understanding of the nature of the farmers' markets during these periods will help us to identify the potential for further market transition.

This chapter looks closely at the development of farmers' markets in three North Korean cities—Shinuiju, Chongjin, and Hyesan—from the 1950s through the 1980s. There are two reasons why we picked farmers' markets in city areas. First, we aim to identify the potential causes at the micro-level for such macro-level change as a market transition. Second, we aim to understand the relative autonomy these cities might enjoy even under such a centralized system as that found in North Korea. We picked the three cities of Shinuiju, Chongjin, and Hyesan for their close proximity to the Chinese border, which makes it relatively easier for us to access information through the North Korean people from these cities who have crossed into China.

We also aim to focus on the distinctive characteristics of each city. Despite the fact that all three are home to their respective provincial governments, their industrial backgrounds differ and make them distinct from each other. The industrial base in Shinuiju is light industry and logistics. Chongjin's industrial base is heavy industry. Hyesan's status was elevated from a town to a city when it became home to the newly established Ryangkang Province, and mainly houses primary industries such as mining and forestry. Another important topic that is undertaken in this research is to identify how these different industrial backgrounds influenced the development of farmers' markets in these regions.

II. Analytical Framework and Use of Data

1. Analytical Framework

In a "classical socialist system," as defined by Janos Kornai, legalized market coordination mechanisms such as farmers' markets are considered to be secondary, playing only a supporting role in ensuring the Communist Party's monopoly of power and their bureaucratic control over the nationalized planned economy.[5] Bureaucratic coordination mechanisms are based on an asymmetrical relationship of power among participants—a vertical linkage between the ruler and the ruled. On the other hand, market coordination mechanisms operate based on horizontal linkages that are established through voluntary transactions between participants. In most classical socialist systems, bureaucratic coordination mechanisms were predominantly favored.

It is, however, also true that they did not ignore market coordination mechanisms as a secondary tool, although the extent to which these were used varied from regime to regime.[6] Because,

---

[5] This management system operates as a subsystem of the socialist structure, controlling individual and organizational activities. Any ongoing relationship involving more than two people or organizations must be governed by established controls. Kornai divides these established controls into bureaucratic, market, self-governing, moral, and familial controls. J. Kornai, *Socialist System: The Political Economy of Communism* (Princeton: Princeton University Press, 1992), 91-109.

[6] For example, following class policies regarding farming communities, farmers' markets repeatedly went through drastic cycles, leading China to implement small-scale management. Cuba did so from the very beginning of socialization, and Romania reformed farmers' markets after suffering an economic crisis in the 1980s. Dorothy J. Solinger, *Chinese Business Under Socialism: The Politics of Domestic Commerce, 1949-1980* (Berkeley: University

theoretically, socialism is in transition from capitalism to communism, a socialist society inevitably requires the existence of a private-
sector economy, the "necessary evil" as a remnant of capitalism,
where market coordination mechanisms are at work.[7] As such, it is
fair to say that such market coordination mechanisms as farmers'
markets, legal or illegal, do not necessarily contradict the official
ideology of socialism.

The problem, however, is that this ideological explanation of
socialism can conceal the problem of inequality in the production
mechanism of the classical socialist system. We believe that the
development of market coordination mechanisms such as farmers'
markets is attributed to the inherent problems of the "shortage
economy" of the classical socialist system and a subsequent ration-

---

of California Press, 1984), ch. 6; Jorge F. Perez-Lopez, *Cuba's Second Economy*
(New Brunswick, NJ: Transaction Publishers, 1995), ch. 3; Horst Brezinski
and Paul Petersen, "The Second Economy in Romania," in Maria Los, ed.,
The Second Economy in Marxist States (New York: St. Martin's Press, 1990).

[7] Between a capitalist society and a socialist society is a revolutionary shift
from the former to the latter. Correspondingly, there is greater political transition, and then there is nothing for the government outside of proletarian
revolutionary autocracy—Paraphrased from Marx's "Kritik des Gothaer
Programms."—Karl Marx, F. Engels, *The Works of Marx* ((in Korean) (Seoul:
Kureum, 1988), 183. Kim Il Sung adopted Marx's social transition theory.
Differences existed, but he designated socialism as "communism's lower
level" and communism as the higher level. He also categorized socialism
into different "levels" such as the institutionalization period, transition, and
complete socialism.

As socialism was separated as a "level" institutionalization and transition
were designated as part of socialism. Kim Il Sung referred to the complete
triumph of socialism during the latter part of the 1980s. Sung Chul Kim,
"Analysis of Kim Jong Il's Understanding of Economics: Possibility and
Methods of Reform," *Research on Modern North Korea* 3, no. 2 (2000), 63-65.
Accordingly, the existence of farmers' markets and similar market measures
at the end of the 1980s did not cause "theoretical" problems.

ing system that tends to be anti-egalitarian. Our first assumption, therefore, follows that given the structure of the classical socialist system, the development of farmers' markets is inevitable.

According to J. Kornai, in a classical socialist system with a planned economy, sellers' control of the market is predominant to that of buyers, which results in "forced adjustment"—for example, forced substitution or stockpiling—of producers' and consumers' choices. Therefore, if a consumer in a shortage economy experiences monetary overhang, and somehow the consumer's demand can be fulfilled at the private-sector level, there arises the possibility that the monetary overhang could be consumed in a legalized free market or a black market.[8] This is the primary reason that market mechanisms such as farmers' markets did not cease to exist in the classical socialist system. As A. Walder points out in his research, when the state rationing system is used as a means to appease a certain group of people and only provides for them to maintain the vertical alignment of power, those who are excluded from the benefits of the state rationing system will tend to depend more on markets, whether they be legal or illegal.[9]

However, the existence of either legal or illegal market coordination mechanisms resulting from the shortage economy does not automatically lead to their proliferation. When one makes that assumption, there is the danger of falling into the trap of mechanical, schematized economic determinism. It also makes it difficult to explain the relative stability in North Korea during the "Arduous

---

[8] Kornai, *The Socialist System*, op. cit., 228-261. Classical theories regarding insufficient economies, J. Kornai, *Economics of Shortage* (Amsterdam: North-Holland, 1980).

[9] Walder called this type of tendency "communist neo-traditionalism." A. Walder, *Communist Neo-Traditionalism: Work and Authority in Chinese Industry* (Berkeley: University of California Press, 1985).

March." It follows, therefore, that proliferation of legal or illegal markets occurs when collective anti-market sentiment, which is continuously forced into the minds of the mass through the official ideology, is weakened. The collective anti-market sentiment is weakened when official ideology fails to pose substantial influence over the mass or when the state adopts market reforms as state policy. In other words, a shift in the minds of actors under the shortage economy is another cause for proliferation of farmers' markets. This is our second assumption, which takes into account the role of actors in explaining the development of farmers' markets.

Even under the economy of shortage, however, as long as economic crisis does not deepen, preventing social dissatisfaction from further spreading, and the bureaucratic system maintains its legitimacy of power, there may not be a shift in the collective mind of the masses that might otherwise force the classical socialist system to change. The expansion of markets in the form of black markets in the classical socialist system represents a shift in the minds of actors. In other words, the expansion of black markets is a phenomenon that can be seen when actors begin to develop political consciousness against the official ideology that leads to changes in their behavior.

Assuming that North Korea fits into Kornai's definition of the classical socialist system, it can also be assumed that North Korea operates under the economic structure of shortage. From 1950 to the 1970s, the shortage economy in North Korea and its selective state rationing system contributed to the development of farmers' markets, but the markets never grew in absence of serious economic crises. Farmers' markets did exist as a form of socialist commerce, but with North Korea's official ideology functioning as a tool to solidify the masses' collective anti-market sentiment, farmers' markets only played a secondary role, complementing the formal, planned economy.[10]

However, we also contend that as North Korea entered the 1980s and its economic situation deteriorated, the inflow of foreign products and the increase in domestic production outside the formal sector led to increased activities in not only farmers' markets but in black markets as well. As the regulations that had previously obstructed the development of spontaneous order disappeared, North Korean residents began to grasp the concepts of a market economy through a process of discovery, setting off the expansion of farmers' markets as well as black markets both within and outside the boundaries of farmers' markets.[11]

We discovered that the most important variable in this process was the significant weakening of the collective anti-market sentiment of the North Korean population. The existence of farmers' markets and the black markets that often shared the same physical boundary in the 1980s was the result of economic undertakings of North Korean people whose desire for economic autonomy grew as the state failed to provide rations. However, the weakening of the people's anti-market sentiment and the proliferation of farmers' markets progressed differently in the three selected cities, according to their socio geographic conditions.

---

[10] Despite their secondary role, the need for farmers' markets as a tool for stimulating production was recognized. "Slight bourgeois, selfishness" was promoted, and Kim Il Sung, in order to suppress left-wing criticism, responded by stating that it was a misanalysis. He spoke of "increasing party enterprise while being frugal on household goods," *Selected Works of Kim Il Sung* 20 (in Korean) (Pyongyang: KWP Publishers, 1982).

[11] For spontaneous order and the process of discovery see F. Haeik, translated into Korean by Park Sang Soo, *Individualism and Economic Order* (in Korean) (Seoul: Center for Free Enterprise, 1998).

2. Use of Materials: Interviews with North Korean Defectors

Given the lack of information available through official North Korean publications, interviews were conducted with North Korean defectors.[12] Defector interviews can be a useful method of gaining a more concrete, in-depth understanding of North Korean society. Particularly for the purpose of this chapter, in which we attempt to identify the dynamics of legal and/or illegal farmers' markets, the closed nature of the North Korean regime makes it extremely difficult to obtain credible information through official publications. It was therefore inevitable that we relied heavily on defector interviews as opposed to site visits or archival research in our effort to reconstruct the history of the development of farmers' markets.

For this chapter, we conducted in-person interviews, which we consider to be more effective than telephone or postal surveys, and both individual and group interviews were conducted. Individual interviews were especially useful in obtaining such information as personal connections, means of making extra, unofficial economic gains using their positions, and other illegal, unofficial economic activities—information North Korean defectors are often reluctant to disclose for various reasons. Since the purpose of the interviews was not for statistical processing, an open, unstructured interview technique was adopted in order to minimize interference by the interviewer and encourage the interviewees to speak freely on their personal experience and feelings using their own language. This type of in-depth interview is also useful in constructing oral history. It is, however, one that takes much time,

---

[12] For this endeavor, two rounds of in-depth interviews were conducted between 2001 and 2003. Of these, forty-nine interviews were chosen for analysis. The basic statistics of these interviewees are listed in the appendix.

as the result can be maximized when there is a certain level of trust built between the interviewer and interviewees.

Despite the positive attributes, one must not overlook the limitations of defector interviews.[13] Discerning whether a defector's view of the North has consciously or unconsciously shifted as a result of their learning or has been embellished after leaving North Korea is not an easy task. Most defectors spend three to four years in China and/or Russia before coming to South Korea, and their experience can affect their perception and attitude toward their understanding and evaluation of North Korea. This opens the possibility that the subjects' memory may be imperfect, and that they could try to intentionally omit or distort information for various personal reasons. In order to resolve this problem, information obtained from the defectors was cross-checked with information provided during other interviews and with other defectors, and was also compared to existing data for verification.

There is also the question of whether defectors can represent the general population of North Korea. There is a good chance that defectors do not represent the average North Korean citizens, but rather, represent the atypical group in the lower social and economic strata. In fact, most defectors who have entered South Korea either have family ties to Korea or overseas Koreans or are considered as "hostile" by North Korean standards.

It is, therefore, difficult to conclude that the results from the defector interviews are representative of the situation in North Korea. For the purposes of this study, however, interview questions were limited to market experiences, and as these defectors bought and sold in local markets, their experiences can be used to

---

13 Walder, *Communist Neo-Traditionalism*, op. cit., 255-269, points out problems with the limitations of a survey conducted on Chinese defectors.

understand the changes in the North's market-based economy. Finally, there is the issue of objectivity of the interpretation. "The politics of interpretation" is practically inevitable in social research, and so the authors of this chapter made conscious efforts to fully recognize their own values or biases that might be present, minimizing their impact on objectivity in order to maximize the persuasiveness of the interpretation of data.

III. Development of Farmers' Markets in the Three Cities: Pre-1970

1. Restrictions on and Justification of Farmers' Markets: Logic and Policy

1) Restricted Role of Farmers' Markets

Following the completion of collectivization of farms, factories and businesses in 1958, the North Korean government established farmers' markets in cities and counties throughout the country. This was based on the recognition that it would be impossible to avoid acknowledging the legality of farmers' markets while promoting production and attempting to ease the lives of its citizens. The North Korean government has always defined farmers' markets as "one form of enterprise where agricultural products and livestock from collective farms and private lots can be sold directly to citizens at a fixed location."[14] This official definition includes

---

[14] Kim Il Sung, "On the Socialist System and Related Theories (1969.3.1) (in Korean)," *Selected Works of Kim Il Sung* 23 (Pyongyang: KWP Publishers, 1983), 465. One example of modern North Korean economics and the very different beginnings of farmers' markets can be found in Dong Ky Lee, "So-called Price Measures in Socialist Society's Farmers' Market (in

restrictions on sellers' and buyers' market participation, items permissible for sales, transaction rules, and the physical boundaries of the marketplace where the goods can be sold. Under the regulatory premises, farmers' markets operating outside the planned economy are officially endorsed as a form of socialist commerce and granted a position as the only legal markets in the unplanned economic realm.

However, even if the farmers' markets are defined on a theoretical level as "unorganized markets" (traditional markets) that are transitory and therefore bound to fade away as productive forces develop in reality, the possibility of private transactions and resultant private gains leading to potential sprouting of spontaneous capitalism cannot be overlooked. While they did not attempt to abolish the farmers' markets, North Korean authorities made sure that the markets did not overly expand, and limited the markets' role as secondary and peripheral to the official planned economy. In order to institutionalize the "regulated proliferation" of farmers' markets, North Korean authorities implemented a number of preparatory measures before establishing the farmers' markets.

2. Isolation of Supply and Demand in Farmers' Markets

Until at least the early part of the 1980s, North Korean farmers' markets did not deviate significantly from the authorities' policy objective of "restricted proliferation." Several explanations can be given here but most of all, it is not unrelated to the fact that North Korean authorities have implemented a number of institutional mechanisms to curtail any undesirable side effects prior to the

Korean)," *Kim Il Sung University Newspaper* (Philosophy, economics) 44, no. 3 (1998).

establishment of farmers' markets. This also means, however, that a cause for tension with the planned sector as the role of the farmers' markets grew out of the authorities' restricted definition can be found in possible malfunctioning of these mechanisms.

First, after the socialist restructuring, North Korean authorities saw to it that there was no chance of a revival of the idea of those outside of the agricultural realm selling at farmers' markets. Of course, the outcome was predictable, that the largest group likely to be upset was the individual trader. Apart from efforts to eliminate this group, the authorities also created consumers' cooperatives in 1946 for small traders and peddlers in cities and rural areas and in 1947 created, on an expansion basis, joint productive bodies comprised of home manufacturers and handicraftsmen who were engaged in both production and consumption activities.

By the time the socialist restructuring was officially announced as completed in 1958, most of these groups were reorganized into consumers' cooperatives and producers' cooperatives and had been incorporated into the official planned economy.[15] Through these measures, the authorities were able to put under control the social class that was by far the largest in terms of number, the most isolated and dispersed given the petty, trifling nature of their economic activities and therefore often out of reach of the state. It is for this reason that there were hardly any peddlers that could be

---

[15] Following liberation, there were three factions of cooperative trade groups. The smallest peddlers were formed as the "Cooperative Trade Group," small-scale, dispersed private businesses operating along streets, or small-time traders (including food) in farming communities formed "Production/Trade Cooperative Group," and the basic city market traders and stores formed localized groups similar to the "Production/Trade Cooperative Group." Kim Young Hee, *Individual Business's Socialistic Restructuring Experience* (in Korean) (Pyongyang: Social Science Printers, 1987), 18-27, 72-76.

seen in cities or in rural areas up until the 1970s, and only by the late 1980s, when the economy had already fallen deep into a crisis, did peddlers and home manufacturing reappear in some city areas where farmers' markets took shape.

Second, in order to repress supply to the farmers' markets, North Korean authorities attempted to control the flow of goods that had the potential to be smuggled into the farmers' markets. This was because immediately after the Korean War, small traders were not only in control of the flow of most grain and agricultural products, but were also engaged in entrepreneurial "small and medium-scale production of daily necessities" in connection with farmers who would often provide necessary raw materials for them. This drove the state to strengthen and expand operations in order to bring individual farms under the umbrella of agricultural cooperatives, so that by 1957 the state was able to ensure that all agricultural products and cereals, with small exceptions, were funneled to the state through the state purchasing mechanism and consumers' cooperatives.

By taking hold of the production base, North Korean authorities were able to control both the volume and type of agricultural products that could be sent to farmers' markets.[16] In addition, as

---

16 Around that time, North Korea's agricultural purchasing was divided into state purchasing and individual purchasing. With state purchasing, obligatory purchasing, purchase by subscription, and free purchasing were all used. Light industry's raw materials and "the most important agricultural products" fall under this system. It follows that grains and cereals, planned production, and distribution fall under obligatory procurement. Individual purchasing including the likes of individual enterprises (and cooperative trade groups) dealt with goods produced in various regions, and in order to establish a fund, the focus was on "all types of agricultural products" not part of the state purchasing scheme. "Expansion of Our Country's Socialist Commerce," in Democratic People's Republic of Korea School of Science

North Korean authorities made sure that any vegetables and agricultural goods produced through side farming at agricultural cooperatives, and not subject to state purchasing, could only be sold via their official sales outlet in cities and towns, the only produce that could be sold at farmers' markets were excess vegetables and other agricultural/livestock products that had been produced individually.

Third, on the premise of a functioning state distribution system for foodstuffs and daily necessities, North Korean authorities banned urban residents from participating in farmers' markets by forbidding the sale of agricultural goods that were subject to state purchasing.[17] Authorities reinforced these efforts institutionally by replacing the markets' grain distribution function with a food rationing system based on state-mandated prices. In 1946, North Korean authorities implemented a state rationing system for limited classes such as workers, students and office workers, gradually expanding over time to cover more people. By November 1957, the Cabinet banned independent sale of grains completely by legislating articles 96 and 102. The state rationing system was fully in place by this time covering everyone except for members of agricultural cooperatives, thereby completing the regime's ban on participation of urban residents in farmers' markets.[18]

Economic Law Research Center, *Building the Socialist Economy in Our Country* (in Korean) (Pyongyang: School of Science Publishing, 1958), 304, 331-332, 347-348.

[17] Through the retail industry's distribution web, this type of consumable distribution could only occur under the state distribution system, of which the state was the sole user. This is an important factor of socialist commerce, that is, "Planned distribution of products for the citizens." Kim Il Sung, "Regarding the Improvement of the Product Distribution Scheme while Increasing Production of the People's Consumables (1958.6.7) (in Korean)," *Selected Works of Kim Il Sung* 12 (Pyongyang: KWP Publishers, 1981), 313.

3. The Shaping of Farmers' Markets: 1950s

1) Spatial Control over Farmers' Markets in Regional Cities

Institutional mechanisms that were meant to encourage limited expansion of farmers' markets also prevented people from participating in other unrestricted markets, eventually integrating these markets into the controlled realm of the state distribution system. First, the authorities reorganized preponderant traditional markets as "people's markets" after Korea was liberated from Japan. At the same time, the authorities reestablished markets by creating permanent markets in city centers, while in city suburbs and rural areas they allowed markets to be set up regularly for a fixed number of days. Through these physically restrictive measures, the state attempted to control the traditional markets.[19] Also, in 1950, a Cabinet resolution restructured people's markets into "rural markets" and established "farmers' markets" in cities where provincial governments are located, allowing only farmers to sell

---

[18] Young Kyu Kim, *Analysis of the Level of North Korean Material Consumption* (in Korean) (Seoul: Institute for Korean Unification,1984), 70. At the same time, it was announced that grain in the possession of individual traders was to be gone by December 1, 1957, and that commercial transactions of grain were to be strictly prohibited (*Rodong Sinmun*, "The Task of Establishing a State-run Monopolized System for the Purchase and Sale of Grain," 10 Nov. 1957). The general rationing system could push for even distribution of consumables to the people during times of war and scarcity; however, during World War II, the Soviets employed a ration system, but black-market and open market prices were set noticeably lower causing the circulation of consumables to focus less on the state stores and more on bazaars. Julie Hessler, "Postwar Normalization and its Limits in the USSR: the Case of Trade," *Europe-Asia Studies* 53, no. 3 (2001), 448.

[19] "Permanent Markets" were "opened 150 days of the year," and part-time markets were markets open less than 150 days. Kim Young Hee, *Individual Business's Socialistic Restructuring Experience* (in Korean), 33-34.

grains and other agricultural produce.[20] This can be considered as reinforcement to the earlier measure of restructuring traditional markets into people's markets as farmers' influence in this traditional arena was still relatively securely in place.

On the other hand, in the post war era the authorities established state-owned stores along the main streets of residential areas in the cities, gradually increasing public access to the stores, and established farmers' markets within the traditional market spaces. For example, if we look at Chongjin or Shinuiju, we can find that while department stores were established in city centers and general stores were specialized into a manufactured goods store, a grocery store, and a seafood store, farmers' markets were allowed to be located in only a few traditional market areas.[21] In light of these moves by the authorities, we can see that not only did the government's control over farmers' markets include systemic measures and subsequent physical restrictions but also decided the actual location of the markets.

2) Conditions of the Farmers' Markets: 1950s

In the latter portion of the 1950s, main farmers' markets in Chongjin included the Kunwha Market in the Sinam district (the central market), the Songpyung Market in the Songpyung district, and the Ingok Market in the Chungam district. The Kunwha and Songpyung markets had been in operation since the Japanese occupation era and were located in downtown. Since they were

---

[20] School of Social Sciences, Economic Research Institute, *Economics I* (in Korean) (Pyongyang: Social Science Printers), 448. In a piece introducing Pyongyang's first farmers' market, this change can be verified. Lee Chun Young, "The Women Welcoming the Farmers' Markets (in Korean)," *Korean Women* (April 1950).

[21] C8, C18-1, *Rodong Sinmun* (15 Mar. 1958), 3.

Chongjin's largest markets, it can be assumed that they were still operating on a permanent basis even after the liberation. Of the two, the Kunwha Market, specializing in seafood trade, was the larger. According to a defector (C18-1), these two markets were very busy even up until the mid-1950s. However, as consumers' cooperatives were established and became active the role of these markets began to wane fast. This was because the consumers' cooperatives offered a wider selection of products and could sell them at lower prices. Also, another reason was that urban residents could more easily access these centrally located department stores, grocery stores, and manufactured goods stores as opposed to the markets. As a result, by 1958, when these two markets were turned into farmers' markets, there were hardly any transactions taking place, significantly reducing the role of these markets (C5, C18-1).

Unlike the other two markets, the Ingok Market was set up as a temporary wartime market by Kunhwa Market traders who had moved to a safer place. As such, the size of the market was much smaller than the other two markets. Nevertheless, most consumer goods were traded through the Ingok Market, and one could even find medicinal supplies within the market (C18, C18-1).[22] As the war came to an end, the wartime boom lasted only so long thereafter, and most refugees moved back to the city, and the Ingok Market was the first of the three markets to dry up. There may have been other regular farmers' markets in areas like the Ranam district, which is located farther away from the city, but this needs to be verified.

---

[22] Because Chongjin was established as a city for heavy industry, it was heavily targeted by the U.S. in attacks on the industrial sector of North Korea. During this upheaval, residents headed to the markets at any break in the action. Kim Shin Jo, *I Speak My Sad History* (in Korean) (Seoul: Dong A Publishers, 1994), 95.

When Korea was liberated from Japan, Shinuiju had two major markets in two different locations, both throwbacks to the era of occupation. The Chaeha Market, which was located in the city, took a direct hit during the war and was put out of operation for some time, but in the 1950s it began operating as a permanent market (S9). The other one, the Namsong District Market, was located on the outskirts of the city and opened regularly for farmers in the vicinity. Unlike the permanent Chaeha Market, it opened every tenth day during the 1950s (S4-I).

According to witnesses, the Chaeha Market had a sign that said "*Chaeha-ri* People's Market" at the entrance until the latter half of the 1950s when it was transformed into a farmers' market. And the market was packed with traders just like Chongjin's Kunwha and Songpyung Markets up until its transition to a farmers' market. It is interesting to look at the case of the Chaeha Market from the time of liberation to the transition to a farmers' market, as this would give insight into the restructuring of unorganized markets. As "socialist restructuring" officially became complete in 1958, stores were set up in the Chaeha Market with signs that read manufactured goods store, dried herbs store, and seafood store. These stores were originally called "consumers" cooperative shops, and used to be owned by individuals until around the liberation.[23]

Hyesan's status was elevated from *eup* (town) to *si* (city) only in 1954, as Ryangkang Province was created and the city became

---

[23] S4-1. This cannot be concretely verified through verbal evidence, but it appears that the same kind of restructuring occurred in Chongjin's Kunwha Market. In 1957 many people from traditional business towns such as Kaesong and Hamhung cities have pictures of permanent markets and markets in farming communities. Larry Resel (pictures), Seung Jong Baek (writing). *West German Master Carpenter Resel's North Korean Retrospective* (in Korean) (Seoul: Hyohyung Press, 2000).

home to its provincial government. As such, Hyesan was considerably less developed than Chongjin or Sinuiju. Perhaps due to these conditions, or perhaps due to the mountainous terrain around the city, by the late 1950s there was only one farmers' market in front of Hyesan Station, the same spot where markets used to be set up during the Japanese occupation era. Although this was the only market in the area and located in the heart of the city, it still opened every tenth day. Based on these facts, one can infer that the farmers' market in Hyesan was decidedly smaller than the farmers' markets in Chongjin or Sineuiju and was not all that active even before it was turned into a farmers' market in 1958 (H7). As we have seen so far, except for the case of Hyesan, where the development of the city (and hence the market) itself lagged much behind that of Chongjin and Shinuiju, traditional markets in the subject areas remained relatively active until at least 1957 whether they were called the "farmers' market" or "people's market."

3) Austerity in Domestic Consumption and Peripherization of Farmers' Markets: 1960s–1970s

(1) Weakening of the State Distribution System and People's Empirical Realization

Production of consumer goods in North Korea came under pressure for various reasons during the 1960s. These factors included the structural restraints of increasing planning, priority investment in the heavy industry sector, and excessive investment in the military sector in accordance with the state economic plans and other distorted resource allocation structures. These factors perpetuated tensions within the North's economic management system. This can be seen, for example, in North Korea's discussions during the late 1960s on the limitations to the strategy for extended economic growth and its coming to grips with a plan to overcome them.[24]

The tensions created within the planned economy in the early 1970s from these problems brought about a weakening of the state distribution system for foodstuffs and daily necessities.[25] Follow-

---

[24] Kim Il Sung criticized that "even in recent times leaders and academics in some sectors ... while reducing the preparations for the expansion of production in order to rebuild, the capacity to increase production in order to develop the economy and increase its size is diminishing. ... Preparations for expansion of industry are slowly decreasing while production speed is falling off." Kim Il Sung, "Regarding Several Theoretical Issues Regarding the Socialist Economy," 444-445. According to one witness, the North's economic tendency during the 1960s and 1970s could be summarized, "The 1960s plan was to eat and survive, from the beginning of the 1970s, there was a lack of daily necessities, and since the middle of the 1970s material and electrical shortages were faced" (E1). Also, in the early 1970s the state looked into a system for selling foodstuffs rather than providing them through a rationing system. Kim Il Sung, "Regarding the System and Method of Government Enterprises as Cooperative Businesses Organize (in Korean) (1985.10.22)," *Selected Works of Kim Il Sung* 39, 243.

[25] The planned procurement scheme for foodstuffs also helped to increase tensions within the economy. One defector stated, "While producing, all the materials concerned with the product are used. For example, all production must be in line, down to the screw, bolt, nut ... Well, with this kind of plan, it is not individual items but themes that collapse. Every few years, many new products come out, so much electricity is needed. While only 1,000,000 kw is available, one and a half, two times that amount is demanded, so that is how the baseline of the plan is set from the top and fed to the lower ranks ... the same with the state stores; people's lifestyles, needs of heavy industry drive decisions ... even in wool production when a certain quota is set, if it causes tensions at the production level, this causes tensions in the state stores as well ... due to their passivity and conservative nature (due to the sharp reprimands that are handed down) the demands of the lower groups cannot be voiced. When plans are handed down that don't line up with the reality of the economy, the plans are set and they turn their backs ... plans are never fully completed ... North Korea has moved toward planned enterprise since the middle of the 1970s. Beyond that, mount the

ing the full implementation of a centralized state distribution system in 1958, the government provided North Korean laborers and workers with an average of 700 grams of food per person per day. However, around 1973, authorities began to withhold two days' worth of food out of every 15 days' rations and set it aside for war preparation. Not only that, but children's supplements were also "reduced according to age." Additional reductions were made under the flag of nationalism, so that by the end of the 1970s, one month's worth of food rations had been reduced by 10-15 percent.[26]

Chollima" (the *Chollima* is a mythical flying horse, and the *Chollima* Movement symbolized increased production) (E4). "While moving toward cooperatization, two years passed and it was impossible for the state plan to call for increases in grain production and then later scale back. Because one year saw a bumper crop, the state plan called for more regardless of whether the next year did well or not. Because of this, living became increasingly difficult" (C17-1). The previous statement (E-4) mentioned the *Chollima* movement. This motivation to increase production included "people's high revolutionary pitch" and according to Kim Il Sung, "Regarding the Complete Manifestation of the Highest Vitality Through the Centralization and Detailing of the People's Economic Plan (in Korean) (1956.9.23)," *Selected Works of Kim Il Sung* 19 (Pyongyang: KWP Publishers, 1982), 461-464; and Kim Il Sung, "Regarding Several Theoretical Problems with the Socialist Economy (in Korean)," 446.

[26] C1, C3-1, C8, S8. According to C8, who worked on a cooperative farm in (A) town in North Ham, as early as December 1969, rations were reduced by two days' worth. It was explained that "every day is 700 g, making one month's ration just over 8 kg, so an additional two day's worth was cut. When the announcement was first made, exactly 700 g were sealed and delivered, out of every 15 deliveries, two were held back, and that was life. After the late 1970s, that announcement went away but even less rations were given. Rather than 700 g, only 589 g per day were given. This was not enough so, many people were borrowing rice. Rations were eaten, rice was given, and some was shared and that was how we lived. Rice was gone after ten days, so there were many people who came to borrow rice" (C3-

During the mid 1970s even city laborers began to see changes in the rationed basic necessities. By 1967, the authorities had already implemented controlled sale of basic non-grain foodstuffs.[27] By 1974, they broadened the list of products that were not allowed for independent sale, thus enhancing their control over the distribution of necessities. In addition, during this time ration cards for foodstuffs, manufactured goods, and fuel began to be issued and a household ration card system was put into effect.[28] The introduction of the card system was indicative of the shortage problem and, in fact, some state-owned stores did fail to carry enough supply for people by around this time.[29] The mid-1970s saw the deterioration of the distribution system for food and daily necessities and urban residents experienced suppressed consumption.

Examining the effects of the weakening distribution system on consumption by the people after the mid-1970s can shed some

---

1). The ration system's announcement created a network of compatriots. Good Friends Network, *North Korean Talk* (in Korean) (Seoul: Paradise Publishers, 2000), 69.

[27] C22-1, who lived in North Ham's (B) town, stated that since October 1967, soybean paste, salt, sugar, and other non-food items could only be purchased in amounts corresponding with the number of mouths to feed in the family.

[28] Purchases were divided between allotted goods received with the ration card and unrestricted goods. Allotted goods were rationed per month or per year, and per person and were available with the ration card at nationalized stores. Unrestricted goods were also available at the national stores, and could be purchased at will. Kim Young Kyu, op. cit., 120-125.

[29] C3-1, C6-1, C10, C14, C17, and more verbal accounts all indicate that the ration card system was implemented around 1975. According to one account, during the 1960s, display items were of high quality, but what was actually purchased was of much lower quality. After 1974, many display items were not even available for purchase. Shoes, socks, school supplies, etc. were not for sale (S12).

light on whether or not they sought out instruments to make their living outside the official state distribution system. Personal experiences of defectors from the Chongjin area can be used to reconstruct a consumption pattern of the people at the time.[30] Local party officials, security agents, "powerful" administrators, and those working in the distribution sector or in state-owned stores, as well as teachers and doctors, were not subjected to food shortages (C4, C14, C17).[31] Unskilled laborers, office workers, and the like faced no particular trauma due to food shortages, but they could purchase only limited amounts of non-grain food items or clothing with the wage they earned (C10, C11).

On the other hand, those in the lowest level of the social strata faced a serious food shortage problem even at the end of the 1960s. For example, those households on collective farms found it difficult to get by only on what was provided by the rationing system (C15). And by the mid 1970s, even those laborers with many children living in urban areas had to live on porridges.[32] Those living in the city would form a rice club so they would take turns receiving contributions from other members of the club.[33]

---

[30] It is not easy to reconstruct the consumer lifestyle of the Shinuiju or Hyesan defectors based on their testimony. That is why only Chongjin is mentioned. It is believed that the consumer lifestyle during the 1960s and 1970s was similar in the three cities.

[31] In the fall, at the outset of kimchi-making season, the collective farms on the outskirts of the city first provide vegetables to the party and government officials. Next are the businesses (C17). C4, who was a doctor, said that there were many opportunities to obtain meat and vegetables needed for medical care through non-official channels.

[32] C14 stated that in the neighborhood where (s)he had previously lived, 3-4 of around 26 households suffered this fate.

[33] Testimony verifies these cases in South Hamkyung's (A) city, and North Hamkyung's (B) town (C3-1, C8). According to C3-1, even worse off than those mentioned above, the "destitute" made up for food shortages by

After the introduction of the ration card system, non-grain food supplies and manufactured goods were hardly made available to ordinary citizens. Notwithstanding their poor quality, soy sauce and soybean paste were still provided through the state distribution system through the end of the 1980s. However, eggs, clothing, shoes, and other products were not always available and could only be bought when stores carried a supply (C3-1, C10, C18). Toward the end of the 1970s, department stores in downtown Chongjin were running out of manufactured goods.[34] Those working on collective farms usually purchased products—cloth, shoes, and clothing—that had been set aside for farmers or bought basic necessities with cash earned from the sale of vegetables. Their conditions, however, were not any better those that of those living in the city (C21-1, C17).

However, overall, the residents of these three cities did not face any major difficulties as a result of the cutback in the rationed goods. Most of those interviewed stated that compared to the 1960s, certain sweets and non-grain foodstuffs were more difficult to come across in state-owned stores during the 1970s; however, most people still found ways to adjust to the reduction in the rationed goods. One interviewee succinctly describes the situation in the 1970s as follows:

> Until the 1970s, things were relatively OK. As long as you
> worked, you still received rations and pay. No one received

---

collecting acorns. In North Hamkyung's (C) town, at the beginning of the 1970s the same situation was faced by those in the lowest class (C1). State distribution varied slightly from region to region.

[34] C17. Goods available for purchase were limited in the department stores. High-grade cloth, wedding gifts, trunks, etc. were available, but the average person rarely needed to make these types of purchases (C14, C18, C21).

more than enough, but no one starved to death either. We just lived somewhere in between these two extremes. Those who worked hard were slightly favored (C-17).

(2) Individual Side Jobs and Peripherization of Farmers' Markets

Despite the shrinking food rations and opportunities to purchase daily necessities, the majority of the interviewees cited the state distribution system as the primary reason people have been able to maintain their subsistence living. Also, goods normally difficult to find in state stores, such as cooking oil, pork, and fish, or luxury items such as alcohol and tobacco, were occasionally provided to people as "gifts" on certain statutory holidays, and these supplied no small amount of supplementary support to people's lives (C8, C10, C14, C21). This is not to say, however, that people did not engage in side jobs to improve their living conditions during the 1960s and 1970s. They were engaged in roughly two types of side jobs.

The first category is linked to the state distribution network or public service facilities. In this category, women earned additional income by working at factories' or enterprises' home manufacturing groups or cooperatives.[35] However, testimonies and the authorities' continued encouragement for such efforts rather show that this type of side jobs was not always popular.[36] A slightly more

---

[35] For example, by-products from Shinuiju's wool spinning factory are gathered and children's clothing, scarves, gloves, etc., are made by small, family-centered working groups (*Rodong Sinmun*, 20 Jan. 1961), 4; *Rodong Sinmun* (8 Nov. 1961), 2, *Chollima* (February 1961), picture archives.

[36] For example, Kim Il Sung, "Regarding Strengthening of Party Activities while Tightening up Household Activities (in Korean) (1965.11.15~17)," *Selected Works of Kim Il Sung* 20 (Pyongyang: KWP Press, 1982), 94-95,

profitable and therefore more aggressively pursued side job was selling dried pollack or dogskin leather for foreign currency, and then purchasing hard-to-find high-quality women's clothing or similar products (C8, C14). Up until the 1970s, however, raising pigs or dogs at home and selling them for a side allowance only applied to those few who were often involved in the public distribution network because "it was not that people had difficulty buying feed for animals, but because the state still provided rations, people were not in such dire need. Although it was no feast we could still eat three square meals a day" (C14).[37]

The other option was to engage in side work that was not linked to the state distribution network. Along this line of work was primarily farmers' participation in farmers' markets, which is partially acknowledged by North Korean authorities. During the mid- to late 1970s, the authorities warned against farmers' engagement in illegal exchanges in the markets,[38] and according to several

---

Selected Works of Kim Il Sung 33 (Pyongyang: KWP Press, 1987), 177-178. C14 hand-knitted gloves and socks, to be sold at the local store. In the neighborhood, there were a few households that carried on this kind of side work. In the early 1970s, money sent from Japan was used to set up a small family cooperative, and one woman from Hamheung was bringing in more income from the cooperative than her husband made as a steel worker. This is one example, but side work that brings in this kind of income was not easy to come by. If it were, it would stand to reason that more women would take their 300 g of food rations and stay at home working. Soon Duk Chung, "Pil Nam's Rainbow-Striped Clothes," Institute for Korean Women's' Social Research, *Lives and Dreams of North Korean Women* (Seoul: Institute for Culture and Society Research, 2000), 130.

[37] Farmers had private lots and raised domestic animals, yet it was difficult to find different side jobs outside the realm of the state purchases. In most districts, chicken, dog, pig, etc., was raised, and wool or animal hide was sold in order to buy wares such as rice bowls or other manufactured goods (E2).

testimonies, at least in Chongjin and Hyesan, this type of trade in the farmers' markets was rare. In Chongjin, for example, the most action one could find was through the elderly selling chili powder, cabbage seeds, taffy, bean pancakes, or some dyes in the farmers' markets for some pocket money.[39] However, Shinuiju was a bit different than Chongjin or Hyesan. Some elderly women in the farmers' markets were nominally "farmers," but in actuality, they were often acting as "middlemen."[40] This phenomenon probably dates back to the Japanese occupation era when Shinuiju was known to be a logistical hub with deep-rooted commercialism in the daily lives of the people.

Apart from this type of side work in the farmers' markets, yet another, more informal type of side job was held by repatriated North Koreans (returnees). Returnees began trading some time in the 1960s, as can be seen in Chongjin and Shinuiju, and it was usually the married women who were active in the markets.[41] These

---

[38] For example, Kim Jong Il criticized that "Some farm workers raise dogs or chicken and sell at high prices in the farmers' market rather than the national procurement organ." Kim Jong Il, "Strengthen Party Guidance over Agricultural Accounting, and Set This Year's Agricultural Yield at a New High (in Korean) (1976.2.6)," *Selected Works of Kim Jong Il* 5 (Pyongyang: KWP Press, 1995), 273. "Regarding a Few Tasks that Party Directors Need to Break Away From (in Korean) (1978.11.10)," *Selected Works of Kim Jong Il* 6 (Pyongyang: KWP Press,1995), 152.

[39] C1, C8, C14, C21-1, C22. In the 1970s in Chongjin's largest downtown market, Ingok Market, elderly peddlers numbered less than 20-30 (C14).

[40] For example, these women would find cooking oil or other hard-to-come-by supplies and introduce the houses that could easily sell them (S12).

[41] When Japanese-Koreans returned to the North from the end of 1959 to the late 1960s, most settled in cities like Pyongyang, Wonsan, Hamheung, Chongjin, and Shinuiju. These people settled in Shinuiju because of its important role in the transport network between the North and China, and because of being a conduit for Chinese troops withdrawing following their

women faced relatively the worst living conditions, and were forced to sell the goods they had brought with them or sell high-quality products their relatives sent them from Japan in order to supplement their needs. They would tend to sell or trade for other products, such as watches, clothing, blankets, sugar, and other goods. These goods were often sold to wealthier families.[42] This type of black market trading was a result of the coinciding interests of those who were financially better off and seeking higher-quality goods and those who are seeking supplementary income.[43] This kind of "black market" sporadically formed as a result of the returnee trade in Chongjin or Shinuiju areas and had therefore nothing to do with the farmers' markets.

Another form of side jobs usually took place at the end of the growing season on collective farms following the division of crops. Poor farmers lacking food supplies or cash would take long-grain

---

participation in the Korean War. Because of this geographic factor, for two or three years following the 1959 famine in China's three northeastern regions, many Chinese and Koreans fled to Shinuiju, leading to the appearance of many Chinese goods at Shinuiju's Jaeha Market. Because many refuge seekers were unable to return home, and rather took up residence in Shinuiju, it became one of the cities not only having many returnees, but also many foreigners (S-4).

[42] S3, C3-1, Kim Mi Ja, "Is Return to Japan Possible?," Institute for Korean Women's Social Research, *Lives and Dreams of North Korean Women* (in Korean) (Seoul: Institute for Culture and Society Research, 2000), 155. These and similar examples are in Chung Soon Duk, "Pil Nam's Rainbow-Striped Clothes," 130-131.

[43] State authorities did not crack down hard on this type of repatriated trader. C3-1, "up until the 1980s there were no traders in North Korea, and repatriates selling goods they had returned with were not thought of that way. When it did come out (their way of life), it was looked upon with understanding." However, since goods sent from Japan were banned across the board from sale in legitimate markets, there were more than a few who were afraid to sell them (C13-1).

rice and sneak into the cities to trade it for glutinous rice in order to acquire food supplies for self-consumption or to make some hard currency. Some instances of this can be verified in Shinuiju, but the practice was not frequent.[44] Rather, it appears that most of these supplementary types of side jobs fell into the legal realm of the informal sector up until the end of the 1970s, and that these activities did not revolve around farmers' markets. While the fact that the state rationing system was maintained throughout this time played a role in the lack of growth in farmers' market, a more fundamental reason can be found in the people's collective anti-market sentiment. This collective anti-market mindset, however, began to weaken as the 1980s rolled in.

(3) State of the Farmers' Markets in the Three Cities and Their Peripherization

As could be expected, there was little change in the role of the markets in the three cities from the end of the 1950s through the 1960s and 1970s. For the most part, farmers' markets in these cities played a peripheral role in the consumer lives of the people. Of the three markets established in the late 1950s in Chongjin, the largest, Kunwha Market, was closed by around the late 1970s, and the Seo-heung Farmers' Market was established.[45] The Songpyung Market was also reduced in size, which left the Ingok Farmers' Market as the largest market. There was also the Banjook Farmers' Market in the same Chungam area and the Ranam Farmers' Market in the Ranam area, but these farmers' markets were on the outskirts of

---

[44] This type of trade was rarely witnessed in Shinuiju in the 1970s; however, it was rumored to have occurred, and glutinous rice traded 2:1 for long-grain rice (S5, S8, S9).

[45] Reports are that the largest general market in Chongjin during the 1970s was the Shinjin Central Market in the Sinam district (C12).

the city and were relatively small. However, as can be seen in the case of the Ingok Farmers' Market, which was opened every tenth day in the early 1970s, one can assume that the other two relatively smaller farmers' markets probably followed the same suit.[46]

In Shinuiju, the Chaeha Market closed down and reopened once or twice before it was finally integrated into the farmers' market in Namsong district in the mid-1970s. However, despite the efforts by the state authorities, people continued to gather around the closed market area and by the end of the 1970s a farmers' market was newly established at the old Chaeha Market site.[47] The farmers' market in the Namsong district continued with business as usual. The Chaeha Market also continued to operate daily, although it was closed during the mobilization period for farming.[48] On the other hand, the Namsong Farmers' Market remained open, and following the closure of the Chaeha Market in the mid-1970s it began to operate on a daily basis (S14).[49]

In Hyesan, there was only one farmers' market up until the end of the 1970s, and it had moved to a location just behind the Hyesan department store sometime during the mid- to late 1970s (H1, H2, H3). As can be seen here, in all three cities, state authorities either

---

[46] C1, C6, C12, C13-1, C14, C15, C18.

[47] The mention of the Chaeha Market in South Korean publications stirred up trouble, and then the market was said to be closed down because it incited individual selfishness (S4, S4-1, S8).

[48] From the rice-planting season to the harvest, May through July, who was allowed to work in the markets during these three months was regulated (S7, S12).

[49] It was reported that during the 1970s, the Namsong District Farmers' Market was transformed from a ten-day market to a daily market. The market continued until the end of the 1970s, and was filled mostly with ethnic Chinese, selling homegrown radishes, lettuce, etc., and Shinuiju farmers selling mountain fruits (S4-1, S8, S14).

closed down or relocated to the outskirts of town the farmers' markets that had been established in downtown areas in old traditional market sites from the Japanese occupation era. These cases well represented the intentions of the authorities to physically separate the farmers' markets from the daily consumer lifestyles of urban residents.

In Shinuiju, the temporary closing of the Chaeha Market seems not unrelated to the peddling by "broker" women. In the cases of Chongjin and Hyesan, government measures against the farmers' markets show that their real perception of the markets differed from their official lines that emphasized the "limited role" of the farmers' markets.

These three cases clearly show that despite the differences in their socio economic and geographic conditions and weakening of the state rationing system, farmers' markets in these areas with a slight exception of Shinuiju only played a limited role on the periphery. This was due to North Korean authorities' partial recognition of the markets but with physical restrictions placed on them, but more importantly, it was also due to the lack of enthusiasm on the part of the urban residents to take an active part in the activities around the farmers' markets. This is an important point as we shall see in the next section on the development of farmers' markets during the 1980s when the government continued to restrict the markets but the markets nevertheless expanded. The markets expanded against government measures in the form of a black market with increased participation by people, which shows that strict government control alone does not fully explain the peripherization of the farmers' markets during the 1970s.

IV. Side Job Activities in the Unregulated Sector, Farmers' Markets and Anti-Market Sentiment in the 1980s

The 1980s led to the failure of the state distribution system, and the collapse of the food rationing system was accompanied by mass starvation that killed hundreds of thousands of people in the 1990s. It can be inferred therefore that in the 1980s, it must have been difficult to make a living relying on the state distribution system alone. In this section, we will look at the state of the functioning of the food and basic necessities distribution system during the 1980s and responses of the people who sought to maintain their living, and how these factors influenced the development of the farmers' markets in the three cities.

1. Worsening State of Food Rationing

North Korea's economic situation gradually worsened from the 1980s on, and people had increasing difficulties purchasing foodstuffs and necessities. By the latter half of the 1980s, with the exception of non-cereal food "gifts" from the state on particular holidays, purchases at state-owned stores in the three cities were limited to soybean paste and soy sauce.[50] Throughout the 1980s the food rationing continued albeit at sub-par level; however, after the nationwide "commandeering" of flood relief supplies to be

---

[50] S4-1, C15. It is not that goods such as workbooks, light bulbs, or glass were not produced in the 1980s. By looking at the example of one state store in Shinuiju, the reason behind the lack of products can be understood: "There were no people who were making purchases at the state store at state-set prices. Goods were not put in display cases, either. They were never for sale. Products were in the storage room, never given to residents. People didn't know if even notebooks had been delivered" (S2).

provided to South Korea in 1984 and requisitioning of supplies in 1989, supposedly in preparation for the Pyongyang Student Festival, people faced great hardships.[51]

In 1984 the North Korean government commandeered mass amount of medical supplies, food, and cloth, and so on to provide to South Korea in flood relief, which put great pressure on people's daily lives, according to the following interviewee.[52]

> When the 1980s came around, particularly in 1984 when we sent flood relief goods to the South, we didn't even have unpolished rice for ourselves but had to give polished rice to the South, which was not easy. Then things worsened at the time of the 13th festival, and then got much worse in 1994 when Kim Il Sung died (S2).

That measures were taken to reduce the number of female employees in factories, enterprises, and businesses after the mid-1980s is also indicative of serious problems with the food rationing system. For example, in 1984 when the Chongjin planning commission's distribution funds were reduced, most positions filled by women whose head-of-household received 700 g of food rations were eliminated (C1). Also, from the mid-1980s at the Shinuiju spinning factory, operations were cut back due to the shortage of

---

[51] C9-1, C11, C19, S2, S6, H1, H2-1. Following the collapse of the global socialist market in 1989, North Korea's propaganda machine announced in the early 1990s that the sudden hardship faced by consumers was mainly due to a U.S. blockade.

[52] Due to assistance given to South Korea, North Korean citizens faced food, and, more seriously, medical supply shortages. From this time on, according to C11, "even doctors became thieves, taking medicines home and selling them in order to eat, not delivering doses, or giving half doses."

raw materials. As pay and rations were delayed by several months, some women were forced to leave their jobs and seek other work (S-5). In addition to these measures, state assignments in offices for women with higher education were significantly reduced as well. These measures reflected the fact that the food rationing system was so deteriorated that the state needed to reclassify many residents as housewives and dependent family members, who were eligible for 300 g of food rations, rather than continue supplying them with the 700 g of food rations allotted for full-time members of the work force.[53]

In the 1980s, especially in light of the obviously weakened food and necessities rationing system in the mid-1980s, people relying only on the state distribution system were faced with considerably more difficulties than in the 1970s, and those seeking to maintain their family's standard of living had no choice but to look for alternative means such as participating in economic activities outside the planned sector.

2. Economic Activities in the Unregulated Sector and the Formation of the Black Market

1) Increase in Illegal Side Job Activities

The deteriorating food situation in the 1980s placed more pressure on the lives of the people. However, the degree to which people felt this pressure was not the same for all households. The amount of food rations provided to each household differed based on one's job or socio economic conditions, and such a system made it more difficult for those on the fringes of society. A tendency to

---

[53] Measures reducing the ration system since the mid-1970s arose again in 1992 in the midst of a considerably worsened foodstuff situation.

participate more actively in economic activities in the unregulated sector, therefore, was more evident among this vulnerable group. There are two types of legal and illegal work.

The primary forms of legal economic activities in the unregulated sector are various types of side jobs held by housewives. Most housewives in the three cities were not enthusiastic about holding side jobs during the 1970s. However, the situation dramatically changed in the 1980s, as unemployed women began to engage in side job activities. These women registered themselves at home manufacturing groups run by the Women's Union or local trade or service management offices, from where they received fabric and thread to produce finished goods at home. They then handed over the finished products to their respective home manufacturing groups for a fee. This type of activity really took off after the "August 3rd People's Consumer Goods Production Movement" (8/3 Movement) was introduced in 1984 (S4-1, S5, S11, H3-1).[54]

Apart from the legal side jobs, illegal types of economic activities also began to flourish since the 1980s. These illegal 'side jobs' are mainly constituted of stealing supplies or raw materials from factories in order to turn out finished products at home, which can later be taken out to the local farming region and secretly traded for rice or corn, or outrightly sold.[55] Usually, laborers in the light industry sector producing necessity goods engaged in this type of

---

[54] Participation in these groups was not compulsory, but rather was up to the individual, and there was also private activity that was not registered with local offices, such as pig farming. However, with difficulties in buying feed and supplies, these types of activity were rare (S10).

[55] Laborers stole raw materials and parts from factories before the 1980s, as well, but it was rare, as it would be criticized by factory workers or in the community as immoral. Also, that type of theft was generally not in order to trade or sell. This type of theft arose in the 1980s.

side job as the situation was especially difficult for these laborers to live on food rations alone.[56]

In Chongjin, similar side job activities began to be seen as early as the first part of the 1980s, which by the end of the decade became rampant.[57] Things were not much different in Shinuiju in the early 1980s, although not to the same extent as was in Chongjin.[58] In the latter half of the 1980s, "destitute people" selling shoes made from materials stolen from the Shinuiju shoe factory were not hard to find in the farmers' market.[59]

Hyesan's experience was considerably different from that of Chongjin or Shinuiju. Toward the end of the 1980s, laborers in the Hyesan textile plant would steal thread, but only a little at a time, and it was very carefully traded (H1). Hyesan's primary factories were its paper mill and textile plant, and neither of these was very large. The small-scale thefts in Hyesan can probably be attributed to the fact that both the size and the number of its factories were considerably less than the other two cities. This passivity of the

---

[56] Workers at light industrial factories producing necessities justified this type of "side work." To expand, "Even when food comes, the rations are not enough to live on. Anyway, at the average house, even when there are not many mouths to feed, dinner must be eaten. Full rations are not given and 10 percent is always stripped away" (C14).

[57] In Chongjin's match factory, bus factory, etc., goods such as wool, matches, enamel, firepans, etc., were stolen (C9-1, C14). At certain enterprises, zinc, mortar, leather, and other goods valued as 8/3 products were not easy to come by, but could be obtained illegally toward the end of the 1980s (C20).

[58] In the late 1970s as well, laborers stealing from Shinuiju's synthetic fiber factory and shoe factory could be found selling their wares in the farming community, but only rarely (S15).

[59] Although it was rare, at this time there were also those who bought cloth, and then after cutting clothing, subcontracted the sewing to other households so that several identical pieces were produced and then sold in the farming community (S3).

Hyesan citizens can also be seen in that most side jobs were in the form of selling firewood or vegetables in the back alleys of local neighborhoods (H2, H3-1).

Examples of secondary illegal activities include farmers entering the city of Shinuiju with agricultural products and going door to door in order to sell or trade them for manufactured goods, or selling moonshine on the main street of town.[60] Another form of this, extremely rare but not unheard of, was for city officials from the supply or customs offices to hoard goods and later sell them at the market (S12, C1). Among these various types of legal and illegal side job activities, illegal side job activities seem more significant in terms of explaining the development of the farmers' markets in the 1980s.

2) Import of Chinese Products and Growth of the Black Market

The increasing illegal activities of factory workers in Chongjin and Shinuiju acted as forces pressuring the growth of black markets on the outskirts of town. Official pressure on farmers' markets during these hard times worked to further the side activities and led to the expansion of the black markets. Other important factors that led to this increasing tendency were the "8/3 Movement" and the opening of trade between China and North Korea in the border region during the mid-1980s.

China's Cultural Revolution had broken ties with North Korea, but following the normalization in 1982, North Korean authorities allowed some trade in the border region. Also, since 1984 officials have allowed ethnic Koreans in China to cross the border for family visits. One consequence of this, despite efforts by North Korean

---

[60] Usually, the farm workers who would bring goods into the city in order to trade or buy products were from a nearby collective farm (S1).

officials to restrict such a development, was a gradual increase of ethnic Korean merchants crossing the border under the guise of family visits bringing in bundles of goods for trade.[61] As a result, by the end of the 1980s, import and circulation of Chinese products had greatly increased.

Chinese products began to come into Chongjin in the mid-1980s. Because of Chongjin's geographic location on the interior of the border region, traders from mostly the Hyeryung and Musan regions visited the city. These traders would bring goods from places such as the Ranam regional farmers' market, mostly Chinese underwear, blankets, and spices, and sell them to willing buyers (C6). They would also make private sales to those who heard of their coming through the rumor mill and sought them out (C13-1). Around the same time, shoes, medicine, and other Chinese products began to make their way illegally into the Chaeha Market in Shinuiju.[62] These ethnic Korean traders stored Chinese goods in homes for unofficial sales or sometimes took them out to a street corner and sold them off. By the end of the 1980s it was not diffi-

---

[61] In one town in the North Ham region, "Many goods from China have been coming in since 1985. Most prevalent were blankets, underwear, head wraps, handkerchiefs, etc." (C3-1). Trade in the border region is introduced in Shim Wui Sub, "Trade Bundles and Farmers' Markets (in Korean)," *Socialism and North Korean Agriculture* (Seoul: Bibong Publishing House, 2002); Lim Keum Sook, "Present Condition and Outlook of Economic Exchange and Trade between Yunbyun and North Korea's Border Region (in Korean)," *Chinese-Korean Family Society's Cultural ascendancy and Expansion Strategy* (Yunbyun: Yunbyun People's Publishing, 2001).

[62] Actually, Chinese products were available in Shinuiju even before 1980. From 1976 until relations were normalized, ethnic Chinese in Shinuiju were allowed one trip across the border every four years. Many took advantage of this and amassed a fortune taking DPRK bicycles or other goods with them, selling them in China and returning with Chinese goods to sell in Shinuiju (S3).

cult to buy Chinese clothes or other Chinese manufactured goods in the farmers' markets (S2, S3, S4-1, S6, S8).

Just as Hyesan had considerably less illegal side job activities by factory workers as compared to the other two cities, there were not many Chinese products coming into Hyesan, even in the mid- to late 1980s, when ethnic Koreans were allowed to cross the border.[63] The authorities clamped down tightly on the illegal sale of Chinese goods in the farmers' markets until the mid-1990s, so that these goods were only sold secretly from behind the closed doors of individual homes (H4, H5, H6, H7).

3) Dual Effects of the 8/3 People's Consumer Goods Production Movement

If the import of goods from China was to be considered the exogenous factor for the growth of black markets in all three cities (although considerably less in Hyesan) in the mid-1980s, then the 8/3 Movement could be considered the endogenous factor. The significant deterioration in the standard of living for urban residents in the three cities during the 1980s drove people to engage in illegal side work in order to preserve their livelihood. But North Korean authorities also made efforts to improve the standard of living for the people. This was, however, mainly because the malfunctioning rationing system impacted the stable supply of labor as well as the authorities' ability for effective on-site management of labor, posing a threat of seriously undermining the state's efforts to implement economic plans. The 8/3 Movement was in recogni-

---

[63] As most ethnic Chinese from here had returned to China, Hyesan's ethnic Chinese population was considerably less than the other two cities, and since Hyesan was a comparatively smaller city, less residents there had relatives in China (H7).

tion of a potential crisis resulting from the chronic shortage problem, and it was the state's answer to the need to expand the production of necessities.

The key behind this movement was to put to use idle workers
and unused, discarded goods or regional raw materials in order to
boost light industrial output, and to use idle city workers and
housewives organized into any number of "production groups" in
order to boost the production of foodstuffs, clothing, etc.[64] This
was not the first time that such mass production movements had
been launched. However, because the past experiences had not
proven effective,[65] the authorities came up with different means to
make this movement into a success. This time, the authorities
established the 8/3 Direct Sales Outlets for all products to be funneled only through this channel and sold at "a price agreed upon
between buyers and sellers," a new provision that was unprecedented.[66] This provision allowed the production and sales of the

---

[64] Kim Jong Il, "Regarding Some Issues of Establishing Production Facilities
for Citizens (in Korean) (1984.8.3)," *Selected Works of Kim Jong Il* 8 (Pyongyang:
KWP Press, 1998), 131-144; Kim Il Sung, "Discussions of the Open Meeting
of the 10th Plenum of the 6th Congress of the Korean Workers Party (in
Korean) (1984.12.10)," *Selected Works of Kim Il Sung* 38 (Pyongyang: KWP
Press, 1992), 403-405.

[65] "Neither the cloth of one loom nor the string of one strip of cloth is to be
discarded, but rather, use everything." Socialism was reformulated to maximize production of light industry in support of daily lives, and organize
lifestyle-supporting side work for housewives. A few examples include
Rodong Sinmun (20 Jan. 1961), 4; *Rodong Sinmun* (15 Jan. 1961), 3; Choi Soo
Ryeon, "Afternoon and Night (in Korean)," Korean Women's Social
Research, *Lives and Dreams of North Korean Women*, 294.

[66] C20 was one who connected to the effort to circulate the goods through the
8/3 Direct Sales Outlets' town stores and cities' district stores; Kook Jung
Won, "Exit from a Dark Tunnel (in Korean)" (Defector's Testimony), see
http://www.nis.go.kr; Park Neung Sook, "Every Time Hong Sung Lee

8/3 Movement products to take place outside the official state plan-ning, which consequently allowed for decision-making processes in this line of production to follow "market-like" profit-seeking principles, although in a very restricted sense.[67]

This regulation helped to increase the productivity of factories through expanded production of 8/3 products by individual pro-duction groups (or 8/3 working groups) and allowed laborers to take a certain portion of profits earned from the sales of these goods. As a result, the 8/3 Movement turned out to be in the inter-est of the state as it helped to decrease the amount of factory theft and other illegal side activities. For example, at one car chassis plant in Chongjin during the mid- to late 1980s, "basic production" was impossible. The daily necessities production team would instead use pieces of left over iron to make shovels or stoves and sell them through the 8/3 Direct Sales Outlets so that the plant could pay and distribute food to its employees with the profits raised from the sales. The 8/3 Movement in this sense helped to provide for factory workers, effectively keeping them under con-trol and preventing their diversion away from their designated workplaces.[68] The same effect could be seen in Shinuiju and Hye-

---

Stands at the Counter (in Korean)," *Chollima* (August, 1995).

[67] This movement brought about "market reform type measures" that were related to the new 1989 "private side work stipulations." Yang Moon Soo, *Structure of the North Korean Economy* (in Korean) (Seoul: Seoul University Press, 2001), 353-356, 364-371. Also, based on E3's comments on the unavoidable planning of the 8/3 production and distribution following the mid- to late 1990s.

[68] The results sought by officials through boosting factory production of 8/3 goods were not just the economic benefit of repressing this illegal "side" work that undermined the planned economy. The political result was considerably more important. Officials were extremely concerned about the likelihood of weakened control over labor and relaxed control over

san (S15, H4) as long as the supply of raw materials for the 8/3 production was guaranteed for the next few years.[69]

As the factories enjoyed a certain degree of flexibility when it came to the production of 8/3 goods, managers and supervisors gradually began to stow away some funds for factory operation or conspire with the direct outlet stores in order to support "back door" businesses by employees. Other illegal means were also employed to divert 8/3 products to be sold at black markets. One example was the unauthorized mass purchase of "zinc tubs" in Chongjin's 8/3 Store to be sold for two to three times the original price in rural areas or exchanged for rice at the cost of a brokerage fee.[70]

The fact that the 8/3 products were not counted toward the official state planning made it easier for factory managers or laborers to divert the goods away from the official distribution channel. Employees from the Chongjin car plant stole car parts and made finished products at home, and there were more of these illegal products in circulation than officially sanctioned products (C2). Chongjin's match factory and Shinuiju's rolling mill saw similar

---

laborers. The reasoning behind the late 1990s' "Arduous March" demanded that workers continue to show up to factories and enterprises, even when there was no work to be done, was that it was a control measure implemented because "if people are too dispersed, to spread out across the country, there is no control mechanism" (C2).

[69] The 8/3 products focused production on those regional factories falling behind in size, equipment, and level of technology. Because procuring the raw materials necessary for the manufacture of many 8/3 products was difficult, many factories ceased production in the late 1980s (H2-1, H-8). Following that, it was relatively easy to come by secondhand work clothes and other supplies with which to make gloves (mainly mittens), rags, etc., and these became the representative products of the 8/3 Movement.

[70] E4 can confirm that this happened in a northern Ham town, not just in the factories in the cities, but in rural areas as well.

cases (C14, S1).[71] The problem with this type of illegal 8/3 product was that they had to be sold outside the direct procurement store, outside the national network. This meant that it could not avoid being filtered into the black market. While the introduction of the 8/3 Movement had the effect of cutting down on illegal side job activities in the unregulated sector, at the same time it also had the effect of driving the growth of the black market.

4) Farmers' Markets and the Binding Power of Anti-Market Sentiment

(1) Conditions at the Farmers' Markets

As the state rationing system deteriorated throughout the 1980s, all three cities saw an increase in side job activities in the unregulated sector and an increase in Chinese manufactured goods and illegal 8/3 products that led to the spread of black markets, although Hyesan was a little slower to change than the other two cities. The farmers' markets in the three cities, however, remained physically separated from the black markets.

In the mid-1980s following the erection of the Kim Jung Sook Heritage Building in Chongjin, the Ingok Market was closed and the Banjook Farmers' Market was moved to Changpyung-ri, where it became the Changpyung Farmers' Market (Chungam Farmers' Market) (C6, C19). Aside from this, physical distribution of markets in Chongjin at the end of the 1980s was the same as in the 1970s.[72] The mid-1980s saw a rise in wholesaling of agricultural

---

[71] There was a slight difference in Hyesan's experience here as well. Toward the end of the 1980s, Hyesan's ironworks factory built a large cage in which scraps were stored, and there were guards who searched employees and their bags when they entered or exited the factory, so there were no 8/3 goods to be found on the market (H4).

[72] Products manufactured by the 8/3 household groups had the same effects

goods in the farmers' markets, but ordinary citizens were rarely seen in the farmers' markets.[73] Only senior citizens were found in the market selling vegetables grown in home plots, or handmade lampshades and other goods, and some Chinese manufactured goods on the outskirts of the market hiding from the eyes of the police.[74]

Shinuiju was slightly different from Chongjin. Due to its location it has had long-standing trade with China, and illegal trade of Chinese manufactured goods was not unusual in the Chaeha Market even in the early 1980s. People knew it as the "manufactured goods black market" and the Namsong Farmers' Market as the place for agricultural and marine products. As the Chinese goods were illegally circulated through the Chaeha Market, the authorities began to control their sales only through the national procurement office while at the same time cracking down on the markets. This drove the black market activities to the Namsong Farmers'

---

as those of the factory products. In all three cities, the movement worked to mobilize housewives. The original goal of the movement was to increase participation in the legal, unregulated sector thereby helping to establish shops in each city, and increasing production in order to relieve stresses on the ration system, and this was effective (H8). Also, by having these groups registered, and controlling the type of business undertaken, the state could control the groups. By fixing production limits and product types, the state could control the production realm as well. The state also retained to power to restrict the ability to amass wealth while assuring that a standard of living was ensured. However, if a household undertook printing, or tofu production, then the printing supplies or beans would have to be directly monitored. The desire to find more of these is what supports the black markets, farmers' markets and other unrestricted markets (C4, C14, C22).

[73] The largest market in the early to mid-1990s, the Namsoo Market, was only a small farmers' market, much like those in other districts, in the 1980s.

[74] For example, potatoes from the Yang River region were trucked into the Ranam Farmers' Market and sold by the bag (C7).

Market, which by the end of the 1980s eventually became the bigger of the two markets.[75]

In addition to this type of illegal activity, illegal transactions between urban residents and the nearby farming community gradually increased so that by the end of the 1980s, South Shinuiju Market (daily market), Rakwon Machinery Market (ten-day market), Majun Market (irregular ten-day market), Namhadong Market, and others had sprung up. None of the markets other than the original two were officially recognized by the state as authorized farmers' markets. By this time, "whale oil" and other non-staple food items, as well as the officially banned sale of bicycles, shoes, and Chinese clothes were all available in these markets.[76] Of course, these were not items that people could easily purchase and were mostly for those who were slightly better off than others. As was the case in Chongjin, the farmers' markets did not see too many ordinary citizens up until the end of the 1980s.

Hyesan's case was different from that of Shinuiju or Chongjin. It was smaller in size and had fewer factories so the illegal trade in manufactured goods was at a minimum. This also made it easier for the state to control any irregularities surrounding the farmers' market. The market remained in only one area, Shinheung District, and always opened on every tenth day. In the 1980s, Hyesan's farmers' market moved four times, from Sungho District → Ryunbong District → Hyewha District → Hyeshin District. This was not because the authorities had a hard time controlling the farmers' market like the Chaeha Market in Shinuiju, but it was more due to

---

[75] Average citizens only go to the farmers' market "for sightseeing on a holiday or some other special occasion" or to buy some particular good that is difficult to come by in the state-run store (C9, C12, C13).

[76] At the end of the 1980s, Chaeha Market was so full of Chinese products, it was known as the "Chinese Hong Kong."

concerns over the deteriorating academic atmosphere at a nearby university, its impact on the business of nearby enterprises, or the negative image the market might give to outsiders (H4, H7).

(2) Anti-Market Sentiment and the Peripherization of Farmers' Markets

In the 1980s, an overall look at the three cities' farmers' markets shows that they played only a peripheral role in the consumer lives of the population. Several causal factors are evident here. The primary reason is the presence of physical restrictions from the state authorities over farmers' markets even up until the end of the 1980s. Another important factor is the continued state rationing system, although not without delays and problems. However, even more important is the anti-market sentiment that subconsciously restricted the actions and perceptions of the people. Farmers' and black markets proliferated during the 1980s, and the following comment by an interviewee from Shinuiju whose residents tend to have a more fundamental understanding of "private commerce" shows how different forces were at work.[77]

> During the 1980s, in the state-run store ... vegetables were occasionally available but manufactured goods were almost completely unavailable. Particularly, necessities such as shoes and socks were rarely available ... which was still bearable. Those with money could buy shoes, socks, and underwear at the marketplace ... people weren't aiming to make a fortune by trading. And there was the burden of the crackdowns. And, the situation was not so bad at the time. There were only a few people who were in it for money (S12).

---

[77] S2, S3, S4, S4-1, S6, S8, S13.

Under the circumstances, up until the 1980s it was only natural for this one woman, who lived through the "post-war recovery" period of the 1950s, to say that although the state rations were not sufficient, one "wouldn't even think" about engaging in side work, even if it was legal (C8). A similar response by another woman from Chongjin, who is a slightly more "standard" type of social character, shows that such activities "did not even cross" her mind. These two testimonies show that a removal of self-perception as an autonomous economic entity is closely related to the collective consciousness of anti-market sentiment, a critical element in ensuring that the principles of the socialist regime are upheld.

> Before the supplies were seriously cut in the 1990s ... I thought that whatever I did, as long as I worked hard, things were going to be OK. Not only me, but everybody probably thought the same. I didn't wish for grand splendor or wealth. All I wanted was to raise my children well to be loyal to the state and turn out to be fine people. This was the ultimate goal and society believed it as well. I didn't particularly look forward to being rich but carried on with whatever tasks had been assigned to me thinking that it's what was meant for my life (C6-1).

The anti-market sentiment internalized by the people is found in the memories of one Heysan woman who engaged in trade during the so-called "Arduous March" in the mid-1990s. She suffered the physical pain and mental anguish in doing trade in the farmers' markets.

> I used to think that I'd be happy with old corn covered with mold if the portion was up to standard. I hadn't even thought of making my own living at that time. Because I lived as I

was taught and that's all I knew ... I just thought that as long as I received 15 days worth of even the moldy corn on time, I would work as I am told to (H1-1).

Such self-denial of the possibility of emerging as an autonomous economic entity lasted at least until around the 1980s. It is also unlikely that although the growth of the farmers' markets really took off in the 1990s such anti-market sentiment faded away in a short period of time.[78] However, it is necessary to recognize the limitations of the food rationing system, the weakening of which eventually worked to chip away the binding power of the anti-market ideology. This is most evident in Shinuiju's case, where the black market gradually encroached upon the legal farmers' market despite strict government control. Such development in the late 1980s was led by people like S2, who are anti-socialist and market-oriented actors, who "dropped out of college in order to make money" and engaged in illegal "side jobs" (but in effect his full-time job).[79]

---

[78] Compared to other border cities, small-scale border trade developed relatively quickly in one particular North Hamkyung town, and one resident stated that "the size of the market was unbelievably big." (C3).

[79] Following communization, when looking at markets, even from the beginning, when vegetable sales appeared, feelings of being "almost criminal" and other feelings of shame and embarrassment were faced by one woman in a farming community in Bulgaria. She faced confusion over her values regarding markets and her still remaining socialist criticism of value and moral standards. At the market level, rational action can take the shape of "free" individuals, and also injustice. Deema Kaneff, "The Shame and Pride of Market Activity: Morality, Identity and Trading in Postsocialist Rural Bulgaria," Ruth Mandel and Caroline Humphrey, eds., *Markets and Moralities* (Oxford: Berg, 2002), 39-43.

V. Conclusion

North Korea completed collectivization of farms and private industries in 1958, and from then until the end of the 1980s farmers' markets were the only legal trade outlet in the unregulated sector. Despite the authorities' official lines allowing "limited use" of the farmers' markets and authorizing partial private sales of agricultural goods to increase farms' incomes and improve the living of the people, strong adherence to the state distribution system for foodstuffs and daily necessities until the 1970s meant that the lives of most urban residents saw little change. On the contrary, farmers' markets in densely populated areas were closed or moved to the outskirts of town. Even when, in the 1970s, measures were taken to reduce food rations and implement ration cards for daily necessities pushing people to the brink of poverty, they still rarely used the farmers' markets.

The physical separation of the farmers' markets from the daily lives of urban residents and the isolation of the farmers' markets can be seen in many rural cities, including the three case cities we looked at. The most important reason behind the inactivity of the farmers' markets was, more than anything, the state's distribution system for food and daily necessitie—a system that, however unable to deliver the necessary amounts, was able to supply rations steadily. Another important factor that cannot be ignored is the effect of the binding power of the collective anti-market mentality that considered traders as the parasitic products of capitalism. Also worth noting is the almost complete lack of hard cash that could be spent on goods outside of food and necessities.

These farmers' markets, shunted to the side as the state distribution system was employed, played only a subsidiary role in the 1980s. As the first half of the 1980s passed, it was slightly more difficult for urban residents to get their share of food and daily rations; however, the same factors that played a role in the 1970s continued to see to it that farmers' markets remained on the periphery. However, in the mid- to late 1980s the farmers' markets had to cope with the development of black markets within its boundary. There are several factors behind this:

1. As time passed, the state distribution system continued to weaken, and the farmers' markets previously pushed to the outskirts of the planned economy arose as a tool for supporting one's livelihood, as theft of goods from factories could be traded for food or other goods;

2. Since the middle of the 1980s, Chinese goods increasingly made their way into the country and a wider range of goods became available in the black market;

3. In the latter half of the decade, 8/3 products previously available only through the state's direct outlet stores slowly made their way into the black market. It became impossible to avoid the illegal distribution of these goods, just as the illegal distribution of grains was under way in farming regions, leading to the emergence of wholesalers connecting the urban residents and farmers through illegal transactions. It goes without saying that the government decided to strongly clamp down on these activities.

From the mid-1980s on, black markets became a normal part of the unregulated economy, and as the illegal trade of these goods expanded, the black market forces tended to penetrate into the legal farmer's markets. The pace at which these emerged and the restrictions by the state varied between the three cities, as did the partial proliferation (partial de-peripherization) of the farmers' markets. Compared to Hyesan, Chongjin, with more emphasis on heavy industry, and Shinuiju, with a focus on light industry but also as an active logistics hub, saw illegal trade of goods in the farmers' markets and surrounding areas driven by factors 1-3 and state restrictions. This was especially true for Shinuiju, with quite a few light industrial facilities.

Many products from these light industry factories were illegally traded through home-based manufacturing related to 1 and Chinese manufactured goods related to 2. Chongjin had more metal and machinery factories, so it saw more of these goods related to 3 illegally traded. On the other hand, Hyesan, heavy on the forestry and mining industries, was less affected by these three factors up until the end of the 1980s, and as such their relative impact on Hyesan's farmers' market was minimal. Also, despite the fact that Hyesan is in the border region, Chinese goods were less prevalent than expected. This is due to the poor distribution and transportation infrastructure of Changbai, the Chinese city with which it could trade. In addition, the smaller size of Hyesan compared to either Shinuiju or Chongjin made the state control over the farmers' markets much more effective.

The mid- to late 1980s saw the peripherization of farmers' markets due to government regulations, while at the same time also saw their de-peripherization driven by the forces of the black markets. The relationship between these two opposing phenomena was attributable to each city's location, industry, size, and other factors. One thing that can be confirmed here is that the presiding factors over the peripherization and de-peripherization of farmers' markets in these three cities were the physical change in the functioning of the state distribution system and the binding power of the intangible anti-market sentiment.

Details of Interviewees

1. Chungjin residents

Interviewee	Sex	Age	Education	Occupation	Political Affiliation	Year of Defection
C1	M	Late 60s	University Graduate	Designer		1990
C2	M	Early 50s	High School Graduate	Trader	Party Member	1997
C3 (C3-1)	F	Mid 40s	High School Graduate	Photographer	Party Member	1997
C4	F	Mid 60s	University Graduate	Doctor		1997
C5	F	Early 60s	University Graduate	Architect	Party Member	1997
C6 (C6-1)	F	Mid 40s	High School Graduate	Daycare Employee		1998
C7	M	Late 40s	High School Graduate	Driver	Party Member	1998
C8	F	Mid 50s	Elite High School Graduate	Support Staff, Daycare Center		1998
C9 (C9-1)	M	Early 50s	High School Graduate	Military-Foreign Capital Trader	Party Member	1998
C10	M	Mid 60s	University Graduate	Retired Designer	Party Member	1998
C11	F	Early 70s	Elite High School Graduate	Retired Restaurant Manager	Party Member	1998
C12	M	Mid 40s	High School Graduate	Driver		1999
C13 (C13-1)	F	Late 30s	High School Graduate	Public Speaking Lecturer		1999

1. Chungjin residents (continued)

Interviewee	Sex	Age	Education	Occupation	Political Affiliation	Year of Defection
C14	F	Mid 40s	High School Graduate	Business Manager	Party Member	1999
C15	M	Mid 40s	Some High school	Technical Lecturer	Party Member	1999
C16	M	Mid 50s	Vocational School Graduate	Material Manager		1999
C17 (C17-1)	M	Early 70s	Elementary School Graduate	Forest Ranger	Ex-Party Member	1999
C18 (C18-1)	M	Mid 60s	University Graduate	Retired Doctor	Party Member	2000
C19	F	Mid 30s	High School Graduate	Technician, Collective Farm		2001
C20	F	Early 40s	Vocational School Graduate	Shopkeeper		2001
C21 (C21-1)	M	Late 60s	University Graduate	Administrator, Collective Farm	Party Member	2001
C22 (C22-1)	F	Mid 60s	University Graduate	Retired Accountant	Party Member	2001

2. Shinuiju residents

Interviewee	Sex	Age	Education	Occupation	Political Affiliation	Year of Defection
S1	M	Late 40s	Military School Graduate	Fatigue Party Leader	Party Member	1992
S2	F	Early 30s	Some University	Accountant		1993

2. Shinuiju residents (continued)

Interviewee	Sex	Age	Education	Occupation	Political Affiliation	Year of Defection
S3	M	Late 60s	Some Middle School	Warehouse Manager		1994
S4 (S4-1)	M	Early 50s	University Graduate	Doctor	Party Member	1996
S5	F	Mid 60s	High School Graduate	Supply Clerk		1996
S6	M	Early 30s	University Graduate	Educator	Party Member	1997
S7	F	Late 40s	High School Graduate	Maintenance Worker		1997
S8	M	Early 60s	University Graduate	Carpenter	Party Member	1997
S9	M	Early 60s	High School Graduate	Foreign Currency Manager	Party Member	1997
S10	F	Early 60s	University Graduate	Maintenance Worker		1997
S11	F	Late 30s	Vocational School Graduate	Statistician		1998
S12	M	Early 50s	High School Graduate	Material Manager		1998
S13	M	Early 30s	High School Graduate	Non-Commissioned Military Officer	Party Member	2000
S14	M	Late 40s	High School Graduate	Material Manager	Party Member	2000
S15	M	Mid 40s	High School Graduate	Laborer	Party Member	2002

3. Hyesan residents

Interviewee	Sex	Age	Education	Occupation	Political Affiliation	Year of Defection
H1 (H1-1)	F	Early 40s	University Graduate	Commentator		1996
H2 (H2-1)	M	Late 30s	University Graduate	Mining Engineer		1997
H3 (H3-1)	F	Early 40s	University Graduate	Educator		1997
H4	F	Late 30s	University Graduate	Director of Inspection Statistics		1997
H5	M	Late 60s	Some Middle School	Retired Materials Procurer	Party Member	1997
H6	F	Mid 60s	Middle School Graduate	Maintenance (Material Manager)	Party Member	1997
H7	M	Mid 60s	University Graduate	Retired Secretary	Party Member	1998
H8	M	Late 30s	University Graduate	Contractor	Party Member	1999

4. Interviewees from other regions

Interviewee	Sex	Age	Education	Occupation	Political Affiliation	Year of Defection
E1	M	Early 60s	University Graduate	Central Organization Management	Party Member	1988
E2	F	Mid 60s	Elite High School Graduate	Retired Cashier		1998
E3	M	Late 40s	University Graduate	Store Owner	Party Member	1998

4. Interviewees from other regions (continued)

Interviewee	Sex	Age	Education	Occupation	Political Affiliation	Year of Defection
E4	M	Late 60s	University Graduate	Store Manager	Party Member	2001

Notes: 1) The first round of interviews was from May 2001–February 2002 (S4, S13, E1), and the second round was from September 2002–March 2003.
2) Interviewees with (-1) indicates a second round of interviews.
3) In the age column, early/mid/late is broken down as 0-3, 4-6, and 7-9.

Bibliography

Chung, Soon Duk, "Pil Nam's Rainbow-Striped Clothes (in Korean)," Institute for Korean Women's Social Research, *Lives and Dreams of North Korean Women* (Seoul: Institute for Culture and Society Research, 2000).

Good Friends Network, *North Korean Talk* (in Korean) (Seoul: Paradise Publishers, 2000).

Hessler, Julie, "Postwar Normalization and its Limits in the USSR: The Case of Trade," *Europe-Asia Studies* 53, no. 3 (2001).

Kaneff, Deema, "The Shame and Pride of Market Activity: Morality, Identity and Trading in Postsocialist Rural Bulgaria," Ruth Mandel and Caroline Humphrey, eds., *Markets and Moralities* (Oxford: Berg, 2002).

Kim Il Sung, "Regarding the Improvement of the Product Distribution Scheme while Increasing Production of the People's Consumables (in Korean) (1958.6.7)," *Selected Works of Kim Il Sung* 12 (Pyongyang: KWP Publishers, 1981).

_____, "Regarding the Complete Manifestation of the Highest Vitality Through the Centralization and Detailing of the People's Economic Plan (in Korean)," *Selected Works of Kim Il Sung* 19 (Pyongyang: KWP Publishers, 1982).

_____, "Regarding Strengthening of Party Activities while Tightening up Household Activities (in Korean)," *Selected Works of Kim Il Sung* 20 (Pyongyang: KWP Press, 1982).

_____, "On the Socialist System and Related Theories (in Korean)," *Selected Works of Kim Il Sung* 23 (Pyongyang: KWP Publishers, 1983).

_____, "On Further Increasing Rural Earnings (in Korean)," *Selected Works of Kim Il Sung* 33 (Pyongyang: KWP Publishers, 1987).

_____, "Discussions of the Open Meeting of the 10th Plenum of the 6th Congress of the Korean Workers Party (in Korean) (1984.12.10)," *Selected Works of Kim Il Sung* 38 (Pyongyang: KWP Press, 1992).

_____, "Regarding the System and Method of Government Enterprises as Cooperative Businesses Organize (in Korean) (1985.10.22)," *Selected Works of Kim Il Sung* 39.

Kim Jong Il, "Strengthen Party Guidance over Agricultural Accounting, and Set This Year's Agricultural Yield at a New High (in Korean) (1976.2.6)," *Selected Works of Kim Jong Il* 5 (Pyongyang: KWP Press, 1995).

_____, "Regarding a Few Tasks that Party Directors need to Break Away From (in Korean) (1978.11.10)," *Selected Works of Kim Jong Il* 6 (Pyongyang: KWP Press, 1995).

Kim, Mi Ja, "Is Return to Japan Possible? (in Korean)," Institute for Korean Women's Social Research, *Lives and Dreams of North Korean Women* (Seoul: Institute for Culture and Society Research, 2000).

Kim, Shin Jo, *I Speak My Sad History* (in Korean) (Seoul: Dong A Publishers, 1994).

Kim, Sung Chul, "Analysis of Kim Jong Il's Understanding of Economics: Possibility and Methods of Reform (in Korean)," *Research on Modern North Korea* 3, no. 2 (2000).

Kim, Won Sam, "Expansion of Socialist Commerce in Our Country (in Korean)," Chosun Democratic People's Republic School of Science, Economics and Law Research Center, *Building a Socialist Economy in our Country* (in Korean) (Pyongyang: School of Science Publishing, 1958).

Kim, Young Hye, *Individual Commerce and Industry's Socialist Remodeling Experience* (in Korean) (Pyongyang: Social Science Publishers: 1987).

Kim, Young Kyu, *Analysis of the Level of North Korean Material Consumption* (in Korean) (Seoul: Institute for Korean Unification, 1984).

Kook, Jung Won, "Exit from a Dark Tunnel (in Korean)" (Defector's Testimony), see http://www.nis.go.kr.

Kornai, J., *Socialist System: The Political Economy of Communism* (Princeton: Princeton University Press, 1992).

Lee, Chun Young, "The Women Welcoming the Farmers' Markets (in Korean)," *Korean Women* (April 1950).

Marx, Karl, F. Engels, *The Works of Marx·Engels* (in Korean) (Seoul: Kureum, 1988).

Park, Neung Sook, "Every Time Hong Sung Hee Stands at the Counter (in Korean)," *Chollima* (August 1995).

Resel, Larry (pictures), Seung Jong Baek (writing). *West German Master Carpenter Resel's North Korean Retrospective* (in Korean) (Seoul: Hyohyung Press, 2000).

Suk, Chang Hee, "A Quarter of Hong Sung Hee's Day behind the Counter (in Korean)," *Chollima* (August 1995).

Walder, A., *Communist Neo-Traditionalism: Work and Authority in Chinese Industry* (Berkeley: University of California Press, 1985).

Yang, Moon Soo, *Structure of the North Korean Economy* (in Korean) (Seoul: Seoul University Press, 2001).

Chapter 4

Changes in North Korea's Corporate Governance

⊣ Moon Soo YANG and Kevin SHEPARD ⊢

I. Introduction

The use of institutional economics for analysis of enterprises is recognized as being a very valuable approach not only to capitalist enterprises, but also to socialist corporate structures. In particular, institutional economics is seen as a valuable tool for analysis of the actions of socialist enterprises exposed to a sharply changing environment brought on by forces such as economic reform and transition, and in evaluating the prospective development paths for such enterprises. It has proven to be very helpful in bringing to light shifts in corporate governance in studies of the former Soviet, Eastern European, and Chinese enterprises, yet there has been very little use of institutional economics in the analysis of the North Korean system. This has led to a void in existing economic research regarding North Korea's enterprises.

The need for more systematic research into the functioning of North Korea's enterprises was further driven by the July 1st (2002) Economic Management Improvement Measures, known as the 7/1 Measures, which led to significant decentralization of economic authority and corporate oversight, along with a sharp increase in management autonomy within individual enterprises. These measures can be seen as the North's first step toward economic reform, and one essential element of these measures was increasing the autonomy of enterprises. Therefore, in order to be more prepared to accommodate and facilitate further North Korean economic reforms in the future, a more systematic arrangement of North Korea's current enterprise activities and operating systems and mapping of the changes that followed the 7/1 Measures are very important subjects for policy makers and academics, alike.

For North Korea, one important matter regarding its system of enterprise management in the process of economic reform and transition is the issue of corporate governance. Up until now, an important factor in the reorganization of the corporate system as part of the North's transformation has been privatization. That said, however, the experiences of transitioning countries have shown that while privatization may be necessary, it is, by itself, an insufficient condition for economic reform. Chinese economic reforms revealed that the issue of corporate governance needs to be tackled before that of privatization.[1]

On a related note, neoclassical economic theory is criticized for its conception that effective corporate governance can be implemented through the establishment of a stock market and the privatization of collective state-owned enterprises. The institutional economic approach recognizes the existence of a variety of alterna-

---

[1] China began economic reforms under the banner "Socialism with Chinese Characteristics" in 1978. Heralded by Deng Xiaoping, these reforms were introduced in phases, first allowing farmers to retain surplus crops, then establishing locally owned industries. This was followed by introducing market functions and demand-led pricing as the government slowly decentralized management authority and encouraged enterprises to adapt to local markets and conditions.

tive transitional corporate governance systems, and emphasizes the importance of understanding the history and traditions of a particular system when it is being evaluated. In the case of North Korea, when seeking a favorable model of corporate governance, this type of institutional economic approach appears to be more valuable due to its ability to recognize and accommodate the unique style of socialism pursued by Pyongyang.

This chapter focuses on an analysis of North Korea's corporate governance after the 1990s. Understanding and organizing the real conditions of corporate governance allows for analysis of the background and factors behind the emergence and maintenance of the North's corporate governance. In addition, this research seeks to explain the meaning of this kind of corporate governance, and at the same time, examine what systematic changes have been under way in the wake of the so-called "7/1 Measures." Institutional economic methodology, and principal-agent theory in particular, are employed in this effort.

II. Scope and Methodology

1. Framework of Analysis

This chapter undertakes analysis of general corporate governance based on institutional economics, and within this field, principal-agent theory. The relationship between principal and agent is one in which an employer, or principal, hires employees, or agents, to work for the principal's best interests, establishing the relationship by way of a written or an assumed contract. Therefore, the principal-agent problem arises when the agent does not work for the best interests of the principal. Generally, common ground can be found where both parties' interests cross paths.

The principal-agent theory can take on all forms of reciprocity, but ordinarily, analysis of a hierarchical relationship is used. In particular, analysis generally seeks to discover what rights the principal holds, for example, the right to use resources, that are entrusted to the agent, what compensation is provided to the agent in order to encourage the agent to work for the best interests of the principal, and what type of formal or informal contract exists that stipulates these conditions. Therefore, principal-agent theory has been extensively used in research involving issues surrounding most enterprises.[2]

This theoretical framework of the principal-agent problem offers a valuable analytical tool for explaining the relationships between socialist governments, enterprises, managers, and laborers. Actually, principal-agent problems can be found repeatedly throughout socialist economies. Myriad negotiations and consultations take place in the relationships between state and enterprise, state and middle management organizations, and middle management organizations and enterprises. D. Granick (1983, 1990), Keun Lee (1991), and Y. Qian (1996) provide many examples of the use of principal-agent theory in discussions on classical socialist economy, and economic reform, enterprises in transition, and corporate governance, in particular.[3]

---

[2] For a more detailed explanation, see Dong-woon Yoo, *Neo-institutional Economics* (Seoul: Sunhaksa, 1999), 261.

[3] D. Granick, "Institutional Innovation and Economic Management: The Soviet Incentive System, 1921 to the Present" in G. Guroff and F. V. Carstensen, eds., *Entrepreneurship in Imperial Russia and the Soviet Union* (Princeton: Princeton University Press, 1983); D. Granick, *Chinese State Enterprises* (Chicago and London: The University of Chicago Press, 1990); Keun Lee, *Chinese Firms and the State in Transition and Agency Problems in the Reform*

2. Research Methodology

This chapter employs both literature reviews and field surveys in gathering data. A unique aspect of corporate governance research is the considerable importance of field surveys. Of course, it is not possible to conduct actual, direct field surveys regarding North Korean enterprises. Therefore, we are left with no option but to rely on surveys of North Korean defectors. For this paper, interviews and written surveys on 165 North Korean defectors were conducted between August 2004 and October 2005. These subjects worked in North Korean enterprises, and basic details of each individual can be found in Table 4.

Table 4. Information on North Korean Defector Interview and Survey Subjects

Categories		Number of Respondents	Percent (%)
Region of Birth	North Hamgyung Province	100	60.6
	Other	65	39.4
	Total	165	100.0
Gender	Male	69	42.1
	Female	95	57.9
	Total	164	100.0
Age Bracket	Less than 30	20	12.1
	30-39	77	46.7
	40-49	48	29.1
	Over 50	20	12.1
	Total	165	100.0

China (New York: M. E. Shape, Inc, 1991); Y. Qian, "Enterprise Reform in China: Agency Problems and Political Control," *Economics of Transition* (June 1996).

Table 4. Information on North Korean Defector Interview and Survey Subjects
(Continued)

Categories		Number of Respondents	Percent (%)
Level of Education	High School Graduate	117	74.5
	Technical School Graduate	22	14.0
	College Graduate	18	11.5
	Total	157	100.0
Era of Defection	Prior to the 7/1 Measures	103	62.8
	After the 7/1 Measures	61	37.2
	Total	164	100.0
Korean Workers' Party Affiliation	Member	38	25.9
	Non-member	109	74.1
	Total	147	100.0

It goes without saying that when using results of defector interviews and surveys, issues such as representativeness and believability could come into play. However, in this case, the author has focused on questions and information related to the subjects' experiences in the North Korean corporate world, conducting "apolitical" interviews and surveys.

III. Changes in North Korea's Corporate Governance

1. Established System of Corporate Governance

North Korea's enterprises are, for the most part, state-owned. While some collective private enterprises exist, they are extremely rare. Therefore, the state's management of enterprises is inevitable. In North Korea, there exists a centrally planned economic system in which the central government exercises decision-making authority and coordinates distribution of resources according to plan under the constraints of the state ownership system. The system evolved through several stages, as the 1958 "Socialist Rebuilding of Production Means" was brought to a close and the "Daean Industrial Management System" was established in 1961, after which the "Unified and Detailed Planning System" was set up in 1964-1965.

The "Daean Industrial Management System" focused on corporate management, and as such, prioritized party leadership rather than administrative guidance. Contrary to the previous system, in which the top manager[4] alone had absolute authority over, and responsibility for, enterprise management, the new system was characterized by a collective leadership by a factory Party committee that oversaw business operations. The organization and execution of the central plan issued by the regime was also physically supported by centrally issued material rations, so what was important about the Daean Industrial Management System was that there was a framework under which the ruling authorities (ministries, management authorities, etc.) took responsibility, and the lower levels (business offices, factories, etc.) were rationed actual materials.

North Korean authorities introduced the "Unified and Detailed Planning System" as "the most correct path to strengthen centralized order in the economic sector." Centralizing economic plans created by establishing one planned system and national planning authority to encompass the whole of the nation meant ensuring uniform, planned enterprises operating under the guidance of the

---

[4] In North Korea, factories and enterprises' top administrators are called *jibaein* (in Korean).

national planning commission's unified leadership. Creating a very detailed plan was a means for the state planning commission to closely tie, directly and in every facet, economic development and administrative activities.[5]

North Korea's national corporate management authority was simplified into a hierarchical pyramid, with the central government's national planning commission at the top, followed by various industry-related ministries, then industrial complexes. Figure 1 shows the central government's planning authority and its control over the entire economy, as well as the scheme in which authority flows down to the individual production units. Actually, a socialist economy is designed to operate as if it were one giant factory encompassing the entirety of the people's economy, and North Korea is no exception to this. Planning authorities prepare planning proposals in order to fulfill national quotas, and then "plan assignments" are handed down to all enterprises. These operation and quota orders are then managed and supervised by the planning authorities.

Decision making regarding corporate activity is firmly in the hands of the central government's planning authorities. Enterprises are told what and how much to produce, who to sell to and at what price, from whom and in what amounts investment and materials can be brought in, how much is to be invested in equipment, how much labor may be employed at what wage, and all other management decisions are made centrally. This kind of decision making equates to top-down arbitrariness at the cost of efficiency.

Along with this, planning authorities provide enterprises with

---

[5] Kim Il Sung, *On the Management of the Socialist Economy* (Pyongyang: Foreign Language Publishing House, 1992), 218-220.

Figure 1. North Korea's Corporate Management Structure

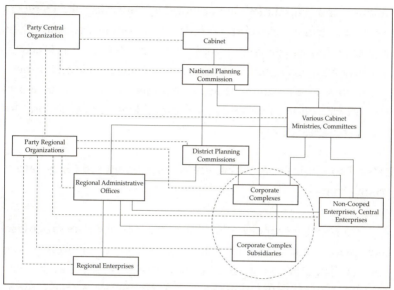

Note: North Korea's corporate management authorities are extremely simplified. From the 1985 establishment of the overall complex enterprise system until the present, this framework has been sustained. Solid lines indicate administrative guidance relations, while broken lines indicate party guidance relations.

Source: Moon-soo Yang, *Structure of the North Korean Economy* (Seoul: Seoul National University Press, 2001).

the necessary raw materials, equipment, and capital. In addition, these authorities direct the enterprises as to where they are to distribute their finished products. If profits are made, they are submitted to the state, and if the business suffers losses, these are, in turn, covered by the state. Under such a system, it is not an overstatement to say that enterprises lack autonomy. Enterprises are simply nothing more than production facilities.

North Korea's system of corporate governance is one based on the *Daean* Industrial Management System and a Unified and Detailed Planning System. An enterprise's proprietary rights lie not within the enterprise, but outside it. Therefore, outside organizations—and central planning authorities, ministries, and committees, in particular—city and town People's Committees, and other regional mid-management organizations are designed to function as overlapping inspection and management organizations. Furthermore, outside management authorities are dispatched to work within enterprises as factory Party committees, further adding to this overlapping design.

2. The Economic Crisis of the 1990s and Changes in Corporate Governance

In a socialist economy, the manner in which business activity takes place—that is, in line with the intentions of the formal system—is diametrically opposed to that which is found in the real world. Looking at the experiences of the former Soviet Union, Eastern Europe, China, and others, business activity did not take place in a manner dictated by political authorities or an official regime. North Korea had a similar experience prior to the economic crisis it faced during the 1990s.

Business activities in the North reflected the following characteristics: First, enterprises would underreport their production capabilities to the planning authorities, while at the same time, inflate requests for "necessary" raw materials. Second, enterprises would hoard more raw materials than they needed. Third, enterprises had no interest in consumer needs, as central planners would decide arbitrarily on product mix. Fourth, even when manufacturing operations were under way, enterprises took no interest in having the necessary goods delivered within the time frame consumers were demanding. Fifth, quantity was important; quality and production cost were not. Sixth, installation of new technology or desire for development was lacking. Seventh, enterprises informally traded materials among themselves. This included black market transactions, as well.[6]

When the bottom fell out of the ongoing economic difficulties during the 1990s, the gap between the official system and reality reached extremely severe levels. As the economic crisis grew, material shortages and the instability of material distribution worsened. Since the central authorities' materials distribution system served as the backbone for the centrally planned economy, as it weakened, the seven trends mentioned above became even more conspicuous in North Korean enterprises. Furthermore, the following unique activity patterns became apparent: First, enterprises gained some amount of autonomy in drawing up operational plans. The central government's plan, especially regarding production quotas and other revisions, came to reflect considerably more input from enterprises. Furthermore, corporate autonomy, from selecting goods for production to setting product prices, grew. This was, in part, due to the government's assessment of an enterprise's performance, which was now being based not only on output quantity, but also on market value of the goods produced. In addition, the state's inability to supply materials according to plan hindered its ability to demand enterprises meet production quotas, furthering decentralization of authority.

From another perspective, the authority of an in-house manager could be said to have strengthened. With the state ration sys-

---

[6] This kind of activity is also noted, to different degrees, in research on enterprises in the former Soviet Union and East Europe. Joseph S. Berliner, *Factory and Management in the USSR* (Cambridge, Mass.: Harvard University Press, 1957); Alec Nove, *The Soviet Economy*, 3rd ed. (London: George Allen & Unwin Ltd, 1968); Janos Kornai, *The Socialist System: The Political Economy of Communism* (Princeton: Princeton University Press, 1992).

tem practically in disrepair, these managers became responsible for the livelihoods of their employees, and the issue of whether production could be sustained came to directly impact the ability of these employees to feed their families. Faced with this, some top managers decided to take the risk of turning to illegal and unofficial trading in order to keep factories up and running.

Market-related business administration activities also increased. As the official materials distribution system was unable to meet the needs of enterprises, these businesses employed myriad unofficial trading schemes in order to procure these materials. They also took to trading left over raw materials among themselves, and took to exchanging finished goods, as well. These goods and materials also appeared regularly in North Korea's black markets.

In addition, some goods other than those assigned to a particular company according to the state plan were produced and unofficially, or more appropriately, illegally sold either to other enterprises or on black markets. When this occurred, prices generally followed market-driven forces of supply and demand, rather than government-set price guidelines. The reason this took place was because of the government's inability to ration necessary materials. Food was also quickly becoming scarcer. Businesses had to become more reliant on their own devices to keep operations running. These enterprises had to dispose of their product, the only resource they had, and the only outlet was to sell to other enterprises or on black markets. These market activities took place among central state enterprises to some extent, but regional or more localized businesses were considerably more active.

The actions of these enterprises can be said to be the progression of unofficial marketization and decentralization. They also meant the collapse of the Daean Industrial Management System and Unified and Detailed Planning System, two core elements of

the North Korean enterprise management system. This is supported by the statements made by North Korean defectors, as shown
in Table 5. In response to a question of whether the leadership of
the Party committee, at the center of the Daean Industrial Management System, amounted to nothing more than a perfunctory role
during the economic crisis of the 1990s, 67 respondents (44.4 percent) strongly agreed, while 53 respondents (35.1 percent) somewhat agreed with the assertion. This means 79.5 percent of the
respondents felt that the Party committee's collective leadership
was nothing more than perfunctory. When asked to agree or dis-
agree with a statement that the central government's materials distribution system, another core element of the Daean Industrial
Management System, had practically collapsed, 86 respondents
(58.1 percent) strongly agreed, while 49 respondents (33.1 percent)
somewhat agreed, for a total of 91.2 percent agreeing that the sys-

Table 5. Collapse of the Daean Work System in the 1990s

(Units: persons, %)

Statement	Strongly Agree	Somewhat Agree	Somewhat Disagree	Strongly Disagree	Total
In the 1990s, the collective leadership of the Party committee, a central component of the Daean Industrial Management System, was nothing more than perfunctory.	67	53	26	5	151 persons
	44.4	35.1	17.2	3.3	100.0 %
In the 1990s, the central authorities' materials distribution system, another central component of the Daean Industrial Management System, practically collapsed.	86	49	10	3	148 persons
	58.1	33.1	6.8	2.0	100.0 %

tem designed for the distribution of raw materials necessary to keep factories up and running had all but collapsed.

The fact that the central authorities were unable to resolve the problems in the materials distribution system essentially meant that they were unable to ensure the essential means of implementing the state's economic plan. At the same time, while demands were being placed on enterprises to meet state-set production quotas, these central authorities were losing their grip on these enterprises, and controlling them became increasingly difficult. This meant that the authority necessary to ensure quotas were met had to be handed over to the enterprises themselves.

Changes in the North Korean corporate governance during the economic crisis of the 1990s, according to defectors with first-hand experience, are shown in Table 6. Here, what can be seen is that 21.2 percent of survey respondents strongly agreed that top managers' authority grew more than that of Party secretaries during this time, while another 34.6 percent somewhat agreed with the statement. Furthermore, 21.7 percent of respondents strongly agreed that the authority of team leaders and office managers increased, while another 45.9 percent somewhat agreed. This goes to show that even within enterprises, real decentralization of power was, to some extent, carried out.

The changes did not stop at decentralization—36.7 percent of respondents strongly agreed that factory and business managers and executives came to see raw materials, equipment, and even finished products not as possessions of the state, but rather, saw them as their own possessions. Another 44.2 percent somewhat agreed with this assertion. Overall, 80.9 percent of these former North Korean employees stated that managers and executives began to see themselves as rightful owners of the factories and enterprises they ran. As such, these managers took extraordinary,

Table 6. Changes in Corporate Governance in the 1990s

(Units: persons, %)

Statement	Strongly Agree	Somewhat Agree	Somewhat Disagree	Strongly Disagree	Total
During the 1990s, tensions often flared between top managers and Party secretaries about factory or enterprise operations.	60	56	28	10	154 persons
	39.0	36.4	18.2	6.5	100.0 %
During the 1990s, managers' authority over a factory or enterprise's economic activities grew more than that of Party secretaries. Of course, basically, the Party secretary's authority was stronger, but the manager's authority grew more than before.	33	54	43	26	156 persons
	21.2	34.6	27.6	16.7	100.0 %
During the 1990s, the authority of team leaders and office managers within a factory or enterprise strengthened more than before.	34	72	33	18	157 persons
	21.7	45.9	21.0	11.5	100.0 %
During the 1990s, factory and business managers and executives came to see raw materials, equipment, and even finished products not as possessions of the state, but rather, saw them as their own possessions, and treated them as such.	54	65	22	6	147 persons
	36.7	44.2	15.0	4.1	100.0 %
During the 1990s, workers welcomed managers scheming or engaging in illegal activities to acquire raw materials and keep factories and enterprises in operation.	49	48	39	17	153 persons
	32.0	31.4	25.5	11.1	100.0%

illegal steps in order to keep operations up and running, and 63.4 percent of respondents believed that these steps were welcomed by the workers, with 32 percent strongly agreeing that laborers welcomed these moves.

During the 1990s, changes in the corporate governance system were confined to shifts toward "insider control."[7] Despite the fact that enterprises were being run by the managers inside them, legal ownership of these enterprises was still in the hands of outside authorities. However, the control mechanism of these outside authorities had weakened, giving local managers relatively more control, and consequently, strengthening their interest in the factory or business they were running.

3. Corporate Governance Following the 7/1 Measures

The most significant change in corporate operations following the 7/1 Measures of 2002 was the expansion of autonomy for these enterprises. This decentralization of the business organization arose in the realms of planning, pricing, and materials acquisition. This was based on an instruction titled "On Strengthening Improvements in Socialist Economic Management to Meet the Demands of the Construction of a Strong and Prosperous Nation," passed down on October 3, 2001, from Kim Jong Il to members of the Party and Cabinet responsible for economic matters.

First, in an attempt to increase efficiency, planning authority regarding goods of low priority in the national economy was shifted away from the centralized state planning authorities, with

---

[7] "Insider control" refers to the autonomy and authority of those managers actually working within a particular enterprise, as opposed to "outsider control" by local and central government oversight authorities.

more authority given to relevant organizations and individual enterprises. In particular, regional economic offices were further empowered to develop plans more in line with the particular characteristics of the province, city, or district under their authority. The methodology employed to evaluate the administrative performance of enterprises was also changed.

An "Income Index"[8] was put in place, employing a system for calculating sales profits plus wages paid to workers. This calculates a business's actual overall profits by excluding all production costs except the cost of labor, which was paid by the state rather than out of corporate funds. This carries important meaning for corporate management because it recognizes profits made from the production and sale of goods above and beyond the state plan. Put differently, it created a legal means for production and market sales outside the state plan.[9] At the same time, following the emergence of general markets, enterprises were given official permission to sell goods there, opening up an avenue for capital gains. Ultimately, production for the purpose of market sales was legalized, as was the actual act of market trading. This laid the groundwork for a whole new realm of corporate activity in North Korea.

The expansion of autonomy for North Korean enterprises brought about changes in the corporate organization, as well. Within a corporation, the authority of the Party secretary was

---

[8] *Bun sooip jipyo* in Korean.

[9] The "Total Profit Index" also had another positive influence. It differs from the previous index in that, first, previously, a factory was evaluated based solely on production, but under the new system, the evaluation takes into account sales. Second, there was previously no accounting for the amount of materials used in production, but under the new system, materials and other costs must be taken into consideration. This means that enterprises now had no choice but to take greater interest in production and management efficiency, and to focus on profit margins.

weakened, while the power of the top manager grew.[10] Of course, this strengthening was a relative measure, and while the position of top manager was strengthened, the actual power afforded to any particular manager was dependent on the circumstances surrounding each individual office. Additionally, in no case did the Party's oversight completely vanish. Just as before, enterprises received their orders through the Party committee and Party secretary, despite any increase in the autonomy or authority of a manager. Despite this, the impact of this transition was not insignificant.[11]

In Table 7, one can easily see the strengthened autonomy of enterprises, as well as the increased authority of managers; 32.8 percent of survey respondents strongly agreed that managerial authority increased more than that of Party secretaries following the 7/1 Measures, with the same number of respondents agreeing to a lesser extent. In addition, 79.6 percent agreed that factory and enterprise autonomy had grown, with 25.4 percent "strongly"

---

[10] The expansion of corporate autonomy and the strengthening of management authority as a result of the 7/1 Measures has been recognized in practically every research undertaken on the subject. For one example, see Ministry of Unification and Korea Institute for National Unification, *North Korea's Economic Reform Tendency* (2005), 24-29.

[11] Defector A, formerly of middle management in an automobile company, stated that they had "changed from collective leadership of the Party committee to a system resembling exclusive supervision by the top manager." Defector B, a former joint-venture executive, stated that one essential factor of the 7/1 Measures was the change from central Party management and a new increase in the authority of managers over labor, as well as materials acquisition and product sales. Defector C worked for the mining materials affairs committee, and heard from the manager of the mine to which (s)he was assigned, "The manager's authority was strengthened." and that the manager was now responsible for production units. All of these testimonies were provided during interviews with the author, and all of these defectors left North Korea after the 7/1 Measures were implemented.

agreeing, and the remaining 54.2 percent "somewhat" in agreement. 25 percent of respondents strongly agreed that the authority of team leaders and office managers increased, as well, while another 45 percent somewhat agreed with this assertion. These survey results indicate that there was real decentralization of authority, both between enterprises and authorities, as well as within enterprises.

Table 7. Changes in Corporate Governance Following the 7/1 Measures (1)

(Units: persons, %)

Statement	Strongly Agree	Somewhat Agree	Somewhat Disagree	Strongly Disagree	Total
Following the 7/1 Measures, the top manager's authority concerning factory and/or enterprise economic activities strengthened more than that of Party secretaries.	20	20	15	6	61 persons
	32.8	32.8	24.6	9.8	100.0%
Following the 7/1 Measures, interference from central or regional party and government offices was reduced, while factory and/or enterprise autonomy was increased.	15	32	10	2	59 persons
	25.4	54.2	16.9	3.4	100.0%
Following the 7/1 Measures, office managers, and team leaders' authority in factories and/or enterprises was greater than before.	15	27	12	6	60 persons
	25.0	45.0	20.0	10.0	100.0%

However, changes did not stop with this decentralization of authority. As can be seen in Table 8, 55.2 percent of survey respondents strongly agreed that following the 7/1 Measures, there was

Table 8. Changes in Corporate Governance Following the 7/1 Measures (2)

(Units: persons, %)

Statement	Strongly Agree	Somewhat Agree	Somewhat Disagree	Strongly Disagree	Total
Following the 7/1 Measures, without direct coercion from the state, factories and/or enterprises were more interested in meeting a profit plan than in meeting individual production targets.	32	22	3	1	58 persons
	55.2	37.9	5.2	1.7	100.0 %
Following the 7/1 Measures, factories and/or enterprises become more interested in earning money than in fulfilling the state plan.	50	6	4	–	60 persons
	83.3	10.0	6.7	–	100.0 %
Following the 7/1 Measures, factory and/or enterprise managers and executives came to see raw materials, equipment, and even finished products not as possessions of the state, but rather, saw them as their own possessions, and treated them as such.	22	28	8	3	61 persons
	36.1	45.9	13.1	4.9	100.0 %
Following the 7/1 Measures, factories and/or enterprises, in an effort to reduce, as much as possible, payments to central or regional authorities, undertook schemes with upper-level Party and government organs, and in this way, were able to reduce payments.	9	27	11	6	53 persons
	17.0	50.9	20.8	11.3	100.0 %

an increased focus on meeting monetary goals rather than production targets, and another 37.9 percent somewhat agreed. Furthermore, an overwhelming 83.3 percent of respondents strongly agreed that factories and enterprises focused more on earning money than on sticking with the state's plan following the economic measures.

Of those polled 50.9 percent somewhat agreed that after the 7/1 Measures, enterprises sought to engage in projects and schemes with upper-level authorities in an effort to reduce the amount of money they would have to pay the government, while another 17 percent strongly agreed that such schemes had been sought. This is not unrelated to the fact that 82 percent believe (36.1 percent "strongly," 45.9 percent "somewhat") that the operators and managers felt even more strongly that raw materials, equipment, and even finished products were not possessions of the state, but rather, their own possessions.

Another factor affecting the change in relations between corporate managers, mid-level authorities, and laborers was the so-called "8/3 Laborer."[12] The 8/3 Laborer could be dismissed from a day of work by paying the factory a set wage. For example, by paying a fee 2-3 times the amount of one's wages, a laborer could

---

[12] The "8/3 Laborer" phenomenon resulted from the "8/3 People's Consumer Goods Production Movement," which was launched by Kim Jong Il after he inspected an exhibition of light industrial products in Pyongyang on August 3, 1984. Impressed by the wide variety of consumer goods produced throughout the country, Kim Jong Il is said to have "set forth important tasks to be fulfilled to make substantial contributions to the improvement of the people's living through an all-people movement for the production of consumer goods" (KCNA, August 3, 2004). The movement called for the establishment of household work units to manufacture wares using locally available materials outside the scope of the central planning authority.

be accounted for as present each day for up to a year without ever even showing up for work. This allowed laborers to forfeit state wages in order to free up their time for market economic activity. In Tables 9 and 10, it can be seen that following the 7/1 Measures, the number of these 8/3 Laborers increased significantly, and that the largest percentage of survey respondents (41.2 percent), answered that around 40 percent of all laborers in the corporate world were taking advantage of this opportunity. The second largest group, 21.6 percent, estimated that 10 percent of workers were 8/3 Laborers.

Table 9. 7/1 Measures and 8/3 Laborers (1)

(Units: persons, %)

Question	Greatly Increased	Slightly Increased	No Significant Change	Slightly Decreased	Greatly Decreased	Total
Following the 7/1 Measure, did the number of 8/3 Laborers increase or decrease?	35	15	3	4	2	59 persons
	59.3	25.4	5.1	6.8	3.4	100.0 %

Table 10. 7/1 Measures and 8/3 Laborers (2)

(Units: persons, %)

Question	5%	10%	20%	30%	40%	Total
When you left North Korea, approximately what percent of factory and/or enterprise workers were 8/3 Laborers?	9	11	5	5	21	51 persons
	17.6	21.6	9.8	9.8	41.2	100.0 %

Note: This question was posed to those defectors who left North Korea after the implementation of the 7/1 Measures.

Ultimately, what can be said to have been the most distinguishing factor of change in North Korean corporate governance, even after the 7/1 Measures, was the increasingly strong authority of those on the inside. Control mechanisms from outside all but disappeared, comparatively strengthening the control held by those inside enterprises. Managers, mid-level authorities, and laborers working within these enterprises increasingly worked together in order to realize their individual interests.

4. The Ripple Effect of Change in Corporate Governance

Insider control became problematic when these managers and executives employed their authority in order to pursue their own personal interests. In the case of socialist, state-owned enterprises, the erosion of so-called "public assets" became an issue. Of course, within North Korea, it is difficult to assess to what extent corporate insiders had felt they had the right to public assets; however, this problem of eroding public assets had developed, at least on a rudimentary level. For example, bribes were paid in order to protect the illegal sale of materials, and here, several types of slush funds could be found. Of the mechanisms employed, one is the so-called "double accounting system."

According to one defector (Defector D), who worked as a manager for a North Korean umbrella manufacturer, "If a manager and bookkeeper are of the same mind, a double accounting system can be created. Of course, the money raised this way is spent on bribes in order to ensure materials can be secured, but if it is discovered during inspections, a punishment is received. I also had a bit of a double accounting system." Another defector (Defector E), this time one who had been an executive in a chemical factory, stated:

The most representative method is the under reporting of actual production. In reality, it is overlooking a certain area when reporting actual production. By doing this, one guarantees products that can be sold at one's own discretion, bringing in cash. In addition, this money is used as a resource to unofficially procure materials. Well, how does a top manager decide to underreport produce? The decision of those within the enterprise is most important. A manager absolutely could not do this alone. A team leader or similar person is needed.

The same defector also stated:

It is almost impossible for a manager to be able to privately hoard money. There are some cases of hoarding by those in charge of foreign currency or materials, but as for the manager, hoarding is impossible without the help of those under [him or her]. Of course, there is embezzlement. But to what extent this takes place is a problem. Everyone does it, so as long as it is not excessive, it is alright. It doesn't matter who it is, everyone is doing the same thing. The law is enforced when it is done in excess.

More blatant experiences were also reported. A former worker from a North Korean clothing factory (Defector F) recollects the following:

Executives from the clothing factory even took Soviet-made sewing machine parts and sold them at the market. They were sold to private handicraft workers. Usually, around 15,000-20,000 won would be received for one unit. Not the whole sewing machine was sold; just the head unit. Because factory production was not maintained, not all the machines were in use. Therefore, there was no big inconvenience even though the machines were sold. For example, with slight tinkering, a machine could be made inoperable, and then paperwork could be forged. The paperwork would read, "the machine broke, and so it was disposed of." Then, a broken or secondhand machine someone brought in would be placed in the factory. This way, the new machine could be sold to an individual, and the used machine would go to the factory. As far as the factory was concerned, it was like swapping an intact machine for an inoperable one. It is ridiculous. This is how individual embezzlement arose.

A private entrepreneur who sold homemade goods in the North (Defector G) gave the following account:

At large corporations such as Kimchaek Ironworks, there are large freezers. They are in the gym. If you work out and sweat a lot, you (can) use this thing made by the state to have a cool drink. Well, this thing does not work this way, and it is used for business, targeting individual sellers of homemade goods. This is unavoidable, as one eats to live here, too. At Kimchaek Ironworks, as well, money was made this way in the summer. This is because in the summer, the ironworks can receive electricity from the state. So, those living in Chungjin City bring their ingredients up to the cooler, waiting in a line several hundred meters long just to put their goods in the freezer. For example, for ice treats, one only has to wait 2-3 hours and they will be all frozen. Then, someone takes their goods back to town and sells them.

IV. Causes and Conditions of Changing Corporate Governance

1. The Principal-Agent Problem

The principal-agent framework is useful for examining the causes and conditions of the changes in North Korea's corporate governance. The principal-agent problem materializes when there is information asymmetry between two parties. When there is a difference in the amount of information held by the principal and by the agent, it is easy for the agent to engage in opportunistic behavior, cutting into the principal's profits.[13] The asymmetry of information makes it impossible for the principal to make an observation on the activities or the endeavors of the agent, thereby rendering the principal incapable of sufficiently understanding the agent or the situation.

There are several factors that can bring about this predicament for the principal. One factor is the element of probability. The outcome that could be produced by the agent may be a result of the agent's ability, but it also may be that of luck. In fact, the only element that the principal could observe well would be the end result; but there also exists the possibility that outside factors, such as weather or any sudden change in circumstances, may have affected the result. Knowing the actual factors that affect the end outcome and judging to what degree the agent is responsible for the outcome is an extremely difficult task.[14]

The inability to draw viable conclusions can also come about

---

[13] For details, see P. R. Gregory and R. C. Stuart, *Comparative Economic Systems*, 7th ed. (Boston: Houghton Mifflin, 2004), 289.

[14] For details, see E. G. Furubotn and R. Richter, *Institution and Economic Theory* (Michigan: University of Michigan Press, 2000), 22-23.

due to the manipulation of a situation by an agent. Originally, in a socialist economy, information was circulated in a controlled manner. Enterprises offered information in the form of reports to higher authorities, and received information in the form of orders passed down from above. Therefore, these higher authorities actually had to rely on the objects of their control, the enterprises, for the information on which their decisions and orders were based. Put another way, when it came to control over information, the enterprises were in a more powerful position than the controlling authorities. This left these enterprises with ample opportunity to distort information in a manner in which to make it most valuable.

For instance, only an enterprise's managers have exact knowledge of a given company's actual production capacity or amounts of raw materials required to produce the final products. Higher authorities can only estimate these figures. This is a prime opportunity for those within the enterprise to manipulate numbers in order to create a more profitable environment for themselves, by understating production capacity, exaggerating material needs, or both. On the other hand, according to the principal-agent theory, the principal has the power of oversight, giving him or her the power to penalize the agent. Therefore, it is assumed that the principal has the power to ensure the agent carries out any agreement.

In order to resolve this sort of principal-agent problem, from the principal's perspective, there must be either a mechanism in place that would allow for oversight of the agent's activities or an incentive system that would automatically lead to the agent pursuing the principal's interests. Here, whether the principal will choose the oversight mechanism or the incentive system depends on the cost and availability of the oversight mechanism. If oversight were to be excessively costly or inefficient, the importance of an incentive system would grow. On the other hand, the principal

2. Problems of Oversight

1) Paralysis of Oversight Functions

As can be seen in Table 11, oversight mechanisms employed by outside offices over enterprises began to fail in the 1990s. In particular, a range of illegal trading and other activities undertaken by managers in order to procure materials began to gain tacit approval.

Table 11. Paralysis of Enterprise Oversight Functions in the 1990s

(Units: persons, %)

Statement	Strongly Agree	Somewhat Agree	Somewhat Disagree	Strongly Disagree	Total
Oversight by each outside inspection office, central ministry, committee, management bureau, etc., oversaw and managed whether factories and/or enterprises were adhering to laws and regulations while carrying out economic activities, but during the economic crisis of the 1990s, this kind of oversight and management was not smoothly accomplished.	39	63	26	21	149 persons
	26.2	42.3	17.4	14.1	100.0 %
During the 1990s, Party secretaries within factories and/or enterprises turned a blind eye to managers engaging in illegal activities or trade in order to procure materials.	44	73	26	10	153 persons
	28.8	47.7	17.0	6.5	100.0%
During the 1990s, city and district administrative economic committees, as well as city, district, and provincial party officials, turned a blind eye to managers engaging in illegal activities or trade in order to procure materials.	28	83	27	10	148 persons
	18.9	56.1	18.2	6.8	100.0 %

Table 11. Paralysis of Enterprise Oversight Functions in the 1990s (Continued)

(Units: persons, %)

Statement	Strongly Agree	Somewhat Agree	Somewhat Disagree	Strongly Disagree	Total
During the 1990s, inspection offices, ministries, committees, management bureaus, etc. turned a blind eye to managers engaging in illegal activities or trade in order to procure materials.	25	68	33	12	138 persons
	18.1	49.3	23.9	8.7	100.0 %

Of survey respondents, 28.8 percent strongly agreed that Party secretaries working in factories and enterprises turned a blind eye to these activities, while another 47.7 percent acknowledged that they somewhat agreed this was the case.[15] Fully 75 percent of the respondents agreed that city and county administrative economic committees, as well as city, county, and provincial Party officials, also turned a blind eye to these activities; 67.4 percent of respondents agreed that this tacit approval took place as high up as inspection offices, ministries, committees, and management bureaus. With these numbers, it is clear that inspection and oversight of enterprises from "outside" offices was not being implemented according to the central government plans.

2) Factors Influencing Oversight Functions

If this were the case, what was it that caused these oversight mechanisms to fail? The biggest reason can be said to have been

---

[15] As Suk-ki Lee (2003) points out, Party secretaries in factories and enterprises were not seen as docile figures. On the one hand, they were workers within the factory or enterprise, but at the same time, they were responsible for oversight and guidance of the managers. In this case, the secretary also takes on the role of the principal's agent in the enterprise.

the escalating cost of inspections. Both the monetary and non-monetary costs necessary for high-level offices to properly investigate the activities of each enterprise grew sharply during the 1990s. The reasons these costs shot up can be largely divided into two causes: the increasing asymmetry of information and the growing incompetence of mid-level inspection offices.

The first cause, the growing asymmetry of information, was also a result of the economic crisis faced during the 1990s. As mentioned, there was ample opportunity for enterprises to distort information provided to the central planning authorities. Furthermore, with the economic crisis, corporate administration data become highly unstable, providing even more impetus to report "creatively."

Before the economic crisis hit, the central authorities guaranteed businesses for a variety of activities, providing the tools necessary for these enterprises to carry out the orders passed down from above. While this guarantee was not sufficient, at least the central government was taking responsibility for them. However, as the economic crisis set in, this situation changed. Serious energy shortages and a lack of raw materials meant that the central government could no longer be responsible for the provision of energy, raw materials, or equipment. This led the central government to call on enterprises to be more self-reliant.

Central planning authorities must observe the activities of enterprises, including endeavors to attain plan goals; but due to the economic crisis, effective observation became increasingly more difficult. Provision of materials and production data became unstable and difficult to verify as the unofficial economic sector, the black market, grew as well. All of these conditions made accurate observation and verification of corporate administrative information an increasingly unattainable goal. Today, the central authorities are even less able than before to obtain concrete data on the activities of North Korean enterprises. Although the authorities still demand data and attempt to keep tabs on corporate activities, it is increasingly difficult to collect valid and accurate information.

A former chemical plant administrator (Defector E) stated, "Socialism is said to be about central control, but in reality, the average person has no idea about much of what goes on, including internal trading within enterprises. Only those in charge are aware of what takes place. This is the path enterprises created in order to survive."

Defector D, the former umbrella factory manager, reported, "Even though someone who came from the higher authorities to inspect the actual conditions would be an expert, [s]he would still not be able to know the exact conditions of the factory better than us." In light of this, it would appear that even though central authorities were making efforts to maintain oversight, their efforts were, in fact, magnifying their inability to accurately verify information provided by the enterprises. This would provide even more incentive to manipulate data for one's own advantage, and was exacerbated further still by the rising costs of oversight.

The second cause was the growing incompetence of mid-level inspection offices. Planning authorities, the principal in this equation, mobilized an array of mid-level inspection offices in an attempt to maintain oversight of businesses, or agents, and get a grip on the growing information asymmetry problem. These mid-level offices included those in the Ministry of Industry, regional administrative offices, and Party organizations within enterprises. However, even under these circumstances, as the mid-level offices also had their own agendas and interests, they also operated as agents of the central planning authorities. This trend continued to grow as the economic crisis grew deeper.

A former leader of an administrative economic committee (Defector H) stated:

> The local industrial bureau of cities' administrative economic committees closed out yearly plans and submitted them to provincial administrative economic committees in order to receive the next year's plan. This process was rife with bribery. It was a kind of lobbying. So, cities and districts that paid many bribes to the provincial offices were given smaller [quotas], and those cities and districts not paying bribes were given more [quotas].

This is one example of lower-level authorities taking on the role of mediator, looking out for the interests of the enterprises when dealing with upper-level authorities. Regional administrative offices are responsible for oversight of enterprises, but at the same time they have a vested interest in whether or not they would submit reports stating that enterprises had met planned quotas. If the evaluation criteria applied to the inspection office were the same as that applied to the enterprises themselves, then naturally it would be in the best interests of both to report that all quotas were met.

Party organizations within corporations, and the Party secretaries in particular, were responsible for carrying out inspections, but there were some limitations. Managers and Party secretaries would meet monthly in district offices to report their status. Administrators and Party secretaries from those enterprises unable to meet quotas would be reprimanded. While obviously shortfalls would be more the responsibility of the manager than the Party secretary, the secretary could not be completely without blame for failures to reach quotas. This meant there was a good possibility of friction between managers and Party secretaries; but at the same time, it meant that, to some extent, their interests aligned in regard to meeting set quotas. Therefore, the criteria for evaluation of both the inspector and inspected were similar, somewhat preventing an inspector from thoroughly observing an enterprise.[16] Not only that, but also because mid-level inspection offices were privy to information that could not be known by higher-level authorities, they were in a position to help enterprises. This pattern also appeared more clearly as the economic crisis deepened and the administrative activities of the enterprises grew more unstable.

The weakening of the mid-level inspection offices is, in part, due to the fact that it was simply not possible for enterprises to meet state-set quotas. At the same time, embezzlement and other forms of corruption also played a role. As enterprises looked toward illegal activities, as it was impossible to produce required goods, it was difficult for them to avoid offering bribes to these inspection authorities. On the one hand, these factors caused the cost associated with oversight after the North's economic crisis to soar. On the other hand, they also reduced the need for such oversight.[17] While the purpose of the principal's oversight is to ensure that the agent is following the conditions of the contract or agreement, overseeing an agent and then punishing that agent based on the results of inspections can actually further complicate a situation.[18] At a time of economic crisis, this could even have a negative

---

[16] When deceiving mid-level administrative offices meant that these administrators could actually profit, enterprises could successfully hide information from authorities. Many ex-Soviet defectors testified to such arrangements. Berliner (1957), 262.

[17] The reduction in benefits and/or results of an inspection means a weakening of the strength of a principal enforcing the implementation of contractual stipulations. This is another possible result of a planned economy's near collapse.

[18] No matter what kind of manager, or to what extent this takes place, illegal

effect on the state.

Before the economic crisis, instances of principal-agent problems existed; but as the crisis mounted, so-called "unofficial corporate activity" spread. It is worth noting that these unofficial activities were undertaken in order to meet state quotas under difficult circumstances, such as the condition of production and reproduction became less stable and more unpredictable. Even if enterprises cannot meet state plan quotas, these unofficial activities are important to employees because they can earn food or basic necessities by selling their product. These days, enterprises have replaced the state as the entity providing workers with daily necessities. This situation also hinders the state's ability to punish other law-breaking entities. If punishment were prescribed, the side effects could end up being greater than the original sin.

Defector E, the administrator from the chemical factory, testified:

> If oversight and inspection were thoroughly carried out, North Korea would be even more crushed. Lax inspection and oversight is necessary if factories are to be operated, allowing workers to show up and collect wages. If every illegal element of an enterprise was to result in punishment, the factory would be unable to operate ... the state cannot provide rations, so where is this wage the manager provides to the workers coming from? Isn't it obvious?

On the one hand, after the 7/1 Measures were introduced, the cost of oversight grew. Enterprises gained considerable autonomy

---

activities are still taking place. Therefore, if oversight and inspection is carried out according to plan, then every corporate administrator would need to be punished.

regarding production, sales, purchases, and other corporate activity, and these activities grew not according to any state plan, but in accordance with the demands of the markets. It should be noted that actually, before the 7/1 Measures, these kinds of activities had emerged in the unofficial realm, but following implementation of the measures, these activities could also be found in the official realms. Furthermore, the state was unable to provide the resources to support corporate activities, leading these enterprises to take matters into their own hands. The further sharpening of asymmetry of information between central authorities and local enterprises leading to an increase in oversight costs was entirely natural, as was the noninterference by central authorities into some realms of business activities.

3. The Issue of Incentives

1) Independent Cost Accounting

The issue of incentives is equally problematic. In North Korea, there is no fully functioning incentive system or enticement program. There is a long history of independent cost accounting in the North. While it is unclear to what lengths it has been implemented, it is known that the system was originally established in 1946. Later, in 1952, 1973, and 1984, regulations related to the system were revised, and the substance of the system was expanded, while at the same time, in reality, the system was nominalized.

Independent Accounting System (IAS)[19] is a system in which state-operated enterprises appropriate their own expenditures

---

[19] The opposite of an independent accounting system is a budgetary system. Enterprises employing this system receive capital according to the state budget, and then finance operations and management with these funds.

based on their revenue, and then submit the remainder of their profits to the state. However, this "completely independent cost accounting system" is merely a concept, and in reality, what the state demands of enterprises is a more "relaxed" version of independent cost accounting. In North Korea, the central theme of this system is how to divide profits between the enterprise and the state. In other words, a given portion of an enterprise's profits would remain with the enterprise, to be spent as fixed-capital investment, floating capital, bonuses, and other expenses. The IAS is related to how the enterprise systematically—or to a certain extent freely—spends this money. Therefore, this accounting system presents the issue of corporate (administrators and laborers) incentives and other material enticements.[20]

During the mid- to late 1980s, a significant chasm developed between the North's purported IAS and the reality of the accounting methods being used. In reality, the amount of profits held onto by businesses was extremely small, as most of the profits were absorbed by the state. The IAS had become entirely nominal. Rather than providing physical enticements or regular autonomy, the state's income was prioritized, and profits were turned over to central authorities, dampening any incentive that the IAS was designed to instill. Actually, what was demanded of enterprises was to treat state capital "preciously," while "fighting" for frugality within the enterprise. These enterprises were to earn profits and turn them directly over to the state.

According to defector testimonies, enterprises were told to employ the independent accounting system. However, in reality, due to an array of restrictive government measures, it was not

---

[20] The use of an independent accounting system is closely related to the issue of to what degree of autonomy enterprises are allowed to operate.

uncommon for the system to be inapplicable. One example given was that, officially, a business bank account was separate from the national treasury; but in reality, money deposited into the account could be freely accessed by the state. During the late 1980s to early 1990s, a visible change took place in the North's accounting processes. From this period on, an unregimented expansion of independent accounting aggressively spread, and its real implementation could be seen on a much broader scale. If businesses were able to produce above and beyond state-set quotas, the businesses could increase operational funds, and administrators' could use their discretion in providing bonuses to workers based on their productivity. However, this was hindered by shortages in state capital and the inability of enterprises to procure necessary materials.[21] Despite these hindrances, the 7/1 Measures did strengthen the independent accounting system in North Korea.[22] The emergence of the "Income Index" marked the real implementation of the new accounting system.[23]

The 7/1 Measures also included instructions for revamping the North's pricing system. This measure eliminated state support

---

[21] Of course, it is true that in socialist enterprises, the independent accounting system is limited from the outset. The reasons for this are, first, the distortion of the macroeconomic pricing mechanisms serve to delegitimize independent accounting and other budgeting systems, and second, the result of this kind of accounting has almost no influence on the current or future position of the business. This is because a business's future production goals are usually not a function of current profits.

[22] On September 2, 2002, North Korean Vice-minister of Trade Yong-seul Kim revealed at a gathering in Tokyo to explain the 7/1 Measures that the two essential elements to this new economic reform were the thorough implementation of the independent accounting system by enterprises and factories, and substantial overhaul of the pricing and income systems.

[23] For details, see Dong-ho Cho, ed., *The Search for a North Korean Economic Development Strategy* (Seoul: Korea Development Institute, 2002), 266.

of pricing and allowed for consideration of the market functions of supply and demand. This also helped to lay the foundation for more thorough implementation of the independent accounting system. The measures allowed wages to actually function more as wages in a market-based economy, allowing real wages to be paid in currency. This too served to support and foster the IAS.[24]

The strengthening of the IAS certainly could be seen in myriad ways, and the contents of the 7/1 Measures served as one way to directly strengthen the system. More than anything, there were several specific points included in the measures that were clearly distinct from the previous system, and were instituted specifically in order to ensure smooth implementation of independent accounting. Despite even these measures, however, limitations existed. Pricing mechanisms were not freed up to the point of eliminating all distortion. Additionally, despite the adoption of the "Total Pricing Index" for evaluation of enterprises, the importance to a socialist economy of evaluating the real material outputs of production complexes could not be completely ignored. Furthermore, shortages of capital and materials, as well as other macroeconomic hurdles, still hindered economic growth.

2) The Issue of Corporate and Labor Incentives

According to J. M. Montias, the following three conditions must be provided in order for upper-level authorities to effectively apply an incentive system so that economic actors within an organization meet the goals assigned or handed down from above:[25]

---

[24] Yun-chul Kim, "Results and Prospects of North Korean Economic Management Reform," Kim, Yun-chul and Park, Soon-sung, eds., *Research on North Korean Economic Reform* (Seoul: Humanitas, 2002), 16.

[25] J. M. Montias, *The Structure of Economic Systems* (New Haven: Yale University Press, 1976), ch. 13.

First, the actor receiving compensation in accordance with the outcome of economic activity must be able to influence that outcome with his/her decisions. This is an issue of the extent to which action (investment) and outcome (yield) are connected—or, to put it another way, the chain of events between input and output. Second, the principal must have the means to be aware of whether or not the agent is carrying out economic activities appropriate for the principal's interests. In other words, an effective system of oversight and supervision must be in place. Third, the incentive offered to the actor from the principal must be of an appropriate value to induce the agent to perform the action directed by the principal.

If these conditions are not sufficiently satisfied, the incentive system will not operate smoothly. In North Korea's case, the collapse of its previously existing incentive system took place in two stages. The first stage of collapse occurred in the 1980s as problems within the North's centrally planned economy became more obvious. The second stage occurred during the 1990s, when the official economy largely contracted, while the unofficial economic sectors quickly expanded.[26] Throughout both of these stages, the failure of the system can be explained by the insufficient existence of the conditions Montias points to as being necessary for effective enticement of economic agents.

First, prior to the 1990s, the distorted, state-set pricing system weakened any link between a business's or laborer's ability, efficiency, or efforts and the actual performance of that business. The same is true of a socialist corporate management system. There is

---

[26] Seung-ryul Oh looks at Montias's theory from the perspective of information flows and transaction costs, and through this framework, explains the collapse of the North Korean incentive system in the 1990s. Oh, Seung-ryul, *North Korea's Economic Change and Incentive System: Prospects for Reform According to the Expansion of the Unofficial Sector* (Seoul: KINU, 1999), 66-69.

no link between incentives and output, and this plays a significant role in the inefficiency of socialist production. Second, the uncertainty and instability of the centrally planned economy weakened oversight functions. The Party and administrative central management organizations had difficulty in supervising the unofficial activities of businesses. Third, distribution of food rations, provision of daily essentials, and guarantees of employment were unrelated to any economic incentives for laborers. Even if they were, the shortages of everyday consumables would have made it impossible to provide sufficient economic incentives to workers.

These factors combined to lead to the weakening of the North's incentive system. In addition, as the 1990s came around, North Korea's already weakened incentive system collapsed under the weight of additional burdens. First, severe energy and materials shortages essentially made workers powerless to produce. In terms of incentives, this would be considered a physical restraint. No efforts of any worker would have any measurable effect on the state of the economy. This meant that there was no longer any reason for the existence of an incentive system. Second, as was explained earlier, the severe economic hardships in the North led to the collapse of the central authorities' information-gathering mechanisms. Third, the collapse of the state rationing network and distribution system, the expansion of black markets, and sharply growing inflation in these black markets meant that the economic guarantees of employment and wages were meaningless to the North Korean worker. Laborers were forced to abandon their work assignments and engage in side jobs or illegal trading in order to maintain their livelihoods.

There are several points in the 7/1 Measures related to the incentive system that are decisively different than the North's previous policy. Most notable is the sharp change in the system of allocation.[27] With the new measures, a worker could completely support oneself and one's family solely on wages, and would no longer be reliant on state rations. This also meant that the livelihood of a worker and his or her family was reliant on the labor they put into their state-assigned job.

Another notable point is that wages now differed according to occupation and position. In addition, the North's contract system was also considerably strengthened.[28] The extent to which an enterprise's production and profit were linked to the wages paid to workers was strengthened to the point that now there is really no comparison with the previous system.

These incentives introduced by the 7/1 Measures were considerably different from the system previously in place. Not only was the link between labor and incentives strengthened, but there was considerable overhaul of remuneration allocation, as well as in other areas, to create a basis on which the new incentive program could be smoothly implemented.

It is impossible not to recognize the potential for increased production due to this strengthening of incentives. However, as the North's economy is practically exhausted, if assistance from outside is not forthcoming, this potential for increased production faces significant barriers. Furthermore, as it becomes increasingly difficult for the state to supply wages and consumables on a regu-

---

[27] The sharp rise in the prices of consumables was centered on commodities and services that had previously been offered at prices so low they were practically free. Food was but one such commodity targeted. This meant that the amount of money a worker budgeted for food, previously around 3.5 percent, now accounted for as much as 50 percent of one's wages.

[28] According to the September 11, 2002, *Choson Sinbo*, Yoo-bong Kim, a worker at one of the North's larger mines, explained that they were producing 300 percent of the monthly quota, and aside from their basic salary (6,000 won), they would receive between 20-30 thousand won in progressive wages.

lar basis, inflation is again on the rise in the North's markets, which, in turn, is again weakening the labor incentive system.

In order to assess the effect of and limitations on the incentive system spelled out in the 7/1 Measures, the three conditions Montias lays out for the effective enticement of labor through incentives should be examined. Through the measures, there is a proportional relationship between action and result, fulfilling the first condition. There is also considerable improvement in the provision of guaranteed economic returns, as stipulated by the third condition. However, even though the first and third conditions have been addressed, ultimately, the improvements are insufficient. This is because some aspects of these conditions remain unchanged, both on an organizational and on a macroeconomic level. Furthermore, the second condition, oversight and supervision, was not addressed at all by the 7/1 Measures.

V. Conclusion: Summary and Policy Recommendations

With the onset of the economic crisis in the 1990s, a tendency toward insider control emerged within North Korea's corporate governance. Some elements of this tendency were present in the North prior to the economic hardships; however, the difficulties that struck in the 1990s brought these elements out in full force. The 7/1 Measures further exacerbated this shift toward decentralization of authority and growing insider control.

As a result, the principal-agent problem emerged on a widespread scale, often with intertwined or overlapping relationships. Relationships between planning authorities and enterprises, as well as planning authorities and mid-level management offices, reflect problems that exist in principal-agent relations, while relationships between mid-level management and enterprises, as well as administrators and labor within businesses and factories, reflect myriad examples of cooperation and collusion. The most significant factor leading to this situation appears to be the failure of the oversight and enticement system.

The increasing cost of oversight was the main cause of the failure of the oversight mechanisms in the North. In addition, this increase in cost was brought on by the worsening asymmetry of information between enterprises and central authorities, as well as the incompetence of mid-level inspection offices. This also resulted, as a secondary impact, in the lessening of the need for such oversight. Therefore, oversight became more relaxed and more perfunctory.

As oversight was reduced, the North Korean authorities turned toward incentives. The 7/1 Measures significantly increased incentives, as they introduced a system of enticement rather than coercion. The implementation of an actual independent accounting system, replacing the largely nominal system previously employed, also served to provide incentives to enterprises and labor. A fundamental framework upon which the system could function was established; however, there were still significant limitations, as macroeconomic handicaps such as capital and material shortages continued to plague the North.

The 7/1 Measures actually further led to the retreat of the North's oversight system. The cost of oversight of enterprises further increased due to these measures. The increased autonomy of enterprises and the expansion of their market activities became legitimized and were considered by the government to be officially sanctioned. Furthermore, this sort of corporate activity emerged out of the self-driven efforts of businesses, rather than any policy shift by central authorities. It was quite natural that information asymmetry between central authorities and enterprises grew, and that this further drove up the cost of oversight. In an effort to reform the economy, one measure to maximize the efficiency of enterprises is the decentralization of authority over business decisions. Therefore, in North Korea's current situation, with practically no systemic protective measures in place and only simplistic decentralization underway, issues of insider control and collaboration between administrators and laborers greatly increase the likelihood of erosion of state capital. Actually, after the 7/1 Measures, this situation could be seen quite clearly in the North. Therefore, decentralization of corporate authority needs to be pursued in conjunction with a revision of the corporate governance system. North Korean authorities need to abandon the current system, within which authority is still centrally controlled by Party organizations, and construct a system of corporate governance in which oversight and evaluation is carried out under a system of tiered administrative control, which would help guarantee corporate efficiency.

Bibliography

Berliner, Joseph S., *Factory and Management in the USSR* (Cambridge, Mass.: Harvard University Press, 1957).

Cho, Dong-ho, ed., *The Search for a North Korean Economic Development Strategy* (in Korean) (Seoul: Korea Development Institute, 2002).

Furubotn, E. G. and R. Richter, *Institution and Economic Theory* (Michigan: University of Michigan Press, 2000).

Granick, D., "Institutional Innovation and Economic Management: The Soviet Incentive System, 1921 to the Present," in Guroff, G. and Carstensen, F. V., eds., *Entrepreneurship in Imperial Russia and the Soviet Union* (Princeton: Princeton University Press, 1983).

_____, *Chinese State Enterprises* (Chicago and London: The University of Chicago Press, 1990).

Gregory, P. R. and R. C. Stuart, *Comparative Economic Systems*, 7th ed. (Boston: Houghton Mifflin, 2004).

Kim, Yun-chul, "Results and Prospects of North Korean Economic Management Reform," in Kim Yun-chul and Park Soon-sung, eds., *Research on North Korean Economic Reform* (in Korean) (Seoul: Humanitas, 2002).

Kornai, Janos, *The Socialist System: The Political Economy of Communism* (Princeton: Princeton University Press, 1992).

Lee, Keun, *Chinese Firms and the State in Transition and Agency Problems in the Reform China* (New York: M. E. Sharpe, 1991).

Lee, Suk-ki, *North Korea's 1990s Economic Crisis and Changes in Enterprise Operations* (in Korean) (Ph.D. Dissertation, Seoul National University, 2003).

Ministry of Unification and Korea Institute for National Unification, *North Korea's Economic Reform Tendency* (in Korean) (2005).

Montias, J. M., *The Structure of Economic Systems* (New Haven: Yale University Press, 1976).

Nove, Alec, *The Soviet Economy*, 3rd ed. (London: George Allen & Unwin Ltd., 1968).

Oh, Seung-ryul, *North Korea's Economic Change and Incentive System: Prospects for Reform According to the Expansion of the Unofficial Sector* (in Korean) (Seoul: KINU, 1999).

Qian, Y., "Enterprise Reform in China: Agency Problems and Political Control," *Economics of Transition* (June 1996).

Yang, Moon-soo, *Structure of the North Korean Economy* (in Korean) (Seoul: Seoul National University Press, 2001).

Yoo, Dong-woon, *Neo-institutional Economics* (in Korean) (Seoul: Sunhaksa, 1999).

Chapter 5

The Pseudo-Market Coordination Regime

⊣ Jung-Chul LEE ⊢

I. An Evolutionary Approach to System Transition

The economy in transition should focus on the most effective way to overcome the transitory recess it is experiencing; in other words, its "valley of tears."[1] It must adopt a tailored strategy that best befits its initial conditions.[2] However, from the experiences of transition economies in the 1990s, important lessons can be drawn: stabilize first, move fast.[3] As "initial conditions" and "stabilizing first," as well as the country's financial capacity, are put under pressure during system transition,[4] the next question is: How do

---

[1] In reference to escape from transition recession caused by role-changing between the winner and the loser in the "valley of tears," see Pradeep K. Mitra and Marcelo Selowsky, "Lessons from a decade of Transition in Eastern Europe and the Former Soviet Union," *IMF, Finance & Development*, Vol. 39, No. 2 (June 2002).

[2] Charles Wyplosz, "Ten Years of Transformation – Macroeconomic Lessons," *World Bank Policy Research Working Paper 2288* (February, 2000), 8.

[3] Ibid., 26-27; Pradeep K. Mitra and Marcelo Selowsky, op. cit., xxii-xxiv.

[4] In a transitional period, chaos prevails in an economy suffering the collapse of the old incentive system and incomplete implementation of a new one. During that period, purchasing power and total demand also shrink in the

we view countries of the old regime that have market economies in all but name? In other words, can we conceptualize the existence of a market in the old regime as "transition?" Naturally, this question leads us to another: How can we evaluate economies that are undergoing a "de facto transition to a market economy," such as North Korea?[5]

If we measure these economies with conventional analytical tools—e.g. price liberalization or privatization—we see that the current economic policy of North Korea is still resisting any systemic change, and thus, belongs to the old regime. Dismantling the old system through price liberalization and privatization cannot

---

course of capital redistribution. In such circumstances, excessive radical price liberalization, decentralization, and even privatization can cause counter reform sentiment by increasing monopoly incomes. The state couldn't avoid financial deficits because of increasing expenditures, but such deficit tended to result in financial insolvency due to the drop of tax revenue. Even though the financial deficit itself was not the cause, there were many cases of vicious downward spirals among deficits, increased issues of currency and inflation. As a consequence, as long as the existence of state systems, which guarantee strong financial capacity and rigid financial regulation, was not presupposed, any result of transition, either radical or gradual, was the last thing to be expected. The dissolution of an old regime was not a guarantee of success of transition.

[5] Moon-soo Yang, "Changing Aspects of North Korean Economy and the Life of the Residents," The Peace Foundation ed., *Current Situation in North Korea and the Life of the Residents* (The 2007 Peace Foundation Forum Presented Materials, Vol. 3, 2007), 15-22; Seok-gi Lee, "Weakened Planned Economy System, Spontaneous Marketization and Changes in Companies' Management Structure: Characteristics and Crisis in North Korean Economy since 1990s," *Trends and Prospects*, No. 62 (2004), 174-181; Young-hoon Lee, "Spontaneous Marketization in North Korea and Development of Economic Reformation," *Research on Unification Affairs*, Vol. 17, No. 2 (2005), 51; Moon-seok Cha, "Dear Leader Replaced by Currency: Market and Market Economy in North Korea," *Discourse 201*, Vol. 10, No. 2 (2007), 78-79.

guarantee transition to a market economy. Worse, under certain conditions, even privatization can be an obstacle to adopting market reforms.[6] The important point is not privatization in form, but a substantial institutional transformation—e.g., new financial institutions, a changed incentive structure, and a change in the government's role in the overall transition process.

The emergence of de facto marketization should not be overestimated to the point it is mistaken for economic transition, but, at the same time, it should not be underestimated as merely an adjusted planning system simply due to the absence of certain free market mechanisms such as privatization or price liberalization. If we more liberally interpret such terms as "new financial institutions," and a "new incentive system," the concept of "transition" can be applied to a much wider spectrum. If we are quick to draw the conclusion that those countries' passive responses to the global market economy indicate the old regime's resistance to reform, we are refusing to accept the probability that there are many different kinds of evolutionary paths in system transition.[7]

This chapter focuses on how the North Korean regime is coping with grassroots transformation, and the role of the regressive market system in the process. This totalitarian regime, once considered monolithic, is now reacting to changes, rather than dictating them. It is accepting new financial institutions and an alternative incentive system, which are, needless to say, contradictory to its traditional mechanisms. A new, market-driven regulation

---

[6] Vito Tanzi and George Tsibouris, "Fiscal Reform Over Ten Years of Transition," IMF (June 2000), 26-29.

[7] This emphasizes the open political-economic approach that micro-evolution and macro-evolution can vary diversely. Referring to the evolutionary standpoint of a political-economy, see Jong-han Kim, "Use of Evolutionary View in Politico-economic Analysis," *Applied Economics*, Vol. 7, No. 1 (2005).

system has also replaced the old system of administrative orders. How do we evaluate and conceptualize these changes in "socialist" North Korea?

Cuba's dollarization and de-dollarization process and Russia's virtual economy provide a very interesting and valuable analogical framework for North Korea's de facto marketization. As such, this chapter first examines how North Korea's dual exchange rate system works in comparison with the dollarization and de-dollarization process in Cuba. Then, through an analysis of Russia's virtual economy, it will examine how a regressive market system took root in North Korea's transitional economy. Based on these analyses, we will make an attempt to interpret North Korea's transition strategy.

II. Cuba's Dual Economy and Russia's Virtual Economy

1. Dollarization and De-dollarization in Cuba and Its Dual Economy

Cuba's dollarization took a different path from that of other, rather conventional, dollarization processes.[8] Normally, dollarization starts with a sharp inflationary trend as sellers begin measuring prices with dollar-equivalents out of fear of undervalued rates.

---

[8] For research on current reforms that dealt with fields such as dollarization in Cuba, see Seong-hyeong Lee, "Success, Problems and Future Prospects of Cuba's Economic Reformation," *Economy and Society*, No. 71 (2006); Yeong-tae Jung, Yeon-cheol Kim, and Sang-hyeon Seo, "Prospect of Change in North Korea from the Viewpoint of Relative Socialism with Focus on the Precedents of Libya and Cuba," *Korea Institute of National Unification Collection*, No. 07-11 (2007); Seok-ho Shin, "Economic Crises and Reformations in North Korea and Cuba," Ph.D. Dissertation, University of North Korean Studies (2008).

As the dollar begins to be used not just for savings, but also as an accounting unit, it begins to be used at exchange values. When this occurs, domestic monetary authorities are no longer able to respond to inflation or dollarization, as the situation normally goes beyond their control. As inflation soars, the government loses purchasing power, tax revenues drop under the Tanzi Effect,[9] and the affected government then increases the issue of currency to repay public loans, leaving no means to respond to soaring inflation and the devaluation of the currency. Finally, the dollar effectively replaces the domestic currency.[10]

The peculiarity of dollarization in Cuba is that the country has two clearly different domestic economic sectors: the dollar sector and the peso sector. Under this dual economy, the monetary authorities legalized dollarization, collecting profits from the dollar economic sector to compensate for its weak domestic economy, and redistributing the wealth.[11] The government entrusted to its

---

[9] The Tanzi Effect (in Argentina, this is often called the "Olivera Effect," in honor of Professor Julio Olivera of the Universidad de Buenos Aires, who also wrote about fiscal lags at about the same time) explains that the real value of tax revenues falls in high inflation as a consequence of the usual time lag in the collection of taxes—for example, between the moment when income is earned and when income tax is paid. With high inflation, this lag means that by the time the government receives the money, its purchasing power has already depreciated, and the money will not go as far in purchasing goods or paying salaries (that often become indexed to inflation faster than taxes). At moderate rates of inflation, the Tanzi Effect is negligible; at triple-digit rates and higher, it can be devastating (Vito Tanzi, *Argentina: An Economic Chronicle, How One of the Richest Countries in the World Lost Its Wealth* (New York: Jorge Pinto Books, 2007), 164).

[10] Arne C. Kildegaard and Robert Orro Fernandez, "Aspect of Dollarization and DE-Dollarization in Cuba," Presented at the Latin American Studies Association Conference, San Juan, PR, March 2006, 3.

[11] Though dollarized economic sectors such as tourism, joint ventures, and

central bank surplus dollars and foreign currency earnings, and collects profits generated when foreign companies pay their employees' dollar wages with pesos.[12] The government then uses the collected dollars in its social service sectors or provides them to some of the less-competitive domestic manufacturing industries at the official 1:1 exchange rate.[13] Setting the official exchange rate at 1:1 is essentially an overvaluation of the Cuban peso. While export

---

exports generally exchange dollars into domestic pesos with the ratio of 1:1, the real market exchange rate is 1:24. Accordingly, when using the ratio of 1:1 in money-changing, they make 24 times as much profit as if they had used the market rate.

[12] In reference to arbitrage or foreign exchange arbitrage in the course of wage payment in foreign-owned enterprises, see Remy Herrera and Paulo Nakatani, "De-Dollarizing Cuba," *International Journal of Political Economy*, Vol. 34, No. 4 (January 2005); Archibald R. M. Ritter, "Survival Strategies and Economic Illegalities in Cuba," *Cuba in Transition*, Vol. 15 (The Fifteenth Annual Meeting of the Association for the Study of the Cuban Economy (October 2005)), 350.

[13] The exchange rate of pesos to dollars rose at the rate of 150:1. The rate had been revaluated seven times in the 1990s alone. C. P. Chandrasekhar, "Cuba; Dealing with the Dollar," *Frontline*, Vol. 16 (April 1999); Now, the rate is stabilized at the level of 24:1. Even though convertible pesos (CUC), which began as a part of de-dollarization in 2004, are exchanged at the ratio of one to one, the exchange rate with domestic pesos was 1:26. But the exchange rate of convertible peso to domestic peso was adjusted to the level of 1:24 as a result of a revaluation of the domestic peso. On the contrary, exchange of domestic pesos into convertible pesos takes a commission of one dollar, making the exchange more disadvantageous. Carmelo Mesa-Lago, "The Cuban Economy in 2006-2007," *Cuba in Transition*, Vol. 17 (The Seventeenth Annual Meeting of the Association for the Study of the Cuban Economy, 2007), 12; in addition, due to discriminatory measures, such as a 15 percent price hike on goods bought with dollars and a collection of a 10 percent exchange commission when dollars were spent, the value of dollar fell about 20 percent (Seong-hyeong Lee, "Success, Problems and Future Prospects of Cuba's Economic Reformation," *Economy and Society*, No. 71 (2006), 221-229).

industries will suffer, such overvaluation provides a de facto subsidy to domestic industries as the state monopolizes certain (dollar) cash-cow sectors, such as the tourism industry.[14] In the dual economy, the Cuban government can protect its less-competitive traditional domestic industries, as well as public sectors such as medical and healthcare services and education, through the above-mentioned intersectoral transfer[15] between the strong dollar sector, which has constant contact with the dollar currency, and the weak peso sector.

It is true that dollarization, in general, has some advantages. It helps stabilize prices, draws foreign investment, balances the budget, and spurs economic growth.[16] However, it is not a suitable alternative for most economies because of its serious drawbacks, such as causing debt deflation and eliminating monetary tools such as seigniorage and inflation tax. However, some have made an interesting argument that Cuba's dollarization is an exceptional case since those drawbacks do not apply.[17]

First, Cuba's central bank functions differently than those of market economies. Under the Cuban planned economy, the government can complement central bank functions by administrative control over wages. The government has little problem regulating commodity prices and quantities through the supply network,

---

[14] Seok-ho Shin, *Economic Crises and Reformations in North Korea and Cuba*, Ph.D. Dissertation, University of North Korean Studies (2008), 172.

[15] When enterprises in dollar-earning sectors send dollars to the central bank, conventional industrial sectors can get authority to import goods with the exchange rate of 1:1. It consequently enables maintenance of the social security system. New enterprises transfer dollars at the cost of managerial autonomy. It is this system that changes enterprise subsidies into inter-enterprise transfers.

[16] Rémy Herrera and Paulo Nakatani, op. cit., 85-86.

[17] Arne C. Kildegaard and Robert Orro Fernandez, op. cit., 4-6.

controlling the prices of imported goods through its state-run retail network, and guaranteeing its central bank's currency sovereignty through the devaluation of the domestic peso against the convertible peso and the dollar.

Second, Cuba's dollarization does not necessarily cause debt deflation. Unlike a free market economy, Cuba spreads its losses throughout the entire economy with the help of the dual exchange rate, and keeps its debt-ridden companies afloat by providing them with the profits from its trade and tourist sectors. In this way, the Cuban government keeps its financial system afloat, and dollarization in Cuba does not automatically lead to debt deflation.

Finally, Cuba cannot count on seigniorage effects, because Cuban-Americans are sending money back to the country as remittances—de facto interest-free loans. In other words, the loss of possible seigniorage during dollarization does not entail any new cost. In addition, it should be noted that the effect of seigniorage is not meaningful in the Cuban case because the prevention of inflation and reduction of liquidity will be at stake as the effect of seigniorage is felt.[18]

Because of this "Cuban exceptionalism," Cuban authorities employ the structuralized dual-currency system in Cuba, even though it is not their preferred strategy.[19] This is because the positive impact, i.e., the transfer of the trade sector's profits to non-trade sectors, is greater than the negative effects of dollarization. It

---

[18] Paul Hare, "Industrial Policy for North Korea: Lessons from Transition," *CERT Discussion Paper* 2007/10 (October 2007), 5; Rémy Herrera and Paulo Nakatani, op. cit., 13-14.

[19] The fact that government debt is not high and private sectors that would disturb governmental sectors are not sufficient provides ground of the high chances of success in stability policy of Cuban authorities. Arne C. Kildegaard and Robert Orro Fernandez, op. cit., 7.

should also be noted that Cuba's de-dollarization in 2004 should not be interpreted as the country gave up its dual-economy strategy.[20] On the contrary, it should be understood as the continuation of the strategy.[21] Seen in this perspective, dollarization in Cuba can be seen as a mechanism that eliminates the need for the direct subsidies and facilitates the government's indirect support of weak industries.

2. Russia's Survival Strategy and the Virtual Economy in the 1990s

The term "virtual economy" was first adopted in analyzing Russia's economy in the late 1990s. One of the characteristics of a conventional planned economy is that the physical transaction price—barter price—is lower than the real market transaction

---

[20] In November 2004, Cuba was forced to use the convertible pesos instead of the dollars while just prohibiting circulation of them. Kildegaard and Fernandez, op. cit., 8. The accomplishment of de-dollarization depends on perception of Cuban people whether they see the convertible peso as means to store value, or not. As Cubans are willing to possess the convertible peso just during the period of transactions, that is, the period when they change currency for goods, the chance of success for de-dollarization is not high. The problem is whether Cubans would possess dollars or euros as the means of preparatory storing. Current weak dollar is just a factor raising the possibility of de-dollarization. But, this, on the other hand, requires examination of the problem of euroization. Archibald R. M. Ritter and Nicholas Rowe, "Cuba: From 'Dollarization' to 'Euroization' or Peso Re-Consolidation," *Latin American Politics and Society*, Vol. 44, No. 2 (March 2002). I agree with the view that the measure for de-dollarization is rather a symbolic reaction to resist the U.S. economic blockade than one to deny dollars as currency. That is, the system of convertible currency is not to deny dollars under the dual economy.

[21] Al Campbell, "Planning in Cuba Today," *International Journal of Political Economy*, Vol. 34, No. 4 (Ontario: Univ. of Ottawa, 2005), 76.

price. In Russia, since the 1990s, however, the physical transaction price has risen higher than the real market price. Clifford Gaddy and Barry Ickes conceptualized this phenomenon as a virtual economy.[22] This concept focuses on where the value is created and how it is distributed in Russia.[23] It drew attention in the discussion over whether the country needed support from the International Monetary Fund (IMF) during the foreign currency crisis. The discussion centered on whether Russian enterprises that did not produce any added value could survive with the help of overvalued physical transaction prices. This issue raised another question: Was the lack of liquidity or the lack of restructuring efforts at the base of Russia's troubled economy?[24]

Recently, Gaddy and Ickes moved their focus from providing theoretical discussion about the virtual economy to proving that values in the resources sector are being redistributed to businesses lacking competitiveness through their analysis of so-called "informal rents," such as price subsidies, excessive costs and bribery. In their view, when ownership of resources is not fully guaranteed, the concerned companies have no choice but to cooperate with the state. Thus, the transfer of "rents" would allow these companies to survive.[25] In this sense, Gaddy and Ickes call today's Russian economy a "resource rent economy." While a virtual economy is

---

[22] Clifford G. Gaddy and Barry W. Ickes, "Russia's Virtual Economy," *Foreign Affairs* (September / October 1998).

[23] Clifford G. Gaddy and Barry W. Ickes, "The Virtual Economy Revisited: Resource Rents and the Russian Economy," *Russia: New Investment Horizons* (Renaissance Capital's 4th Annual Equity Conference, 2005b), 1.

[24] Sophie Brana and Mathilde Maurel, "Barter in Russia: Liquidity Shortage versus Lack of Restructuring" (William Davidson Institute Working Papers Series No. 271, 1999).

[25] Clifford G. Gaddy and Barry W. Ickes, "Resource Rents and the Russian Economy," *Eurasian Geography and Economics*, Vol. 46, No. 8 (2005a), 570-571.

focused on the restructuring of uncompetitive businesses, the transfer of value from the resources sector to the domestic economy characterizes a resource rent economy.[26] However, in principle, the two concepts are the same.

A virtual economy is different, not just from a conventional planned economy, but also from a market economy. Once the import market is opened, quality goods can be imported at reasonable prices, and they compete with products made by domestic companies. When this occurs, it is likely that domestic manufacturers lose out from this kind of competition due to their inefficiency. The government has no choice but to help these domestic manufacturers to survive in order to secure domestic employment and prevent the collapse of domestic industry. Thus, it allows replacing taxes and wages with physical goods as a means for businesses to dispose of their goods, which could not be realized otherwise. Normally, such transactions are made at prices higher than the market value. Workers either accept payment arrears to avoid unemployment or choose to receive overvalued goods as wages. Put another way, it is as if the state, industry, and labor all join in the plot; all the players give tacit consent to stay the course out of fear of facing a more adverse situation that other reform efforts might cause. They are all trapped in the situation.[27] To understand this mechanism, see Tables 12, 13, and 14, showing the before-and-after effects of market opening.[28]

---

[26] The resources export sector creates much profit, but does not provide jobs. Job creation, on the contrary, falls to the domestic industries. Therefore, it is necessary to transfer acquired resource rent to domestic industries for the good of protection of the domestic industries and job creation.

[27] Ibid., 14-15.

[28] Ibid., 3-16.

3. A Balanced Model in the Central Planning Economy Era

Let's assume that the raw materials sector (G) produces 100 units with the input of 50 labor units (L). Competitive commercial goods (M) and uncompetitive conventional goods (MV) each use 50 units of raw materials and 25 units of labor to produce 100 units of output. Additionally, there are 100 workers (or labor units) and 100 pensioners in this economic system. In this case, the 100 units of G's output are used as intermediate goods in producing M and MV, which, in turn, produce 100 and 200 units of final goods, respectively. The 200 units of output in this model are distributed to 100 workers and 100 pensioners, keeping a balance between them. M is purchased with cash in the market; MV is purchased by the state and distributed in-kind.

Table 12. Planned Economic Era-Units In-kind

	G	M	MV	F(C)	Sum
G	0	50	50		100
M	0	0	0	100	100
MV	0	0	0	100	100
L	50	25	25		100

Notes: G=Resources Sector; M=(Competitive) Commercial Goods; MV=Old (Communist) Industrial Goods; F(C)=Final Goods; L=Worker(s)

Now let's take a price-based approach. M is purchased by pensioners using currency. If the price of PG=PM and is 1, and the price of WG=WL is 0.5, the whole economy maintains a balance as we see in Table 13. Workers purchase M in the market with L50—their total wages. Among Pr 150, the government's tax revenue, 50 units are transferred to pensioners as their currency income, the rest (100 units) is purchased by the state to be distributed to workers and pensioners in-kind. Currency is not needed in transactions between businesses (G transaction) or in the in-kind distribution.

Table 13. Planned Economic Era-Price Units

	G	M	MV	F(C)
G	0	50	50	0
M	0	0	0	100
MV	0	0	0	100
L	25(=50*0.5)	12.5(=25*0.5)	12.5(=25*0.5)	
Pr	75(=100–25)	37.5(=100–50–12.5)	37.5(=100–50–12.5)	
Sum	100	100	100	200

Note: Pr=Profit (However, as they are all state-run enterprises, it is practically the same as tax).

4. The Virtual Economy Following the Transition of the Russian Economy

When an economy moves toward marketization, the above-mentioned MV sector loses its competitiveness. While PM=PG will still be 1 even in the free price and trade system, the prices in the conventional communist industry sector will be PMV=0.5, because of the flood of low-priced imported goods.[29] At this price of 0.5 (total 50) the MV sector cannot sustain manufacturing cost of 75 (raw materials, or G sector price of 50 and labor cost 12.5). There are two alternatives: one is to allow the bankruptcy of MV sector

---

[29] For example, the Trabant of East Germany was a very excellent car of high quality, but it could not compete in either price or quality against Western cars, which rushed in after the reform in East Germany. The company went bankrupt because it could not overcome the situation in which the production cost exceeded the market price after the wave of reform. Almost all industries in the former socialist economies faced similar fates.

and accept the decrease in gross product. It is a part of the "creative destruction" theory positing that a certain period of transitory recession is inevitable during system transition.

The other option is the "virtual economy" strategy. The most important goal of this strategy is to keep the MV sector alive. To that end, the government chooses in-kind distribution of the products from the MV sector, rather than exposing MV to an open market. In other words, the products of the MV sector are valued higher than the market price when they are used in calculating for in-kind distribution. Workers choose to get paid in-kind for fear of losing their jobs, while the government collects (overvalued) tax in-kind in order to maintain full employment and avoids de-industrialization of domestic enterprises.

In this case, the G sector, which supplies the MV sector with raw materials, also gets paid in-kind. The G sector could itself provide its products at normal market prices if it were to export them, but, instead, it does business with the uncompetitive MV sector and accepts its products as payment, thus transferring its produced value to the MV sector. It is the de facto transfer of resource rent.

Then, the G sector uses the currency of 50—the payment for the intermediate goods which it supplies—for workers' wages and tax payments to the state with the 50 units in-kind that it received from MV as payment for the intermediate goods. Under the condition that it allows G to pay the tax in-kind, the state demands that G receive the payment in-kind from the MV sector.

In the end, 50 G-sector employees and 25 M-sector employees, together with 25 pensioners, receive payment in currency, while 25 MV-sector employees and 75 (50+25) pensioners receive in-kinds. As a result, there will be a difference in incomes between the 100 people who receive their wages and pensions in currency and the

100 people who receive theirs in-kind, because the real value of the in-kind goods is only half its nominal value. In this case, F(C), gross product, is 200 units, but this national economy is overstated in numbers. As MV is already realized in the market at half its value, the nominal 100k has an actual value of only 50m; the possessors of in-kind goods lose half of their nominal assets in reality. Such payment in-kind worked as social security for the recipients during the socialist planning era, but now it has exactly the opposite effect. What it does, in fact, is making the sector that lacks value-creating capacity looks like a value creator.

Table 14. Virtual Economy

	G	M	MV	F(C)	**Sum**
G	0	50	50		100
M	0	0	0	100m	100
MV	0	0	0	100k	100
L	50m	25m	25k		100
Pr	50k	25m	25k		100
Sum	100	100	100	200	

Note: m=Currency Unit; k=Unit of In-kind Goods

Thus, it will be a successful transition if the government can renovate the MV sector while helping MV's manufacturing industries and workers survive by transferring the values created by the G sector to them. In this way, the "valley of tears" can be minimized. However, it is commonly agreed that this pseudo-subsidy system is more likely to expose the MV and G sectors to moral hazard rather than streamline the transition to a market economy. It is only pseudo-reformation, resisting real reforms by maintaining soft budget restrictions. Figure 2 shows a simplified version of the situation in a single manufacturing industry, instead of the M

Figure 2. Virtual Economy vs. Real Economy

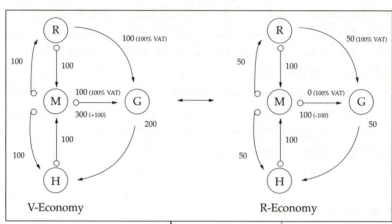

		Virtual	Real
Total Sales		400	200
Total Profits		200	0
Profit Rate (%)		50%	0
Total Value-Added (GDP)		300	100
Industrial Output		400	200
Budget Size			
	Planned	200	100
	As Implemented	67	50
Household Income			
	Accrued	300	200
	Actual	100	100
Arrears			
	Wages	67	50
	Inter-Enterprise	None	50
	Tax	None	50
	Budget	133	50

Source: Gaddy & Ickes, www.uh.edu/~vlazarev/4389/VirtEcon.htm (2008/03/20).

and MV sectors:

A virtual economy is a system that circulates the actual final goods of a certain important industry at a price that cannot be realized in a real market in order to keep the industry alive, even when it has lost its competitiveness. The companies that actually create value cannot help but agree to accept in-kind transactions because the government usually holds a substantial share of these enterprises' assets, and workers accept payments in-kind out of their fear of unemployment. It is like a market-regulating system in that there is no administrative intervention from the state.

A virtual economy that works as a survival strategy by transferring resource rent can be useful in terms of economic sovereignty, as it helps to avoid large-scale destabilization often brought on by market reform, and can aid in stabilizing the macro-economy.[30] As for effectiveness, however, it hinders the transition to a market economy. It is a regressive transitory system that has both bright and dark sides.

III. Changes in North Korea's Price System and Its Dual Economy Strategy

The common element of dual and virtual economies is that the value-creating sector and value-consuming sector are separate. The values created in the former are transferred to the latter by indirect "regulation" by the state. What is different from the former system is that the process is run not by administrative orders from the government, but rather, by utilizing market mechanisms.[31]

---

[30] Clifford G. Gaddy and Barry W. Ickes, op. cit., 570.
[31] The following argument shows that North Korea has loosened controls

Controversy is inevitable during this economic transition because of the value transfer and redistribution through the pseudo-market system.

The North Korean regime suggested five principles of price control through its so-called "July 1st Economic Management Improvement Measures (7/1 Measures)" in 2002, and subsequently changed the relative prices of all essential goods in the country.[32] The measures included abandoning the subsidy-based pricing policy, replacing coal with rice as its relative price standard,[33] linking the domestic rice price with the international rice price, allowing the coexistence of state-regulated prices and market prices, and unifying price composition by revoking indirect taxes.[34] The mea-

---

over market prices through administrative means:

"The current realities of regional market management show that establishing price limits with an administrative character or simple way of publicly announced pricing cannot affect fluctuation in market price. In this situation, bodies of the central bank work directly to affect market prices economically, with one mind among financial and market management bodies ... Bodies of the central bank, beginning with the head office ... must be prepared for business conditions to affect regional markets within their respective regions, recognizing the fact that dynamics of regional markets affect currency management," (Seong-hyeong Lee, "Success, Problems and Future Prospects of Cuba's Economic Reformation," *Economy and Society*, No. 71 (2006), 37).

[32] Ihk-pyo Hong, Yong-sueng Dong, and Jung-chul Lee, "North Korea's Price Management and Commercial Distribution System: Current Status and Reform Tasks," Korea Institute for International Economic Policy, *Policy Analyses*, No. 04-15 (2004), 97-106.

[33] "In former days, we had adopted primary resources such as coal and electricity as the starting point for establishing price ... It is right to take the price of food, which comprises the basis of material life, as the starting point for all prices in every respect" (*Monthly Chosun*, 2003: 88-97).

[34] Transaction incomes, which were de facto indirect taxes, and profits from state-run enterprises, which took on the character of enterprise income

sures led to the redefinition of relative prices of all products. At the same time, North Korean authorities allowed the possession of dollars and other foreign currency in unlimited amounts. On the street, people are allowed to use their dollars for transactions. Moreover, dollars can be used in direct transactions in markets where prices are displayed in foreign currency.[35] Banking organizations can legally receive dollar currency and so-called "dollarization" measures were made official.

At the time, North Korean authorities normalized the exchange rate at $1:150 won.[36] Based on their decision to link the domestic rice price to the international (Chinese) rice price, the exchange rate was close to the rate set at the international price (Beijing wholesale price) of 0.29 dollar, compared to the North Korean farmers' market price of 44 won, as we see in Table 15. The exact figures are not known, as North Korean authorities have not

---

taxes, were unified, and came to be paid solely under the name of profits of state-run enterprises with the concept of enterprise income taxes, (Young-soo Kim, "Profit of State-run Companies and Some Questions about Its Legal Mobilization," *Economic Research*, No. 1 (Pyongyang: Science Encyclopedia Publishing House, 2004), 24).

[35] In some cases, foreigners purchased goods in a domestic-customers-only market in dollars and received the change in North Korean currency, won. According to the testimony of a Canadian who visited Pyongyang June 12-23, 2007, he paid six euros and received the change in North Korean won while purchasing goods at the official exchange rate.

[36] North Korea adjusted the currency at the rate of 150 won to the U.S. dollar from 2.2:1 at the time of July 1st Measures. The exchange rate is given at the (fixed) rate of about 150 won to foreigners. North Korean people have been allowed to exchange unlimited amounts of dollars in conformity with the rule of the floating exchange rate system for domestic use since 2003, when the possession of dollars was legalized. Actually, in front of general markets, there is a separate domestic-customers-only exchange house. Here, dollars are subject to an exchange rate of 1:3,000.

Table 15. North Korean Price of Rice Compared to the International Price

(Unit: USD)

Period	International Rice Price	North Korean Rice Price
2002	0.289	0.29 (44 won at an exchange rate of 150 won)
Aug. 2004	0.35	0.33
Jun. 2005	0.40	0.38
Apr. 2006	0.36	0.36
Oct. 2007	0.38	0.39

	Feb.2002	Feb. 2003	Aug. 2004	Jun. 2005	Apr. 2006	Oct. 2007
Rice (1kg)	48-55 (won)	130-150	780	950	900	1,300
Exchange Rate (Won per dollar)	220 (won)	670	2,300	2,500	2,500	3,300

Notes: 1) Year 2002 is the base period; the price since 2002 is based on North Korea's composite market prices; the average price was used as there were differences in prices among the regions

2) The 2007 price is from the Sinuiju market as of October 17; the Pyungsung market price was 1,300 won as of November.

3) The international rice price is based on the wholesale price of Chinese rough rice.

4) The 2002 price is based on the wholesale price at Jilin Province Food Center.[37]

5) The 2004 price is based on the wholesale price of rough rice (Japonica) in April, 2,890 yuan, which was a record high in food wholesale markets around China.

6) The 2006 price is based on the Beijing Xinfadi Farm Produce Wholesale Market price of rough rice.[38]

7) The 2007 price is based on Beijing Xinfadi wholesale price of 2.80 yuan; Jinxiudadi wholesale price of 2.96 yuan (=0.39 USD).

---

[37] Seung-ho Ryu, "Changes in Exchange Rates and Suggestions since North Korea's 'Measures for Economic Reformation'," *Exim Overseas Economic Review* (December 2003), 65.

[38] See documents available at http://agre.krei.re.kr/file/pdfsource/245918p .pdf.

released details on how they reached the rate, but they seem to set their official fixed exchange rate based on a certain standard band.

However, in general markets—local markets legalized since March 2003—there has been a quasi-official exchange rate based on a floating exchange rate system.[39] As seen in Table 15, changes in rice price in North Korea are usually made according to changes in the exchange rate. In other words, the North Korean rice price in dollars follows the changes in the international (Chinese) rice price, indicating that the domestic exchange rate also follows this change. It is important to note that North Korean authorities virtually accept the floating exchange rate system. When the possession and transaction of dollars was illegal (prior to the 7/1 Measures), the "market exchange rate" meant the black market rate. However, now there are two official exchanges rates: one is the official fixed exchange rate, and the other is the floating rate in the actual market, which is the quasi-official rate; the black market rate also exists, but the difference between it and the quasi-official rate is minimal.

What is interesting about the North Korean economy is that there is incentive for the state to drive up inflation. In North Korea, debt deflation caused by inflation does not cause financial crisis as in the other market economies. Instead, it brings benefits to the state as it reduces the state-owned enterprises' debts. This is possible because the financial sector is controlled by the state and acts as its policy arm.

The North Korean economy has a dual economic structure: one is the dollar currency economic sector, with a fixed 1:150

---

[39] In December 2002, North Korea designated the euro as a settlement currency, instead of the U.S. dollar. However, dollar transactions were not criminalized. This can be considered as just a symbolic measure, as was seen in Cuba.

exchange rate, and the other is the won currency economic sector, with a floating exchange rate of around 1:3,000. The difference between the rates is about 1:20—close to Cuba's 1:24 difference. Figure 3 shows how dollarization and the dual economy work in North Korea.

Figure 3. Flow of Dual Economy in North Korea

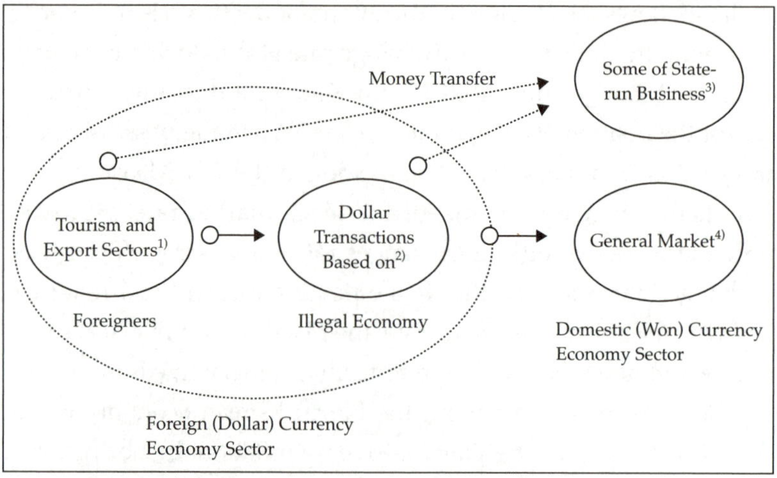

Notes: 1) Special Economic Zones (Kaesong, Geumgangsan)
    1:150 Exchange Rates, Wages based on won currency, Direct dollar transactions
   2) 1:3,000+α Exchange Rate
   3) Imports raw materials at 1:150 exchange rate
   4) Won-based transaction after money exchange at 1:3,000 rate

The mechanisms of North Korea's dual economy can easily be understood if we look at the case of workers in the "special economic zone" sector, such as the Kaesong Industrial Complex. When a South Korean company pays a North Korean employee a monthly wage of 50 dollars for his or her work, it pays an additional 7.5 dollars (15 percent of the wage) into a social security fund. In other words, the South Korean company provides the

North Korean government 57.5 dollars per employee, and North Korean authorities take 7.5 dollars from the wage. Then, the employee receives 5 percent of the wage (2.5 dollars in this case) in won currency after exchange, at the rate of 1:150—the official exchange rate.

Then, North Korea's Central Special Direct General Bureau, or CSDGB, takes the remainder of the workers' wages and deposits them into a Koryo Commercial Joint Company account, which, in turn, imports goods with the money and distributes them through supply stations and stores. Considering that North Korean residents in other regions buy the same goods in regional markets at the exchange rate of 1:3,000, such distribution has the same effect for Kaesong workers, who are buying the same imported goods at the same 1:3,000 domestic exchange rate.[40] Through this mechanism, the 40 dollars is virtually exchanged at the quasi-official rate with the same effect as when the workers possess dollars.[41]

IV. Relevance of the Virtual Economy to North Korea

Hans-Jurgen Wagener argues that a virtual economy could be a transition strategy, but that it is more likely to be a trap than a transition, because it is difficult to break free of this path.[42] Thus, if

---

[40] Calculated at the conversion rate of 3,000 won to the dollar, laborers in Gaesong would be paid the equivalent of 120 thousand won. As of the end of 2007, the average wage in Gaesong Industrial Complex is approximately 100 thousand won.

[41] The state tries to remove dollars from circulation. But, this cannot deprive residents of the dollar effect they enjoy.

[42] Hans-Jurgen Wagener, "The Virtual Economy as Intermediate Stage in Russian Transformation," Frankfurt Institute for Transformation Dissuasion Paper, No 3/01, 17.

a virtual economy is ever used as a "strategy," it will be more useful as a survival strategy for a country that faces marketization from below, rather than as a transition strategy.[43]

Based on the above premise, I will discuss the relevance of a virtual economy to North Korea's current situation in three aspects: relations among the companies, the form of transactions, and labor relations. First, is there a transfer of resource rent on the company level? If there is, value-creating units must exist in North Korea, and the created values must be transferred. It is true that there are combined groups of companies that independently perform the functions of planning, production, distribution, and even financing, thus transferring value internally. One such example is Myohyang Group, which consists of the Koryo Hotel, several manufacturing plants and a Workers' Party business unit ("Office No. 38"). It should be noted that with the help of its exclusive access to foreign currency, the group transfers the value it creates to the state. However, the exact routes of value (the unofficial rent) transfer are not known. Thus, the term "virtual economy" cannot be applied to North Korea as long as we only consider the transfer of resource rent as its unique trait.

Next are transactions in-kind. In this case, we need a new approach to the non-cash account system that the North Korean regime favors. In the past, the non-cash account system worked as a management system for control by the won, but the non-cash account system of today exists only as a means to include transactions in kind in financial accounting.[44] In other words, it works to prevent any illegal cash transactions between companies, thus,

---

[43] Clifford G. Gaddy and Barry W. Ickes, 2005a, op. cit., 570.

[44] Young-eui Hong, "Concentration of Currency on Banks in a Major Way to Secure the Circulation," No. 4 (Pyongyang: Science Encyclopedia Publishing House, 2006), 26; Seok-gi Lee, op. cit., 177.

securing tax revenue. The non-cash account system in the past aided the supply of raw materials by guaranteeing in-kind transactions and prices lower than those found in the market. However, because market trading, especially of raw materials, is now permitted, such a non-cash accounting system is used as a "forced transaction," in which goods are traded at prices higher than those found in markets.[45]

Lacking sufficient liquidity, companies would seek to realize the value of their products through the markets, even at a price lower than the assigned in-kind value or planned price. As a result, the market price can be lower than the in-kind price. Under current conditions, in which "companies use the cash only for their own profits, illegal transactions, divert it to other uses, or simply waste it," and, "import materials without any cash and make banks pay for them," or, "illegally trade goods even when they have enough cash," a non-cash accounting system became the means for letting incompetent domestic companies trade their products at prices higher than the market, with the help of governmental intervention.[46]

Consumer goods, among others, were allowed to be imported and traded without limitation as the general market in North Korea was revitalized.[47] At Pyongyang's Tongil Street Market, 2,000 ven-

---

[45] All kinds of exchanges of supplies are allowed, such as direct exchanges between two factories or companies, circular exchanges among three or more factories or companies, and third-party with other companies. It should be noted that these exchanges give wholesale businesses chances to distribute production goods, (Dong-myeong Shim, "Dependence on Regional Resources is an Important Means of the Development of Regional Industries," *Economic Research*, No. 1 (Pyongyang: Science Encyclopedia Publishing House, 2004), 19. In relation to other markets for exchanges of supplies and production goods, see Hong and Dong, et. al., op. cit., 123-125).

[46] Young-eui Hong, op. cit., 26-27.

dors sold their mostly imported goods to as many as 100,000 people per day.[48] Faced with this kind of situation, there is no way to sell low-quality domestic consumer goods other than using the state-run store network. The products of domestic companies can be traded either through state-run stores as in-kind goods, or as wage payments in-kind. For instance, in many cases, state enterprises' workers receive payment in-kind rather than wages. The virtual economy is more relevant to North Korea's situation when it comes to consumer goods.

On the other hand, unpaid wages and payment in-kind are already commonplace among North Korean workers. There are three ways for North Korean workers to collect their incomes, the first of which is payment in dollars. In this case, the workers earn dollars either directly from a market transaction, or indirectly for services related to market trading. The second way is for the workers, such as those in export factories or manufacturing plants, to receive wages in domestic won. These workers get paid around 20,000-30,000 won per month.[49] The last method of compensation is payment in-kind. Workers in regional companies earn around 2,000 won per month in cash, with the remainder of their compensation provided as payment in-kind. The in-kind goods in this case are from the factory in which they work or goods the companies imported to serve as payment to their workers. If we estimate the

---

[47] A policy to make a new market for imports, where transactions are conducted only in domestic won, has merit in that it could reduce competition for dollar holdings and facilitate currency exchanges. However, it also suffers the weakness that it is difficult to adjust the fluctuations in exchange rates to the changes of domestic currency prices.

[48] An interview with a manager of Tongil Street Market (June, 22, 2007).

[49] Materials gathered during a visit to North Korea by a group from the *Joongang Ilbo* in May 2005. While there are some variations, wages are known to rise to as high as 100,000 won.

price of such goods at an exchange rate of 1:3,000, the real wages of the state workers are much higher than 2,000 won per month, but the quality of the goods they receive are lower than that of the goods found in the markets.

Whether the virtual economy is taking root in North Korea is difficult to judge, due to the paucity of economic information on the country. In terms of resource rent transfer, there is no more evidence than the existence of unofficial rents. In terms of transactions with actual goods, however, the current state-run distribution network must compete with the quasi-private distribution network, which is organized by market forces. If this trend continues and the authorities do not opt for administrative crackdown measures on the growth of such markets, evolution toward a virtual economy could be inevitable.

V. Conclusion

This chapter focused on the fact that the North Korean economy works in two different ways through de facto "dollarization": the dollar (or trade) sector and the domestic sector. This policy allows surplus dollars in the dollarized sector to be deposited in a central fund. The government can then collect dollar wages paid to the employees of foreign-run businesses, and then transfer that money at official exchange rates to the state sector, which lacks competitiveness. At the same time, by legalizing dollar transactions, the government allows residents to exchange their dollars at quasi-official exchange rates (about 20-30 times higher than official rates). This measure ensures that the state maintains dollar liquidity. The sectors that need imported supplies, such as medical, public health, and educational services, are allowed to use preferential exchange rates in order to maintain the social welfare system.

In this sense, the dual economy strategy based on dollarization and dual exchange rates is a way for the North Korean regime to finance its nontrade sectors in a situation where direct subsidies have been abolished. The country's direct support for companies is thus replaced with value transfer between companies in order to keep conventional industries and the social welfare system alive. Part of the collected income from the foreign currency economy is used to compensate the weak won. It is another way of income redistribution using financial means and market regulation, as opposed to direct intervention.

The dollarization policy will not lead to the weakening of economic sovereignty because North Korea is maintaining the state-run industrial structure, and still has many planned economic measures in hand. Yet, inflation caused by dollarization or marketization has raised the need for protection of conventional industries and uncompetitive companies. It would be unhelpful to return to the former price subsidy system because that would undermine the fruits of economic reform, which has been in place since the announcement of the 7/1 Measures.

One of the alternatives for North Korea is a type of virtual economy strategy. Such a strategy would ease the transfer of goods from uncompetitive sectors at prices higher than those in the markets in order to maintain production in various sectors. The state wants to give those sectors more time to build competitive strength. In this way, the government can stabilize the economy and avoid unemployment problems.

Although in-kind transactions and payment in-kind are remnants of an outdated planned economy, they became integral parts of the survival strategy for North Korea. If we consider current in-kind transactions as a "home front supply operation" of the past, we will fail to grasp the changes in the North Korean regime. It can be seen as a way of dealing with uncompetitive domestic products when Chinese products are flooding the North Korean markets. At least in this sense, it can be said that the virtual economy might be taking root in North Korea.

The reform that got under way in North Korea with the launch of the 7/1 Measures may be no more than meaningless patchwork change,[50] and is too early to determine whether North Korea is adopting a virtual economy strategy in its reform process; however, it is a framework worth considering, since North Korean authorities are employing a nonadministrative market regulation system, and regressive marketization is apparent. This framework can be useful as a "pseudo-market survival strategy" to at least manage the challenges of market transformation, if not as a transition strategy.

Bibliography

English-language Publications

Brana, Sophie and Mathilde Maurel, "Barter in Russia: Liquidity Shortage versus Lack of Restructuring," William Davidson Institute Working Papers Series No. 271 (1999).

Campbell, Al, "Planning in Cuba Today," *International Journal of Political Economy*, Vol. 34, No. 4, Ontario: Univ. of Ottawa (2005).

Chandrasekhar, C.P. "Cuba; Dealing with the Dollar," *Frontline*, vol. 16 (India, 1999).

Gaddy, Clifford G. and Barry W. Ickes. "Russia's Virtual Economy," *Foreign Affairs*, September/October (1998).

---

[50] Kyoung-hoon Lim, "North Korea's Economic Reformation: Evaluations and Future Prospects," *Korean Politics Studies*, Vol. 16, No. 1 (2007), 299.

_____. "Resource Rents and the Russian Economy," *Eurasian Geography and Economics*, Vol. 46, No. 8 (2005a).

_____. "The Virtual Economy Revisited: Resource Rents and the Russian Economy," *Russia: New Investment Horizons*, Renaissance Capital's 4th Annual Equity Conference (2005b).

Halpern, László, "Is Exchange Rate Regime Relevant for Transition from Plan to Market?" *Experience of Transition Economies and Implications for North Korea* (International Conference on Transition organized by SNU, KIEP and SKRI, 2008).

Hare, Paul, "Industrial Policy for North Korea: Lessons from Transition," CERT Discussion Paper 2007/10 (2007).

Herrera, Rémy and Paulo Nakatani, "De-Dollarizing Cuba," *International Journal of Political Economy*, Vol. 34, No. 4. Ontario: Univ. of Ottawa (2005).

Kildegaard, Arne C. and Robert Orro Fernandez, "Aspect of Dollarization and DE-Dollarization in Cuba," LASA 2006 (San Juan, 2006).

Mesa-Lago, Carmelo, "The Cuban Economy in 2006-2007," *Cuba in Transition*, Vol. 17 (The Seventeenth Annual Meeting of the Association for the Study of the Cuban Economy, 2007).

Mitra, Pradeep K. and Marcelo Selowsky, eds., *Transition: The First Ten Years* (Washington, D.C.: World Bank, 2002).

Mitra, Pradeep K. and Marcelo Selowsky, "Lessons from a Decade of Transition in Eastern Europe and the Former Soviet Union," IMF, *Finance & Development*, Vol. 39, No. 2 (2002).

Ritter, Archibald R.M., "Survival Strategies and Economic Illegalities in Cuba," *Cuba in Transition*, Vol. 15 (The Fifteenth Annual Meeting of the Association for the Study of the Cuban Economy, 2005).

Ritter, Archibald R.M. and Nicholas Rowe, "Cuba: From 'Dollarization' to 'Euroization' or Peso Re-Consolidation," *Latin American Politics and Society*, Vol. 44, No. 2 (2002).

Tanzi, Vito and George Tsibouris, "Fiscal Reform over Ten Years of Transition," IMF (2000).

Wagener, Hans-Jürgen, "The Virtual Economy as Intermediate Stage in

Russian Transformation," Frankfurt Institute for Transformations Studies Working Paper No. 3/01 (2001).

Wyplosz, Charles, "Ten Years of Transformation—Macroeconomic Lessons" (World Bank Policy Research Working Paper 2288, 2000).

Korean-language Publications

Cha, Moon-seok, "Dear Leader Replaced by Currency: Market and Market Economy in North Korea," *Discourse 201*, Vol. 10, No. 2 (2007).

Hahm, Seong-joon, "Characteristics and Roles of Regional Accounting Computation," *Economic Research*, No. 4 (Pyongyang: Science Encyclopedia Publishing House, 2006).

Hong, Ihk-pyo, Yong-sueng Dong, and Jung-chul Lee, "North Korea's Price Management and Commercial Distribution System: Current Status and Reform Tasks," Korea Institute for International Economic Policy, *Policy Analyses*, No. 04-15 (2004).

Hong, Young-eui, "Concentration of Currency on Banks in a Major Way to Secure the Circulation," No. 4 (Pyongyang: Science Encyclopedia Publishing House, 2006).

Jung, Yeong-tae, Yeon-cheol Kim, and Sang-hyeon Seo, "Prospect of Change in North Korea from the Viewpoint of Relative Socialism with Focus on the Precedents of Libya and Cuba" (Korea Institute of National Unification Collection, No. 07-11, 2007).

Kang, Il-cheon, "A Tentative Analysis of Recent Economic Measures in South Korea 1," *KDI Review of the North Korean Economy* (October 2002).

Kim, Jong-han, "Use of Evolutional View in Politico-economic Analysis," *Applied Economics*, Vol. 7, No. 1 (2005).

Kim, Young-soo, "Profit of State-run Companies and Some Questions about Its Legal Mobilization," *Economic Research*, No. 1 (Pyongyang: Science Encyclopedia Publishing House, 2004).

Lee, Seok-gi, "Weakened Planned Economy System, Spontaneous Marketization and Changes in Companies' Management Structure: Characteristics and Crisis in North Korean Economy since 1990s," *Trends and Prospects*, No. 62 (2004).

Lee, Seong-hyeong, "Success, Problems and Future Prospects of Cuba's Economic Reformation," *Economy and Society*, No. 71 (2006).

Lee, Won-kyeong, "Several Fundamental Questions in Current National Currency Regulation," *Economic Research*, No. 2 (Pyongyang: Science Encyclopedia Publishing House, 2006).

Lee, Young-hoon, "Spontaneous Marketization in North Korea and Development of Economic Reformation," *Research on Unification Affairs*, Vol. 17, No. 2 (2005).

Lim, Kyoung-hoon, "North Korea's Economic Reformation: Evaluations and Future Prospects," *Korean Politics Studies*, Vol. 16, No. 1 (2007).

Moon, Seong-min, "Recent Changes in North Korea's Finance and Reformation Mission," *BOK Institute Working Papers*, No. 236 (2007).

Ryu, Seung-ho, "Changes in Exchange Rates and Suggestions since North Korea's 'Measures for Economic Reformation'," *Exim Overseas Economic Review* (December 2003).

Shim, Dong-myeong, "Dependence on Regional Resources is an Important Means of the Development of Regional Industries," *Economic Research*, No. 1 (Pyongyang: Science Encyclopedia Publishing House, 2004).

Shin, Dong-jin, "Possibility and Problems of Currency Unification between South Korea and North Korea," *The Possibility of Currency Unification between South Korea and North Korea: Problems and Prospects* (Research Institute of Peace Studies Journal, No.12, 2003).

Shin, Seok-ho, "Economic Crises and Reformations in North Korea and Cuba," Ph.D. Dissertation, University of North Korean Studies (2008).

Yang, Moon-soo, "Changing Aspects of North Korean Economy and the Life of the Residents," The Peace Foundation, ed., *Current Situation in North Korea and the Life of the Residents* (The 2007 Peace Foundation Forum Presented Materials, Vol. 3, 2007).

Yoon, Young-soon, "Comprehensive Accounting and Its System," *Economic*

Research, No. 4 (Pyongyang: Science Encyclopedia Publishing House, 2006).

Web Sites

http://www.ucm.es/info/ec/jec9/pdf/A03%20-%20Herrera,%20R%E9 my%20y%20Nakatani,%20Paulo.pdf [Herrera, Remy and Paulo Nakatani, "The Cuban Dollarization"(2004)].

http://www.worldbank.org/html/prddr/trans/so99/pgs20-22.htm [Sutela, Pekka, "Russia: Rise of a Dual Economy"(2007)].

Chapter 6

North Korea's Transition to a Market-Oriented Economy: Lessons from Other Transitional Economies*

⊣ Phillip H. PARK ⊢

I. Introduction

1. Essential Conditions for the DPRK's Economic Reform

So far, the Democratic People's Republic of Korea (DPRK, North Korea) has built its economy according to a self-reliant development strategy. This does not mean that the DPRK's economy has either changed or needs reform. In fact, the DPRK applied reform measures (adjustment, in their terms) to its economy when its leadership viewed them as necessary.[1] These reform measures in the past were not intended for systemic or fundamental change, as they were partial measures that were only intended to provide temporary relief: patchwork measures for short-term fixes. However, as the DPRK's economic situation deteriorated to the point of

---

* This article was presented at a conference sponsored by University of Vienna's East Asian Economy and Society on February 14, 2009.

[1] Phillip Park, "The Future of the D.P.R.K." *Journal of Contemporary Asia*, vol. 31, No. 1 (2001), 111-112.

collapse in the 1990s, the DPRK adopted and initiated reform measures that seemed to have gone beyond these simple repairs.

Known as the "7/1 Measures" as they was announced on July 1, 2002, the measures can be distinguished from past partial reform measures, which were only limited to technical areas within the system, because the 7/1 Measures promoted reforms in the general price system and the usage of commodities-currency exchange of market system.[2] Some view the 7/1 Measures as being similar to the measures adopted by China when it began its economic reform in the early 1980s; others argue that the measures are not intended for fundamental reform, but rather, just more patchwork to save the existing central planning system.[3]

Nonetheless, whether the measures were intended to introduce fundamental reform or to merely patch up the central planning system, their success will depend on improving relations with the United States. The United States has imposed economic sanctions on the DPRK since the establishment of the republic in 1948, and lists the DPRK as an enemy state. As such, the DPRK, a small and poor country in the Far East, has been confronting the United States, the world's superpower, diplomatically and militarily for more than five decades. This is an awesome and almost impossible task for a small and poor country to withstand; during the Cold War, the DPRK received assistance from the Soviet Union and China, but still had to spend more than 30 percent of its budget on defense in order to confront the United States militarily. Under these circumstances, although North Korea made serious

---

[2] Chung, Young Chul, *Bukhanui KahyuckKabang: yeechungchunryukkwa Silisahoechooui (Economic Reform in North Korea: Dual Strategies and Pragmatism)* (Seoul: Sunin, 2004), 135.

[3] Kim, Yeon Chul, and Park Soon Sung, eds., *Bukhan Kyungjae Yeonkoo (Study of North Korean Economic Reform)* (Seoul: Humanitas, 2002), 17.

efforts, economic rationalization such as raising efficiency by sound resource allocation did not have a proper place in North Korea.

Moreover, the collapse of the Soviet Union and the socialist bloc in the 1990s accentuated the plight of the DPRK's economy. The DPRK was neither a satellite state of the Soviet Union nor a member state of the communist economic bloc, the Council for Mutual Economic Assistance (CMEA), but the Soviet Union was like a strut to the DPRK as the Soviets provided (at bargain prices) vital natural resources such as oil and coal that were essential for the DPRK's industrial development and gave military assistance and aid to the DPRK, thereby helping the DPRK to stand against the United States. The problems and contradictions related to the DPRK's economy exploded when the Soviet Union collapsed. The DPRK alone had to stand against the United States. On top of this crisis, natural disasters such as torrential floods and drought hit North Korea periodically, further debilitating its feeble and fragile economy.[4]

Consequently, the DPRK's economy took a nosedive. The country even experienced a famine. Nevertheless, the DPRK's relations with the United States have not improved, but rather, became even worse after the collapse of the Soviet Union. Fearing proliferation of weapons of mass destruction (WMD), the United States planned to carry out a preemptive strike on the suspected North Korean nuclear site at Yongbyon, and since the DPRK vowed to retaliate, the Korean Peninsula was on the brink of war. The imminent war was avoided due to the intervention of former U.S. presi-

---

[4] For fuller discussion of North Korea's economic crisis in the 1990s, please refer to Phillip Park's *Self-Reliance or Self-Destruction?* (New York: Routledge, 2002).

dent Jimmy Carter, who traveled to the DPRK and negotiated with the then supreme leader of the North, Kim Il Sung, to resolve the nuclear crisis.

The talks between the United States and the DPRK went on for two years and both countries finally came up with the Agreed Framework to resolve the crisis. Nonetheless, the Agreed Framework did not get off the ground as the ultraconservative George W. Bush became the 42nd president of the United States of America and designated the DPRK as a member of the "axis of evil," along with Iraq and Syria. That meant an escalation of tension between the U.S. and the DPRK, and it put an enormous burden and pressure on the North, which now had to channel more resources to the military amid a comprehensive economic crisis.

The DPRK came up with its own solution to overcome the comprehensive crisis; its "Military-first Politics." What does this mean? And what is North Korea trying to accomplish through it? The term and motivation for coming up with such a policy will be explained later in the chapter, but in terms of economics, it simply means the military gets priority in national budget allocation. And thus, as the DPRK pushes for this policy, it would likely cause an enormous distortion in the already nonfunctional planned economy. However, come to think of it, for a small and a poor country like North Korea to stand against the superpower of the world for more than five decades can only be described as a "mission impossible." For the DPRK to have meaningful economic reform and a viable economy, improving relations with the United States is not only a helpful, but also an essential condition; therefore, whether the DPRK is able to improve relations with the United States or not will determine whether or not the DPRK will launch genuine reform. If U.S.-DPRK relations were to normalize, then we can expect a genuine economic reform in the DPRK and its accelerated transition to a market-oriented economy.

The DPRK is the latest and the last country trying to transition from central planning to a market-oriented economy. After the fall of the Soviet Union in 1989, almost all the countries in the Soviet bloc went through economic transition from socialist to market-oriented economies. The transition economies in Europe include roughly 26 countries with a total population of 413 million people. The largest state by far is the Russian Federation, with 148 million people, while the smallest is Estonia, with only one million inhabitants. When we include all the countries in economic transition to market-oriented economies, such as China (with a population of 1.4 billion), Vietnam (75 million), and Mongolia (2.3 million), then more than a quarter of the entire population of the world has gone through economic transition.

Although there are many countries in transition, only two major strategies of transition have been subscribed to by the countries in transition. Broadly speaking, they are a simultaneous reform strategy known as Shock Therapy or Big Bang, which was mainly applied to the former Soviet Union, central, and Eastern European countries, and a sequential or incremental reform strategy, which China and Vietnam adopted as their major strategy. In this chapter, we will make a critical assessment of both strategies by evaluating actual experiences of those countries that adopted each respective strategy, and also analyzing their theoretical foundation. We will then seek lessons and implications that can be applied to the Democratic People's Republic of Korea.

II. Shock Therapy and Big Bang Approach: Experiences and Performances during the Transition

1. Rapid Inflation

Those countries that adopted and followed the Shock Therapy strategy, such as Russia and the former Soviet bloc countries, commonly experienced rapid and explosive price rises, or hyper-inflation. The government lost control over the level of prices (see Table 16), and price mechanisms consequently did not function properly. The systematic change from central planning to a market-oriented economy, intended to improve economic efficiency in resource allocation and thus accelerate growth, had the opposite effect. What happened?

Unlike a market economy, the price neither plays a role in allocating resources according to the principle of scarcity nor is determined by interaction between supply and demand in the centrally planned economy. Just like all other economic phenomena, prices have been centrally managed under socialism. Furthermore, prices, once determined, are not changed for a long time.[5] Stability means that prices neither reflect the current relationship between demand and supply nor respond to a change in costs; hence, inflation is not considered to be a critical problem or a symptom of economic crisis in the centrally planned economy. Incidentally, with the possible exception of Hungary, which adopted a partial price liberalization policy even before the collapse of the Soviet Union and the Eastern socialist bloc countries, inflation was not a serious problem in most of the socialist economies. However, after the

---

[5] János Kornai, *The Socialist System: The Political Economy of Communism* (Princeton: Princeton University Press, 1992), 149-150.

demise of the Soviet Union, the situation changed drastically; inflation became the most critical and the urgent economic problem.

The first reform policy that was implemented by those countries adopting the Shock Therapy strategy was price liberalization. This policy was implemented simultaneously; all the mechanisms and devices that controlled prices were either eliminated or lifted across the board overnight (the Big Bang). As a result of this simultaneous and across-the-board price liberalization, hyperinflation occurred in all the countries that adopted this policy. Temporary inflation could happen in any country that goes through economic transition. In addition, inflation also occurs when an economy heats up. Nevertheless, as we consider its duration and magnitude, the inflation that occurred in the transition economies of the former socialist countries of the Eastern bloc were unprecedented (see Table 16). According to the Shock Therapy or the Big Bang theory, the price liberalization policy was implemented in order to improve economic efficiency by ensuring proper resource allocation and thus to accelerate economic growth.[6]

Table 16. Annual Percentage Rates of Inflation, 1990-1995

	1990	1991	1992	1993	1994	1995
Russia	5.6	92.7	1353.0	896.0	303.0	190.0
Ukraine	4.0	91.2	1210.0	4735.0	842.0	375.0
Uzbekistan	3.1	82.2	645.0	534.0	746.0	315.0
Romania	5.1	174.5	210.9	256.0	131.0	32.3
Hungary	29.0	34.2	22.9	22.5	19.0	28.2

Source: World Bank, World Development Report 1996 (New York: Oxford University Press, 1997).

---

[6] Naomi Klein, *The Shock Doctrine: The Rise of Disaster Capitalism* (New York: Picador, 2008), 61-62.

However, this policy had the diametrically opposite effect. As a result of price liberalization policy, relative prices fluctuated erratically. The erratic fluctuation of relative prices distorted the whole price mechanism and had a direct effect on long-term investment; people were afraid to invest and would not make a long-term investment due to future price uncertainty. Moreover, when producers faced inflation, they would not sell their products because prices would rise as time went by. As relative prices fluctuated erratically, long-term investment decision making became impossible, and distribution of income became arbitrary. As a result, investment collapsed, output and income fell sharply, and growth rates became negative. The acute macroeconomic instability created by rapid inflation undermined the entire effort.

Let us examine the causes of rapid inflation, which uniformly occurred in the countries adopting the Shock Therapy strategy, in more detail. First of all, as Kornai pointed out, the socialist planned economies suffered from the problem of chronic shortage.[7] Why did they suffer from chronic shortage? The problem of chronic shortage stemmed from the socialist economic development strategy. In order to catch up with more-advanced countries in the West, the socialist countries adopted an economic development strategy that prioritized development of the industrial sector over the agricultural sector, and heavy industry over light industry.

Yevgeni Preobrazhensky and Grigori Fel'dman provided a theoretical basis for this kind of development strategy; Preobrazhensky argued that in order to channel more investment into industry, the terms of trade between the agricultural sector and industrial sector should be arranged in such a way that it benefits and favors

---

[7] János Kornai, *Economics of Shortage Volume A* (Amsterdam: North Holland Press, 1980), 27.

the industrial sector. In other words, the necessary funds for industrial-sector investment should be found by turning trade against the agricultural sector (exploiting the agricultural sector).[8]

Fel'dman proved mathematically that faster growth could be attained by channeling more investment into the capital goods industry instead of the consumer goods industry.[9] Since the former socialist countries closely followed a growth strategy based on the theories of Preobrazhensky and Fel'dman, the people's consumption was inevitably repressed as these countries put more investment in development of the industrial sector, and heavy industries in particular.

This kind of development strategy, consequently, caused shortages throughout the rest of the economy. The shortage problem was particularly acute in intermediary goods industries, and the shortage of intermediary goods caused inefficiency in capital goods industries because capital goods industries could not produce final goods without intermediary goods.[10] As we can see, shortage was a chronic problem in the socialist economies, and because of this chronic shortage problem, the price of goods, and especially the price of consumer goods, would likely explode when price liberalization policy materialized across the board simultaneously.

Second, price liberalization policy was implemented in places where competition was an exception rather than a rule. Enterprises under the planned economy were like monopolies because having more than one supplier for each good was considered to be

---

[8] Tom Bottomore, ed., *A Dictionary of Marxian Thought* (Oxford: Blackwell, 2001), 442.

[9] Robert Wellington Campbell, *The Failure of Soviet Economic Planning: System, Performance, Reform* (Bloomington: Indiana University Press, 1992), 35-36.

[10] Kornai, *The Socialist System*, op. cit., 273-275.

an excess in a planned economy. After the collapse of the system, they were able to retain and secure their position as monopolists. These enterprises could not set prices as they liked under the planned economy because prices were arbitrarily set by the state, but by using their position as monopolists, they could set prices as they liked under the free market system of price liberalization.

Third, during the transition period, the government usually expanded the monetary base in order to fill the budget deficit, and this became one of the direct causes of inflation. It was indeed what happened in most of the transitional economies of our concern. There were several causes of budget deficit that occurred in these countries, but two stood out among others: First, as state-owned enterprises were privatized, the government lost its main source of income, but its expenditures had not been reduced because the government took expansionary and growth stimulus measures to stimulate growth during the transition period. Second, the first cause mentioned above could be compensated for if these countries had well-established tax legislation and enforcement systems, but they were conspicuously missing in most of the transition economies. The poor tax system exacerbated the already meager government income situation, and inflation inevitably occurred as the government printed money to compensate for its budget deficit.[11]

2. GDP and Economic Growth during the Transition Period

It was believed that the transition from central planning to a more market-oriented economic system would result in faster eco-

---

[11] Keith Griffin, *Studies in Globalization and Economic Transitions* (New York: St. Martin's Press, 1996), 177-178.

nomic growth and a rapid improvement in the standard of living for the great majority of the population. However, this belief and expectation turned out to be seriously flawed. Economic output collapsed (see Table 17) in most transitional economies, social services also diminished or collapsed as a result, and many several hundred people became impoverished. Since the combined population of Russia and the Ukraine comprises approximately 70 percent of the all the Commonwealth of Independent States (CIS, hereafter), let us briefly consider the two countries' economic performance in terms of GDP growth. As we can see from Table 17, Russia's real Gross Domestic Product (Gross Domestic Product minus inflation) in 1999 was about 50 percent of that in 1990, the year liberalization policy was implemented based on Shock Therapy or the Big Bang strategy. In the case of the Ukraine, the situation was even worse; the Ukraine's GDP in 1999 was less than 40 percent of that in 1990. As can be seen in Table 17, only Hungary recovered to the same GDP level, but as we consider that Hungary's economic reform started as early as the mid-1980s, its recovery could be considered neither impressive nor different.

The fall in output and income was largely due to the collapse in aggregate demand and in particular to a sharp fall in invest-

Table 17. Cumulative Change in Real GDP, 1990-1999

(index: 1990=100)

	1990	1991	1992	1993	1994	1995	1996	1997	1998	1999
Russia	100	94.4	76.1	68.1	60.2	57.7	55.8	56.2	53.5	55.2
Ukraine	100	89.3	74.2	63.7	49.1	43.0	38.8	37.4	36.7	36.6
Uzbekistan	100	99.5	88.4	86.5	82.9	82.1	83.3	85.4	89.2	93.0
Romania	100	87.1	79.4	80.6	83.8	89.8	93.3	87.7	82.9	80.3
Hungary	100	88.1	85.4	84.9	87.4	88.7	89.9	94.0	98.6	103.0

Source: Calculated based on IMF World Outlook Database May 2001, Real Gross Domestic Product (developing and transition countries).

Table 18. Total Investment in 1990 and 1995 (% of GDP)

	1990	1995
Russia	30.1	25
Ukraine	27.5	n.a.
Uzbekistan	32.2	23
Romania	30.2	26
Hungary	25.4	23

Source: World Bank, World Development Report 1996.

ment. As we can see from Table 18, Russia's aggregate investment fell about 5 percent (from 30.1 percent to 25 percent of GDP) during the 1990-1995 period, but real GDP fell 38.7 percent. The advocates of the Shock Therapy-based reform strategy always pointed out that investment under socialist rule was inefficient (meaning high input, less output) and distorted toward development of the capital goods industry. They also argued that, as free market would ensure efficiency of investment and sound resource allocation, total product as measured by real GDP should also increase. In the context of their argument, reduction of investment in the transition economies such as Russia could not be considered bad, but rather, sound policy that could ensure efficiency. However, reduction of investment during the transition period did not bring positive results. As we can see from Tables 17 and 18, there is a direct relationship between total investment and total product. In the case of Hungary, the total investment decreased from 25.4 percent of the GDP in 1990 to 23 percent of the GDP in 1995, just 2.5 percent, but the GDP decreased by 11.3 percent during the same period. In the case of Uzbekistan, the total investment decreased by 8.8 percent, but the GDP decreased by 17.8 percent. Romania had a similar story; its total investment decreased by 3.8 percent, but its GDP decreased by 10.2 percent.

3. Income Distribution and Poverty

During the transition, not only did income level fall, but there was also a horrendous increase in inequality in the distribution of income (see Table 19). Before the process of economic reform began, the centrally planned economies enjoyed a relatively egalitarian distribution of income compared both to the developing economies and to the advanced market economies; nonetheless, the income differential widened considerably in these countries after they adopted the simultaneous reform strategy of the Shock Therapy or Big Bang. For instance, Russia's Gini coefficient in 1987, before it adopted reform measures based on the Shock Therapy strategy, was 0.24, but in 1998, eight years after the reform, the coefficient increased to 0.49, matched evenly with that of Brazil, one of the most inequalitarian countries in the world. Income distribution worsened uniformly among most of the transitional economies.

There were several reasons for the deteriorating income distribution, but unfair distribution of productive assets was one of the most important contributing factors in worsening income distribution in the transition economies. The transition also had been accompanied by an increase in inequality in the distribution of productive assets. Prior to the reforms, most productive assets were owned either by the state or by collective institutions; consequently, the distribution of wealth among households was relatively equal. However, when state-owned enterprises had been sold to the private sector from the beginning of 1991, societies became highly polarized between a relatively small wealthy capitalist class and the majority of people who owned almost no assets.

After the collapse of the socialist system, the once socially owned assets were distributed to individuals according to free market privatization measures. Nonetheless, these individuals sold their shares for food as their economic situation worsened. Others tried to run enterprises, but soon after, many had to file for bankruptcy because they were inexperienced and unskilled at running and managing business enterprises. The methods of privatization differed from country to country, but as we can see from Table 19, income polarization occurred as a result of implementing privatization policy in transition economies.

Table 19. Income Distribution (1987-1988, 1996)

	Gini coefficient 1987-88	Gini coefficient 1996	% change
Russia	0.24-0.34	0.50	47-108
Ukraine	0.26	0.33	27
Uzbekistan	0.29	0.34	17
Romania	0.25	0.28	12
Hungary	0.21	0.31	48

Source: World Bank, World Development Report 2000/2001.

The combination of a fall in average income and a rise in inequality resulted in a substantial increase in the incidence of income poverty. Using a poverty line of $4 a day (in 1990 purchasing power parity dollars), the UNDP estimates that poverty in Eastern Europe and the CIS countries increased from 4 percent of the population in 1988 to 32 percent in 1994, or from 13.6 million people to 119.2 million. As incidents of poverty increased, people's average food consumption also decreased. In Russia, it was found that approximately 10 percent of the total households suffered from chronic malnutrition.[12] In particular, the children of poor families seemed to suffer; according to the United Nations Development

---

[12] S. Clark, "New Forms of Employment and Household Survival Strategies in Russia," Coventry, ISITO, 186.

Programme's study, which covered all transition economies, the number of stunted children under the age of two increased from 9.4 percent in 1992 to 15.2 percent in 1994[13] (see Table 20).

Table 20. Population in Poverty

	Year	Percentage
Russia	1994	30.9
Ukraine	1995	31.7
Uzbekistan	1993-94	29
Romania	1994	21.5
Hungary	1989-94	25

Source: World Bank. World Development Report 2000/2001.

The decline in average incomes, the rise in income inequalities, the increase in insecurity, uncertainty, and unemployment, and the deterioration of social services, including health services, led to a sharp decline in birth rates in almost all the transition economies and a rise in mortality rates in many countries (see Table 21). There may be a clear association between the extent of the decline in average incomes and the sharpness of the fall in birth rates. Marriage rates fell, married couples postponed having children, and more and more women had to resort to abortion. In other parts of the world, a decline in the birth rate is a sign of improved economic conditions, but in transition economies, the sharp decline of the birth rate was a sign of acute economic distress. The transition to a market economy has thus been accompanied by a dramatic decline in income and demographic collapse.

---

[13] UNDP, 1999 Human Development Report for Central and Eastern Europe and the CIS, New York, UNDP, 23.

Table 21. Death and Birth Rate, 1980 and 1995 (Per 1,000 people)

	Crude 1980	Death Rate 1995	Change	Crude 1980	Birth Rate 1995	Change
Russia	11	15	+4	16	9	-7
Ukraine	11	14	+3	15	10	-5
Uzbekistan	8	6	-2	34	29	-5
Romania	10	12	+2	18	11	-7
Hungary	14	14	0	21	16	-5

Source: World Bank, World Development Indicators 1997: World Bank 1997.

4. The Collapse of the Social Safety Net and Its Consequences

Privatization policy, the other important measure of the Shock Therapy or Big Bang strategy, was implemented along with price liberalization policy in a way to minimize government intervention and reduce social spending on education, health care, and other services pertaining to the social safety net. In the spirit of the Big Bang and the Shock Therapy, this policy was implemented abruptly, and intended to cause short and brief pain to the people. This pain supposedly lasted a short period of time, but it did not end for nearly a decade and caused a great deal of demographic deterioration of the people in the transition economies. For instance, life expectancy at birth for people in the transition economies shortened across the board (see Table 22).

The abrupt collapse of the social safety net was accompanied by an increase in crime. For instance, the incidence of murder in Russia increased from 15,600 in 1990 to 31,100 in 1999, a twofold increase. Moreover, death caused by homicide doubled during the 1990-1994 period. The rate did decrease during the 1995-1999 periods, but was still 59 percent higher than that of 1990, the year the Shock Therapy strategy-based privatization policy began. In 1999,

Table 22. Life Expectancy at Birth, Comparing 1980 and 1995

	Male 1980	1995	Change	Female 1980	1995	Change
Russia	62	58	-4	73	72	-1
Ukraine	65	64	-1	74	74	0
Uzbekistan	64	66	2	71	72	1
Romania	67	66	-1	72	74	2
Hungary	66	66	0	73	74	1

Source: World Bank, World Development Indicator 1997: World Bank 1997.

death by homicide in Russia was 25.9 per 1,000 people; this figure is three times more than that of the United States, 25 times more than that of England, and as many as 40 times more than that of Japan.

Education in the transition economies also deteriorated considerably. For instance, according to one study conducted in 1994, 21 percent of those students age 15 to 19 years old either did not graduate from high school or did not attend school. This figure was approximately a 5 percent increase from the same study conducted in 1989, the year before the transition policy was implemented.[14] Insecurity and mental panic caused by the collapse of the social safety net caused an increase in the rate of suicide, as well (see Table 23). The average rate of suicide in the European Union (EU) for males and females is 20 per 10,000 people. With the exception of Uzbekistan, most of the transition economies' suicide rates were extremely high, compared to the EU.

As we have seen above, abrupt transition to a free market economy, which was recommended by neoclassical/liberal econo-

---

[14] Michael Ellman, "Transition Economies" in Ha-Joon Chang, *Rethinking Development Economics* (London: Anthem Press, 2003), 191.

Table 23. Number of Suicides (1989-1993)

(Per 100,000 people)

	Male	Female
Russia	66	13
Ukraine	38	9
Uzbekistan	9	3
Hungary	55	18
Belarus	49	10

Source: U.N. Development Programme. Human Development Report 1997.

mists/advocates, was in actuality harmful to many people in the transition. Most transition economies of Russia and the CIS countries bottomed out and began to recover in the beginning of the 21st century, but as former World Bank vice president Joseph Stigliz described, "the last decade" could be aptly described as "the lost decade."[15] As we have seen above, the performance of those countries that adopted simultaneous reform based on Shock Therapy and the Big Bang without exception were miserable. This indicated the failure of the simultaneous reform strategy. In the next section, let us make an assessment of this simultaneous reform strategy by analyzing its theoretical foundation.

III. Assessment of Shock Therapy and the Big Bang Strategy

The central idea in Shock Therapy and the Big Bang strategy is that in order to achieve a complete transition from a centrally

---

[15] Joseph Stiglitz, "Whither Reform? Ten Years of the Transition." Keynote Address at the World Bank Annual Conference on Development Economics, Washington, D.C., April 28-30, 1999.

planned economy to a market-guided economy, simultaneous reform should be applied to all the sectors of the economy (the Big Bang). According to neoclassical/liberal economists, it is expected that a certain degree of pain should accompany this kind of simultaneous reform, but the pain should last only a short period of time and the gain from the reform should override the pain (the Shock Therapy). It is believed that the gain from the reform is determined by the general equilibrium in which supply equals demand. Moreover, according to these people, a market is efficient only if there are well-defined property rights.[16]

Accordingly, there are three requirements for the Shock Therapy strategy to function properly. First, state-owned enterprises (SOEs) must be privatized because the SOEs are perceived to be the source of inefficiency. Second, all the prices must be liberalized simultaneously in order to ensure the proper functioning of price signals so that resource allocation is carried out according to price signals, so the economy becomes efficient. Third, as the market economy functions properly, it attracts foreign investment and would lessen the pain that is accompanied by price and market liberalization.[17]

Hence, the goal of the Shock Therapy approach in the former Soviet republics and Eastern Europe was to transform as fast as possible planned economies into market economies characterized by neoclassical general equilibrium conditions. Consistent with neoclassical economics, the details of transitions and the historical factors were considered to be relatively unimportant. Rather, impor-

---

[16] Anders Aslund, Peter Boone, and Simon Johnson, "How to Stabilize: Lessons from Post-Communist Countries," Brookings Paper on Economic Activity, 1996, 217-18.

[17] Aslund, ibid., 218-219.

tance was placed upon the desired end result of the process—having a market economy in general equilibrium. Institutions were torn down overnight, and it was expected that the institutions of capitalism would quickly emerge to take the place of old institutions. These reforms included such things as privatization of state enterprises, the immediate dismantling of central planning and controls, the comprehensive and instantaneous liberalization of prices, foreign and domestic, and the use of foreign capital to ease the pain of adjustment. The prescriptions of Shock Therapy or Big Bang are not only similar to the so-called Washington Consensus (WC),[18] but resonate the basic tenets of the WC, and probably could be categorized as an extreme version of the WC.

The reform packages offered by international development agencies such as the IMF are based on recommendations and prescriptions based on the WC; however, it is the exception rather than the rule that the country receiving the IMF's rescue package and following its conditionalities indeed recovers from economic crisis. For this reason, critics such as Joseph Stiglitz consistently argue for lessening and changing the IMF's conditionalities. Nonetheless, the neoclassical/liberal economists insist that adopting and observing the conditionalities to destroy socialist institutions as quickly as possible is the only way to attain genuine market reform. Since they try to apply their belief to almost all the countries that seek or need a reform, the implementation of simultaneous reform strategy can be viewed as an ideological inclination rather than an economic necessity. However, in order to realize

---

[18] John Williamson, "What Washington Means by Policy Reform," Chapter 2 from *Latin American Adjustment: How Much Has Happened?* edited by John Williamson. Published April 1990, and November 2002 (Internet version: http://www.iie.com/publications/papers/paper.cfm?researchid=486).

economic transition, one needs much more than just simultaneous price liberalization and privatization of SOEs, including establishment of legislation to support proper functioning of market mechanisms, and development of networks of buyers and sellers relying on market mechanisms, and a competitive environment to ensure market mechanisms are sustained. This can not be done instantaneously.[19]

Society is an organism that consists of different but interrelated cells; thus, changing society through economic reform means changing an interrelated, complex system and definitely requires considerable time. As Nobel laureate Kenneth Arrow once argued, since economic change, whether it is a fundamental reform or merely fine-tuning, is a path-dependent process, and expectations change only slowly; reform requires time to be effective.[20] If one ignores this fact, and tries to change everything at once, she or he is bound to face failure. And, it was indeed exactly what happened in Russia and the CIS countries. In these countries, price liberalization and privatization of publicly owned assets were implemented simultaneously across the board and these became a direct cause of rapid inflation. Since the rapid inflation distorted relative prices and had a harmful effect on investment, the economies became disarrayed and dysfunctional. In the next section, let us take a close look at the reform experience of China and Vietnam, two countries that adopted sequential reform instead of simultaneous reform.

---

[19] Keith Griffin, "Economic Policy during the Transition to a Market Oriented Economy," Working Paper 1998, Department of Economics-University of California, Riverside, 28-29.

[20] Kenneth J. Arrow, "The Place of Institutions in the Economy: A Theoretical Perspective," in Hayami Yujiro's *The Institutional Foundations of East Asian Economic Development*: Proceedings of the IEA Conference held in Tokyo, Japan 1998.

IV. Sequential Reform of China and Vietnam

The most significant difference between the transition experiences of China and Vietnam and that of Russia is macroeconomic stability. As we can see from Table 24 below, with the exception of the years 1988 and 1989, inflation did not become a significant problem in China. The inflation that occurred in 1988 and 1989 was due to excess supply, but it was soon under control due to the government's active intervention policies, such as contractionary macro and monetary policy.[21]

Table 24. Annual Rate of Inflation in China (1981-1991)

Year	1981	1982	1983	1984	1985	1986	1987	1988	1989	1990	1991
Rate	2.6	2.0	1.9	2.8	11.9	7.0	8.8	20.7	16.7	2.2	3.0

Source: UN World Economic Survey 1992.

Vietnam did experience hyperinflation before its reform policy, "Doi Moi," was officially implemented, but hyperinflation went down to a moderate level after the implementation of "Doi Moi." The reason for relative macroeconomic stability in China and Vietnam in comparison with Russia and the CIS countries can be found in the fact that the transition strategy of Shock Therapy and the Big Bang, such as rapid price liberalization and simultaneous privatization, were not adopted and implemented in either China or Vietnam. In the spirit of Shock Therapy and Big Bang, and based on the assumption that adoption of capitalism should be prioritized in the transition from a centrally planned economy to a market-guided economy, reform measures undermining the basis of a socialist planned economy and changing property relations

---

[21] Griffin, *Studies in Globalization and Economic Transitions*, op. cit., 180.

from state and collectives to an individual level were implemented simultaneously and across the board in Russia and the CIS countries. However, as we saw in the previous section, those reform policies caused macroeconomic instability and price explosion, in particular; this price explosion in turn caused a drastic fall in consumption, and contraction of consumption in turn had a negative impact on overall investment; a fall in investment in turn caused a downfall of GDP. A vicious cycle was formed and it lasted for nearly a decade.

In China and Vietnam, instead of the reform measures that pushed for price liberalization and changed property ownership simultaneously across the board, reform policies were implemented selectively to increase production in the areas where elasticity of supply was high.[22] For instance, as farmers' incentives were restricted under the socialist planned economy, elasticity of supply should be high in the agricultural sector if a reform policy was implemented to change the socialist primitive accumulation in which the terms of trade were adverse to the agricultural sector. As such, the reform policy was first implemented in the agricultural sector. As farmers now had incentive to increase their agricultural production, they produced more output, and consequently, the agricultural producers' income also increased. More importantly, China's overall production increased as there was more food to consume. Agriculture was not the only example of this sequential reform. The supply elasticity is also high in small and medium-size enterprises because they do not require large amounts of start-up capital. They also do not necessarily require imported technolo-

---

[22] Keith Griffin, "Relative Price and Investment: An Essay on Resource Allocation," Working Paper, Department of Economics-University of California, Riverside, October 2004, 6.

gy, but rather, can be started by utilizing domestic technology. Hence, the priority of reform should be given to such enterprises, as well.

This was, indeed, the case in China. In the Chinese reform process, small and medium-size local enterprises, and so-called "township village enterprises (TVEs)" were encouraged to form and the Chinese government provided institutional support such as reforming legislative procedures for these enterprises to be formed and to prosper. With this kind of institutional support, the TVEs were established in great numbers and they became not only the symbol of Chinese reform but also the backbone of reform, as they are currently responsible more than half of all industrial production in China.[23] Moreover, as China prioritized reform in the sectors that had high supply elasticity, and as they performed well, China was able to maintain a high employment level and also increase people's income level during the reform process. As people's incomes steadily increased, they saved more than before, and this in turn increased the pool of investment.

The relationship between saving and investment is extremely important, and deserves a detailed explanation. In the case of China, domestic saving increased and it had a direct effect on the increase in investment. Why would domestic saving increase in the first place? There are several reasons for this. First, Chinese people had a positive outlook for China's economy. Without a positive outlook, they would not deposit their money in banks. However, it is important to point out that this positive outlook would not develop without macroeconomic stability. Second, the Chinese government implemented a high interest-rate policy to encourage

---

[23] Barry Naughton, "Chinese Institutional Innovation and Privatization from Below," *American Economic Review*, vol. 84, No. 2 (1994), 266-270.

domestic saving.[24] Since people did not have other alternative opportunities for utilizing their money for investment due to inadequate development of the financial market in China, they saved their money in banks. Nonetheless, it is important to reemphasize that without macroeconomic stability, and price stability in particular, people would not form the positive outlook necessary for China's economy and would not deposit their money in banks even if the government encouraged them to do so.

From the analysis above, we can make the following conclusions: First of all, since reorganization of production, which serves as a basis for change in property relations and ownership, and increase of efficiency can only be achieved through growth, maintaining growth during the transition period has enormous significance. In order to achieve high rates of growth, a high level of investment should be maintained because high levels of investment enable outputs to move according to price signals, and this, in turn, causes a swift increase in production by ensuring profit opportunity. In contrast, reduction in production makes reform difficult as it decreases incentive for investment. In other words, the effectiveness of price liberalization and relative price change are determined by the rate of investment during the transition period. As was seen in the previous section, if reform strategy is limited only to price liberalization, people's employment and income would be reduced. As reduction in these areas occurs, investment is also reduced as a consequence, and finally, growth suffers. Reduction in growth decreased economic flexibility and delayed necessary changes in production composition that were

---

[24] Louis Kuijs, "Investment and Saving in China," World Bank Policy Research Working Paper 3633, June 2005. Accessed at http://www-wds .worldbank.org/servlet/WDSContentServer/WDSP/IB/2005/06/14/0000 16406_20050614112417/Rendered/PDF/wps3633.pdf.

needed for changes in property relations/ownership. For these reasons, reform priority should be given to the areas that have high elasticity of supply, and high levels of investment should be maintained during the entire transition period.

In addition to these requirements, the importance of the initial period of reform should also be pointed out. In order to achieve genuine reform, the support and participation of the people are essential. This is especially important in the initial period of reform because one of the most important objectives of the reform is to change the people's way of thinking or culture that had been harnessed during the centrally planned economy to one that is compatible with a market economy. Therefore, without people's active cooperation and participation, reform cannot be permeated throughout the general population and the objectives of reform cannot be fulfilled.[25]

The different results between China (and Vietnam), which opted for a sequential or incremental reform strategy, and Russia, which adopted the simultaneous reform strategy, are remarkable. China and Vietnam were able to earn agreement and participation from the general population and could achieve annual growth rates of 10.7 percent and 8.1 percent, respectively, from the initial period of reform to the present, while Russia experienced an annual growth rate of negative 6.3 percent during the start of reform from the early 1990s to the end of the decade. The population growth reflects a similar story; Vietnam's and China's population grew at annual rates of 2.1 percent and 1.2 percent, respectively, for the 1990 period, while Russia's population decreased at an annual rate of 0.1 percent for the same period (see Table 25).

---

25 Carl Riskin, Zhao Renwei, and Li Shi, *China's Retreat from Equality: Income Distribution and Economic Transition* (New York: M. E. Sharpe, 2001), 102-104.

Table 25. Comparison of Major Macro Indicators: Vietnam, China, and Russia

Countries/Indicators	Vietnam	China	Russia
Population, 1999 (unit: millions)	77.6	1286.0	148.4
Population Growth Rate (1990-1999)	2.1	1.2	-0.1
GDP Growth (1990-1999)	8.1%	10.7%	-6.3%
GDP per Capita Growth (1990-1999)	6.3%	10.4%	-7.0%
Cumulative Change in Per Capita Income (1990-1999)	63%	104%	-70%

Source: World Bank, World Development Report 2001.

V. The Role of Government in Transition Economies

The advocates of Shock Therapy and the Big Bang strategy basically believe in laissez-faire economics, in which government has a minimal role in the economy; hence they implemented policy measures to rescind government power and influence from the market. As we have seen, the result of adopting such a strategy was devastating for the people in the transitional economies. On the other hand, the countries that adopted a sequential or an incremental strategy of reform prospered. The advocates of simultaneous reform strategy defend their position by arguing that the initial conditions were different in China and Vietnam than those of Russia and the CIS countries.[26] China and Vietnam, they argued, had much more surplus labor in the rural sector than Russia and the CIS countries had.[27] They also argued that the discovery of oil

---

[26] Aslund, "How to Stabilize: Lessons from Post-Communist Countries," op. cit., 227.

[27] Stephen Parker, Gavin Tritt, and Wing Thye Woo, "Some Lessons from the Comparison of Transitions in Asia and Eastern Europe," in Wing Thye Woo, Stephen Parker, and Jeffrey Sachs, eds., *Economies in Transition:*

in Vietnam has had a positive effect on its economic development and it was another factor that distinguished Vietnam from other transition economies.

It was true that both China and Vietnam had surplus labor in the rural sector, but surplus labor itself is considered to be a problem that needs to be overcome, not a cause of successful reform in development economics. Furthermore, oil was indeed discovered in Vietnam, but the size of Vietnam's oil reserve is insignificant compared to oil wells in the CIS countries such as Azerbaijan, Kazakhstan, or Russia. As we take these factors into consideration, instead of differences in economic structure and initial conditions, what set China and Vietnam apart from Russia and the CIS countries were the policies that were adopted. Then, what role should government play during transition?

First of all, as was pointed out previously, the government of a transition economy should create an environment that supports macroeconomic stability, so that proper functioning of price signals is ensured; therefore, preventing rapid inflation is one of the essential prerequisites for success of reform. The government should implement contractionary monetary policy along with its cautious effort to avoid deficits in the public sector in order to keep inflation under control at all times. However, these measures are only some of the necessary conditions for creating an environment that supports macroeconomic stability. In order for the government to fulfill sufficient conditions to avoid rapid inflation, it should have well-defined and established tax legislation and an enforcement system. Second, market institutions should be established sequentially according to the priority of the reform. In this respect, the simultaneous reform that was implemented in Russia

Comparing Asia and Europe (Cambridge: MIT Press, 1997), 6.

and the CIS countries in the hope of obtaining a free market as quickly as possible by minimizing the role of government was a mere fantasy.

The government should play several key roles to support markets and ensure they function properly. For instance, the government should establish legislation to promote legal transactions while preventing illegal transactions. Competition is vitally important for proper market functioning, but unfair competition such as oligopoly and monopoly should be prevented. Since it was observed that information and wealth were not normally distributed fairly to the market participants in the transition economies, the emergence of unfair competition such as oligopoly and monopoly were rampant in such economies. Without government regulation of such unfair competition, the market would not ensure appropriate resource allocation, and thus it could not promote efficiency.

The government should also ensure that public goods that are usually undersupplied and disproportionately distributed in the market economy are adequately and equally provided to all during the transition period in order to promote growth while preventing poverty. The market fails when it comes to externalities. Since the benefit of having education and health care is not only limited to the individual who receives such services, but also extends to the society in which the individual belongs, they are considered to be positive externalities. However, when these services were privatized in the countries that adopted the simultaneous reform strategy, the price of education and health care services rose and many people could not afford them. Apparently, in the cases of Russia and the CIS countries, this kind of privatization had cost society not only a great deal of havoc, but also human lives.

Third, the government should establish a new set of property relations. From the experiences of Russia and the CIS countries, we have learned that privatization is an extremely complex process, and just pushing for a policy of privatization of SOEs without establishing a new set of property relations could cause serious problems to arise.[28] For instance, in the case of Russia, most privatization took the form of management-employee buyout; in this kind of privatization, employees and managers of the SOE were given the resources to buy their enterprises. The idea was to give an individual an equal footing with everyone else in the society. Nevertheless, there seemed to be two outstanding problems associated with this kind of privatization scheme.

First, those people who were endowed with relatively better machines and facilities could purchase better machines and facilities, and they performed better than those people who were endowed with relatively worse machines and facilities. Second, since this kind of privatization materialized without a complete change of institutions, workers sold their shares to the former managers of the socialist era, and once again these former managers became owners and managers of the privatized enterprises. This is called "nomenklatura privatization," and since this kind of privatization was mainly used for enriching the owners and managers of enterprises, it did more harm than good to the workers in general.[29]

Instituting a new set of property relations is one of the most

---

[28] Yalmaz Akyuz, "Reform and Crisis in the Transition Economics," UNCTA, *Privatization in the Transition Process: Recent Experiences in Eastern Europe* (New York: United Nations, 1994), 6.

[29] Wing Thye Woo, "Improving Enterprise Performance in Transition Economics," in Wing Thye Woo, Stephen Parker, and Jeffrey Sachs, eds., *Economies in Transition: Comparing Asia and Europe* (Cambridge, Mass.: MIT Press, 1997), 313.

important factors in a transition strategy. However, this does not only mean privatizing SOEs. Rather than privatizing SOEs, creating an environment in which newly established enterprises can grow and be successful should have been a priority in the transition strategy. As we can see from the above, contrary to the Shock Therapy advocates' prescription of a small or minimum government role, a government has many roles to play during the economic transition. The government of a transition economy must implement a monetary policy to bring inflation under control, establish legislation to collect taxes, create an environment that supports the growth of newly established enterprises, and set up public goods that are undersupplied to create positive externalities for society as a whole. Whether a government can play the aforementioned roles depended on whether the government had autonomy during the transition period. This becomes clear as we compare the different transition experiences of Russia and China.

The transition strategy of the Shock Therapy and the Big Bang transitions was the one-size-fits-all uniform strategy that neoclassical/liberal economists and the international development agencies such as the IMF and the World Bank tried to impose on virtually all the countries that attempted to make the transition from a centrally planned economy to a market-guided economy. It was indeed true that the former Soviet Union, before it collapsed, was in dire economic straits and was faced with many economic difficulties. However, the former Soviet Union, on the other hand, had tremendous economic resources that were not correctly utilized. Had the reform proceeded in a direction toward fully utilizing these resources efficiently, the former Soviet Union would have overcome its difficulties and enjoyed economic growth and development. Nonetheless, as the government dissolved and the former Soviet Union collapsed, chaos reigned over the situation.

What actually happened under Mikhael Gorbachev's *perestroika* and *glasnost* was destruction of the state and its organs, which eventually led to not only the collapse of the socialist system, but also the collapse of the entire state. Gorbachev was not alone in engineering the collapse. Incidentally, Gorbachev was heavily supported and advised by the United States and the U.S.' sovietological institutions; for them, the Soviet Union was an evil empire that needed to vanish. After the Soviet Union collapsed, foreign advisory groups played a significant and sometimes a dominant role in implementing the Shock Therapy/Big Bang transition strategy in Russia, and consequently, the government's role in transition diminished.[30]

On the contrary, the Chinese and Vietnamese governments never lost control and played a dominant role during their economic transition period. In fact, as we have seen above, their economic reforms could be characterized as having been engineered by the states. The state-led transition is not panacea; sometimes it became a cause and a source of corruption. However, by ensuring a socio-political stability, the state in control reduced uncertainty, which could be one of the most serious problems and obstacles faced during economic reform and transition. Moreover, stable governance enabled a certain degree of social integration, so that people from different backgrounds could also participate in reform.

The criticisms of China peaked during the Tiananmen Square incident in 1989, but the Chinese government was neither shaken nor influenced by the criticisms. Instead, the Chinese government continued its reform process at its own pace. By and large, the institutional change was implemented incrementally to suit peo-

---

[30] Peter Nolan, "China's Rise, Russia's Fall," *Journal of Peasant Studies*, vol. 24, Nos. 1 & 2 (1997), 242.

ple's needs and pace. As such, it enabled liberation of potentialities that were embedded in the Chinese economy, and China was able to achieve a sustained annual growth rate of nearly 10 percent for the last two decades. As we compare the transition experiences of Russia and China, a clear lesson can be drawn and applied to the DPRK. The DPRK government should be in firm control to provide socio-political stability and implement a reform policy according to the needs and pace of the people, so that growth and development potentialities embedded in North Korea an be realized.

VI. The Prospects for Economic Reform in the DPRK

So far, the DPRK has tried to build an independent socialist economy based on self-reliant *Juche* ideology, but this does not mean that the economy has never changed and maintained a strict and rigid central planning system; several times in the past, the regime implemented reform measures as it deemed necessary. Those were not full-scale measures that could change the entire system, but rather, selective and partial ones that were only intended to amend and fix the system.[31] The contradictions of the DPRK's economy have accumulated since the 1970s and were accentuated in the 1990s. Since the mid-1990s, the DPRK experienced economic crisis and, as a consequence, several thousands of people are suffering from starvation. In order to cope with this kind of crisis, the DPRK regime implemented far-reaching economic reform measures on July 1, 2002. This was called the "7/1 Measures" in the DPRK; since the "7/1 Measures" seemed to be

---

[31] Phillip Park, "The Future of the D.P.R.K.," *Journal of Contemporary Asia*, vol. 31, No. 1 (2001), 111-2.

going beyond the selective and partial measures of the past as the introduction of markets and the increased usage of commodities-currency exchange were included. However, the real challenge for the DPRK would be whether it can change the current institutions according to the needs of reform. In order to assess such feasibility, let us first take a close look at the DPRK's self-reliant development strategy.

1. Self-Reliant Development Strategy

The DPRK's self-reliant development strategy is based on Juche ideology. The ideology has historical roots. As a small state surrounded by the big powers, the DPRK had to face challenges from outside pressures. For instance, after the Korean War, the Soviet Union tried to make the DPRK its satellite state as it pressured the DPRK to join CMEA. During the Sino-Soviet dispute, the DPRK received pressure from both China and the Soviet Union to join each respective side. On top of these pressures, the DPRK is always pressured by the U.S.-ROK military alliance. Furthermore, as the world's superpower, the United States' containment policy toward the DPRK, and economic embargo in particular, put the DPRK in a position to rely on its own resources to develop its economy and to survive.

It should be pointed out that these external pressures are some of the most important causes for solidifying internal unity in the DPRK. Against this background, the DPRK chose an unbalanced growth strategy called, "giving priority to the development of heavy industry while simultaneously developing light industry and agriculture."[32] What it meant was to give investment priority

---

[32] Hui-gak Hwang, "*Bukhanui Kyungjaechimche*" (North Korea's Economic

to the development of heavy industries, and also develop light industry and agriculture by employing resources generated from mass-mobilization movements such as the *Chollima* movement.[33]

The DPRK strategy seemed to work fine in the initial period (see Table 26). Nonetheless, this kind of unbalanced growth strategy could not be continued. Without concomitant growth of light (consumer) industry, heavy industry could not grow any further and the whole economy ceased to grow as the impact of diminishing returns kicks in. Moreover, the DPRK's self-reliant development strategy was not implemented in such a way as to nurture the capability to be self-sufficient, but rather, implemented in such a way as to be physically self-sufficient, autarky. Among other factors, food must be self-sufficient in an autarkic system. Suffering from a labor shortage due to the tremendous human loss during the Korean War and millions of people having taken exodus to the South, the DPRK developed its agriculture in a capital-intensive way rather than in a labor-intensive way.

Table 26. The DPRK's GDP Growth (Selected Years from the 1946-1960 Period)

	1946	1949	1953	1956	1959	1960
Per Capita Income (%)	100	209	145	319	636	683
Industrial Production (%)	100	337	216	615	–	2100
Production Materials (%)	100	375	158	640	–	–
Raw Materials (%)	100	288	285	598	–	–

Source: Scalapino and Lee, *Communism in Korea*, p. 1223.

Stagnation), *Bukhansahoejui Kyungjaeui Chimchewa Daeeung* (North Korean Socialist Economy's Stagnation and Response) (Seoul: Kyungnam University Press, 1995), 5.

[33] Ellen Brun and Jacques Hersh, *Socialist Korea* (New York and London: Monthly Review Press, 1976), 90.

As such, each sector of the DPRK economy became highly interdependent. The agricultural sector needed inputs such as tractors and chemical fertilizers from the industrial sector to operate, and the industrial sector, in turn, needed food supplies from the agricultural sector to maintain its livelihood. However, given the high interdependency between industry and agriculture, dislocations in one sector are likely to translate into dislocations in the other sector. This kind of high degree of interdependency could spell disaster when external shock is introduced to the system. This was indeed what happened to the DPRK in the mid-1990s. Together with bad weather, the cessation of crude oil supply from the Soviet Union hit the DPRK's agricultural sector first, and then the shock transferred to the industrial sector, setting off a vicious downward spiral of economic setback.[34]

2. Evaluation of Kim Il Sungism and North Korea's Current Regime

The self-reliant development strategy is uniquely tied to the DPRK's particular environment and history. But, achieving self-sufficiency in a country like North Korea is a nearly impossible task. For instance, achieving food self-sufficiency in a state in which only 20 percent of the land is arable is an extremely difficult, if not an impossible, task. Nevertheless, even critics of the DPRK's economy agreed that the DPRK did achieve tremendous economic growth for a sustained period of nearly 20 years from the end of the Korean War to the mid-1970s. This was feasible because the DPRK regime set economic growth as the priority, and was able to generate investment for a sustained period of time. In fact, the DPRK received heavy economic assistance and aid from the Soviet

---

[34] Park, *Self-Reliance or Self-Destruction?* op. cit., 98-110.

Union after the War and channeled those resources to investment for the development of heavy industry.

When economic assistance and aid from the Soviet Union stopped due to the DPRK's refusal to join CMEA, the DPRK had to generate needed investment for the development of heavy industry by turning trade against the agricultural sector. Although this kind of sacrificing of the agricultural sector in order to generate funds for development of heavy industry was in the same line with Preobrezhensky's theory of socialist primitive accumulation that justifies exploitation of the peasant class, the DPRK did not have much choice since it had a closed economy in which trade did not play any significant role in generating much needed funds. The DPRK claimed that since the beginning of the 1970s, such a policy was changed to benefit the agricultural sector. Since the DPRK has not published any official data to confirm its claim, we do not know whether the claim is true. However, if it were indeed true, then the questions are where did the DPRK find necessary funds to make investment in both industrial and agricultural sectors, and were they sustainable? In order to shed light on these questions, let us take a close look at what happened in and out of the DPRK since the early 1960s, when economic assistance and aid from the Soviet Union ceased.

In the 1960s, the DPRK faced not only an investment crisis, but also a security crisis. In 1961, there was a military coup d'etat in South Korea and the military government of South Korea declared that the ROK was an anti-communist state and targeted the DPRK as the number-one enemy. In the following year, there was the Cuban Missile Crisis, which confirmed the DPRK's suspicion that the Soviet Union could not be depended on. Furthermore, as the Sino-Soviet dispute became an intense confrontation in the mid-1960s, the DPRK's sense of isolation grew even more.

The DPRK's response was to strengthen *Juche*, the self-reliance. This time, self-reliance was not only limited to the economy, but also extended to defense. Deemphasizing the current economic development and opting instead for the line of "simultaneously carrying on the building up of the economy and defense," the strengthening of national defense was initiated. Publicly announced in 1962 and officially adopted in 1966, this "line of simultaneously carrying on the building up of the economy and defense" was a response formed out of the supremacy of ideology-oriented strategy as championed by Kim Il Sung.

Hampered with limited resources and adhering to the stratagems of self-sufficiency, this line that simultaneously pursued the strengthening of national defense and rapid economic growth became, in reality, the fortification of the worker's ideological thought processes and the maximization of the mass mobilization. With the looming external threat, and in order to mobilize the internal resources as greatly as possible, the collectivistic solidarity within (the society) had to be further bolstered, and to do so, the political leadership of the party had to be maximally flexed. Kim Il Song's response to external threats was to discipline the revolutionary ideology and put emphasis on strengthening the party. This naturally led to reinforcement of mass mobilization to extract necessary funds for investment. By mass mobilization, it meant more reliance on moral incentives instead of physical incentives, urging workers to work harder.

As the DPRK reliance on mass mobilization to generate necessary funds for investment continued, it inevitably faced problems. Among others, diminishing returns was the most outstanding problem. The law of diminishing returns is a classic economic concept that states as more investment in an area is made, overall return on that investment increases at a declining rate, assuming that all variables remain fixed. To continue to invest after a certain point (which varies from context to context) is to receive a decreasing return on that input.[35] The law of diminishing returns has broader applications than economics. In fact, it is one of the most widely recognized economic principles outside the economic classroom and certainly applies to the realm of moral incentives as well as physical incentives. As the DPRK's dependence on mass mobilization to generate necessary funds for investment continued since the *Chollima* movement started in 1957, the law of diminishing returns had kicked in, and return from mass mobilization was not significant, meaning that North Korea was still faced with economic and security crises. As such, the party looked into means of forming the entirety of the society into an organic unit in order to overcome undying crises. This led to the latticing of the unified solidarity of the *Suryong* (the supreme leader), the party, and the mass into a singular organism.

The monolithic system of *Suryong* signified the birth of an organic social structure. The *Suryong* system that was founded in 1967 was very much the birth of an organic entity with Kim Il Sung, as the *Suryong*, at the center with all the components of society organized into concentric units surrounding him. And the connective that linked all the various components was Kim Il Sung's ideology, or Kim Il Sung's revolutionary tradition. Since 1967, the DPRK has claimed that North Korean society is one organic entity. As we consider the facts that the DPRK continues to exist despite the collapse of the Soviet Union and the entire Eastern socialist bloc, and is able to weather military confrontation with the world's superpower, the United States of America, for

---

[35] Accessed on January 5, 2007, at http://searchcrm.techtarget.com/sDefinition/ 0,,sid11_gci1216814,00.html.

more than five decades, there might be a kernel of truth to their claim. Nonetheless, the real problem will likely begin when the military confrontation with the United States is over, and the DPRK tries to develop its economy as a normal nation.

There has been considerable improvement in relations between the DPRK and the United States. The two countries finally broke their stalemate in 2008 as the United States removed the DPRK from the list of terrorist-sponsoring countries. Under the new U.S. administration of Barack Obama, further improvement of the U.S.-DPRK relationship is expected as both countries have realized that stalemate or worsening the relationship is not in the interest of either country. As the relationship improves, the United States would lift the economic embargo that has been imposed upon the DPRK since the inception of the republic in 1948, and finally, the two countries' relations would be normalized. This will provide a completely different playing field for the DPRK; in fact, there will be different rules of the game as the DPRK will be playing a completely different ball game. Is the DPRK ready for such a drastic change?

So, for more than three decades, the establishment and the intensification of the monolithic system of *Suryong* transformed North Korean society into a single unitary organizational society and forged an organic state based on the unification of the leader and the ideology. However, the *Suryong* system faced a crisis in 1994 as the supreme leader himself passed away. The death of Kim Il Sung was one of the biggest watershed events in the DPRK because (among many things) the DPRK had never experienced a power change since the inception of the republic in 1948. No one could predict what effect the death of Kim Il Sung would have on the country. There were other adverse events that further compounded the situation; the Soviet Union and the Eastern socialist bloc collapsed, tensions with the United States escalated as the DPRK's nuclear development became a hot security issue, and the country was undergoing an acute food shortage crisis. It was observed that many defectors were crossing the border and social order seemed to be unraveling. As such, cracks were beginning to appear in the collectivity and organizational ability demanded by the monolithic system of *Suryong*.

Kim Jong Il, who had just inherited the *Suryong* system of which he had been one of the chief architects, had little choice but to reinforce the existing system. But he put a little twist in it. After the conclusion of the so-called "Arduous March," which lasted from 1994 to 1998, Kim Jong Il introduced "Military-First Politics." "Military-First Politics" is not, as some have mistakenly labeled it, a political system that is dependent on the military. The "Military-First Politics" came about as a result of Kim Il Sung's death, the collapse of socialism, the security threat surrounding the nuclear weapons issues with the United States and the economic crisis within the system. Basically, what Kim Jong Il tried to do with the "Military-First Politics" was two-fold. First, he tried to manage and resolve the security crisis by reinforcing the military; this inevitably meant channeling more resources to the military. However, it was a mighty difficult task since the DPRK had meager resources and was already suffering from an acute economic crisis. Kim Jong Il needed a rationale to channel more resources to the military and found that rationale in his "Military-First Politics."

Second, Kim Jong Il tried to utilize military soldiers to reconstruct the collapsed economy from the very forefront, and also aimed to reorganize the workers, the farmers, and the urban workers as well as the entire society. In the DPRK, the military had not only been active in its traditional role as an armed force, but as a source of labor as well. In fact, the military was a "uniformed labor force," and with the crisis of the 1990s, their dual role as military and labor force only became more pronounced. As we can see, the "Military-First Politics" is not politics dependent on the armed forces, but North Korea's own unique governing practice that sought to overcome the crisis of the 1990s. The monolithic system of *Suryong* is supposedly the collectivization of the entire society in which the supreme leader, the party, and the mass form the revolutionary *Juche*, and it uses this as the organizing and disciplining principle of the entire society.

In the crisis of the 1990s, the only unit that still managed to maintain its organizational, disciplinary and self-sacrificial capabilities was the military. Also, the military was perceived to be a unit that could absolutely obey the orders of the supreme commander and exhibited the ideal examples demanded by the monolithic system of *Suryong*. At a time when the party organizations were debilitating and had a difficult time managing the crises in the 1990s, the military was the sole unit capable of socially reconstructing the collectivity and organizational capacity called for by the monolithic system of *Suryong*. North Korea strengthened its monolithic system while it was going through crises in the 1990s. The North Korean system resembles the "war economy" of the Soviet Union during the Russian civil war. The war economy only lasted for three short years, but the DPRK's war economy has been ongoing for several decades. As a consequence, the DPRK's institutionalization of the monolithic system of *Suryong* hardens over time.

The institutional system of North Korea deserves some credit since the DPRK, while awkwardly, has been able to weather hardships and challenges until now, but the question is whether the institutional system of North Korea is fitting for the new environment that it will face after normalization of its relationship with the United States and the rest of the world becomes a reality. The answer to that question is obviously negative. The DPRK has begun to experiment with new institutions. The 7/1 Measures have introduced pragmatic policies such as the separation of powers, deregulation, material incentives, and other concepts as means for promoting economic growth. The most dramatic change has been the introduction of the market and the increased usage of commodities-currency exchange. As people from the Old Institutional School would point out, setting up a new institution will take a long time because changing people's habits, customs, and culture, hardened in the old institution, is difficult and time consuming. In this perspective, the DPRK regime should be a leading force in transition to a market-oriented economy and must continue its experiment with setting up new institutions because a market-oriented economy is neither created naturally nor instantly by a big bang.

Bibliography

Akyuz, Yalmaz, "Reform and Crisis in the Transition Economics," UNCTA, *Privatization in the Transition Process: Recent Experiences in Eastern Europe* (New York: United Nations, 1994).

Arrow, Kenneth J. "The Place of Institutions in the Economy: A Theoretical Perspective," in Hayami, Yujiro, *The Institutional Foundations of East Asian Economic Development* (Proceedings of the IEA Conference held in Tokyo, Japan 1998).

Aslund, Anders, Peter Boone, and Simon Johnson, "How to Stabilize: Lessons from Post-Communist Countries." Brookings Paper on Economic Activity, 1996.

Bottomore, Tom, ed., *A Dictionary of Marxian Thought* (Oxford: Blackwell, 2001).

Brun, Ellen and Jacques Hersh, *Socialist Korea* (New York and London: Monthly Review Press, 1976).

Campbell, Robert Wellington, *The Failure of Soviet Economic Planning: System, Performance, Reform* (Bloomington: Indiana University Press, 1992).

Chung, Young Chul, *Bukhanui KahyuckKabang: yeechungchunryukkwa Silisahoechooui* (Economic Reform in North Korea: Dual Strategies and Pragmatism), (Seoul: Sunin, 2004).

Clark, S., *New Forms of Employment and Household Survival Strategies in Russia*, Coventry, ISITO, 1999.

Ellman, Michael, "Transition Economies," in Ha-Joon Chang, *Rethinking Development Economics* (London: Anthem Press, 2003).

Griffin, Keith, "Economic Policy during the Transition to a Market Oriented Economy," Working Paper, Department of Economics, University of California, Riverside, 1998.

_____, "Relative Price and Investment: An Essay on Resource Allocation," Working Paper, Department of Economics, University of California, Riverside, October 2004.

_____, *Studies in Globalization and Economic Transitions* (New York: St. Martin's Press, 1996).

Hwang, Hui-gak, "Bukhanui Kyungjaechimche" (North Korea's Economic Stagnation), *Bukhansahoejui Kyungjaeui Chimchewa Daeeung* (North Korean Socialist Economy's Stagnation and Response) (Seoul: Kyungnam University Press, 1995).

Kim, Dong Nam, *'Widaehan ryongdoja Kim Jong Il tongji ui sonkun chongchi nun sahoejuui kyongje kangkuk kunsol ui kyolchong jok dambo* (The Army Centered Politics of the Supreme Leader Kim Jong Il is the Decisive Collateral in the Construction of Socialist Economic Power Nation).' Kyongje yongu, vol. 2 (2002).

Kim, Yeon Chul and Soon Sung Park, eds., *Bukhan Kyungjae Yeonkoo* (Study of North Korean Economic Reform) (Seoul: Humanitas, 2002).

Klein, Naomi, *The Shock Doctrine: The Rise of Disaster Capitalism* (New York: Picador, 2008).

Kornai, Janos, *Economics of Shortage Volume A* (Amsterdam: North Holland

Press, 1980).

_____, *The Socialist System: The Political Economy of Communism* (Princeton: Princeton University Press, 1992).

Kuijs, Louis, "Investment and Saving in China," World Bank Policy Research Working Paper 3633, June 2005. Accessed at http://www-wds.worldbank.org/servlet/WDSContentServer/WDSP/IB/2005/06/14/000016406_20050614112417/Rendered/PDF/wps3633.pdf.

Naughton, B., "Chinese Institutional Innovation and Privatization from Below," *American Economic Review*, vol. 84, No. 2, 1994.

Nolan, Peter, "China's Rise, Russia's Fall," *Journal of Peasant Studies* 24(1-2), 1997.

Park, Phillip, "The Future of the D.P.R.K." *Journal of Contemporary Asia,* vol. 31, No. 1 (2001).

_____, *Self-Reliance or Self-Destruction?* (New York: Routledge, 2002).

Riskin, Carl, Renwei Zhao, and Shi Li, *China's Retreat from Equality: Income Distribution and Economic Transition* (New York: M.E. Sharpe, 2001).

Stiglitz, Joseph, "Whither Reform? Ten Years of the Transition." Keynote Address at the World Bank Annual Conference on Development Economics, Washington, D.C., April 28-30, 1999.

Williamson, John, "What Washington Means by Policy Reform" Chapter 2 from *Latin American Adjustment: How Much Has Happened?* Edited by John Williamson, Published April 1990 and November 2002. Accessed at http://www.iie.com/publications/papers/paper.cfm?researchid=486.

Woo, Wing Thye, Stephen Parker, and Jeffrey Sachs, eds., *Economies in Transition: Comparing Asia and Europe* (Cambridge, MA: MIT Press, 1997).

Chapter 7

Human Resource Development and International Cooperation

⌐ Jong Dae SHIN and Dean J. OUELLETTE* ⌐

I. Introduction

Undoubtedly, there has been heated scholarly and policy-oriented discussion on development assistance—that is, beyond humanitarian assistance—to North Korea in relation to economic development or economic modernization of the country. Such discussion begs two critical questions: First, to what extent does Pyongyang possess internal capacity-building to lead the development assistance provided by the international community for economic development? Second, what effort is North Korea making to improve its capacity-building?[1]

---

* The authors would like to acknowledge the assistance of Michael Spavor in researching this study.

[1] For more detailed discussion on development cooperation, see Sherman Robinson, "Foreign Aid and Development: Summary and Synthesis," in Finn Trap, ed., *Foreign Aid and Development* (London: Routledge, 2000); World Bank, *Assessing Aid: What Works, What Doesn't, and Why* (New York: Oxford University Press, 1998). In addition, for a discussion on problems relevant to North Korean development cooperation, see Dae-Kyu Yoon and Eul Chul Lim, eds. *The New Paradigm for Economic Reform: Theory and Practice of Development Cooperation for North Korea* (in Korean) (Paju: Hanul, 2006);

Development cooperation is most successful when a recipient country actively requests development cooperation to supplement its lacking internal capacity while simultaneously operating its own meaningful economic reform programs. International transfer of technology and knowledge effectively leads to tangible outcomes when the technology and know-how can be applied and widely used in a recipient country. A recipient country's active engagement in adapting technical assistance from the outside world and persistent desire for domestic reform or transformation are yardsticks for measuring the level of success of the development cooperation. Stated more succinctly, a recipient country's capacity-building (and its effort to increase the internal capacity) is a prerequisite for making development cooperation most fruitful. In this vein, we may posit that the expected outcomes of the international community's development assistance to North Korea will largely vary depending upon the country's internal capacity-building.

As understood, capacity-building encompasses governance (system), market openness, and investment/spending in education, all of which are—or should be—considered as crucial factors affecting outcomes of the development cooperation. In particular, governance (a government's capability to accommodate and utilize the development assistance provided by the international community in a realm of the development cooperation) can be

Bradley O. Babson, "The International Financial Institutions and the DPRK: Prospects and Constraints," *North Pacific Policy Papers*, No. 9, Institute of Asian Research, University of British Columbia, 2002, 10-11; and Bradley O. Babson, "Designing Public Capital Mobilization Strategies for DPRK," a paper presented at the conference "Peaceful Resolution with North Korea: Towards a New International Engagement Framework," Washington, D.C., February 12-13, 2004.

generally judged by looking at the capability of policy implementation, the levels of rule of law and corruption, and the sensitivity of public opinion.

In general, North Korea has a low savings rate, high dependence on commodities for export revenue, a small domestic market, underdeveloped economic institutions, low technology and skill, and a lack of private/independent entrepreneurs—all archetypal features of an underdeveloped country. Given these conditions, it is no surprise that socialist North Korea relies on a state-initiated and government-centered development strategy for economic development and modernization. The effect of such a development strategy is swayed by the capability of the state and expansion of human resources. As a number of former communist nations' transformation of political and economic systems have shown, in order to make the transition from a planned to a market-oriented economy, and in turn, have the process lead to economic development, human resources that play a crucial role in the transformation process are critical. In other words, the development of human resources, which allows for the enhancement of the performance of governmental institutions, is the foremost task for underdeveloped countries like North Korea to effectively accommodate development assistance, and thereby develop its economy.[2]

---

[2] As former World Bank staff member notes, "The potential utility of a [DPRK] relationship with the [World] Bank should not be measured primarily by its direct financial contribution. Indeed, the primary value of engagement with the World Bank from North Korea's perspective would likely derive from two other sources: the policy advice and technical assistance that the Bank could provide; and the Bank's capacity to coordinate and potentially catalyze other sources of official aid. ... A key question is to what extent the DPRK government will mobilize its capacities in order to articulate a strategy for economic development and international assistance." Daniel Morrow, "Possible World Bank Assistance to North Korea:

Indeed, North Korea has made calls for development assistance,[3] and continues to participate in a modest level of such cooperative programs. What, then, is the status or the level of human resources of North Korea? We may answer this question by exploring the data of international humanitarian organizations and nongovernmental organizations (NGOs) involved in humanitarian assistance to North Korea or their elementary development cooperation with North Korea.[4] In addition, we could infer the level of

---

Issues and Challenges," *Asian Perspective*, vol. 30, No. 3 (2006), 37-67. Likewise, another specialist notes the following: "The already delayed work on professional training and institutional development issues needs to begin now. With the absence of quick and high quality international support from the IFIs [international financial institutions], the UNDP, and other groups, the DPRK may be unable to sustain the sorts of policy initiatives needed to get growth underway, irrespective of whether its policies focus on economic integration with the ROK or on a wider array of strategic economic partnerships." Thomas F. McCarthy, "The Management of Economic Development Assistance in the Democratic People's Republic of Korea," *Asian Perspective*, vol. 26, No. 1 (2002), 143-144; see also Babson, "The International Financial Institutions and the DPRK"; and Babson, "Designing Public Capital Mobilization Strategies."

[3] In particular—and most radically—requesting resident humanitarian NGOs to shift their programming to development assistance or leave. "The DPRK Government requested its donors to end humanitarian aid for the first time in 2004 and finally enforced it by instruction in August 2005. This move was strongly questioned by the donor community not because of the demand to move on from humanitarian aid to development aid, but as the argument was clearly mixed with considerations related to internal security and the desire to reduce scrutiny by international aid agencies in general and the presence of expatriate aid workers in DPRK in particular." European Commission, Directorate-General for Humanitarian Aid (ECHO), "Humanitarian Aid in Favour of Vulnerable Groups in DPRK," November 30, 2006. "UNICEF Stays on in DPRK," *Korea Herald*, November 16, 2005.

[4] At this stage, it is not reasonable to say that North Korean development cooperation reaches to a substantial level; yet it is also true that assistance

human resources through investigating some of the experiences of advanced countries that have cooperated in capacity-building and knowledge-sharing projects with North Korea. This chapter directs higher attention to Swiss and Canadian development assistance toward North Korea, focusing particularly on human resource development. In doing so, the authors attempt to estimate the current status of human resources of North Korea; determine specific areas in which the DPRK and other nations have cooperated; gauge Pyongyang's attitude toward the development of human resources and the obstacles North Korea faces and/or places when it comes to such development cooperation; and make practical suggestions for the improvement of North Korea's human resources.

II. Current Status of Human Resource Development of North Korea and International Cooperation

As economic systemic transformations of some former communist countries showed, human resources established in an early stage of the transformation substantially contributed to the speed of the transformation and to its success. During the Cold War, the personnel involved in the Soviet culture, intelligence, and science exchange programs had supported the Soviet's transformation and have played a central role in transforming the USSR after the end of the Cold War. Much the same can be said about China and Vietnam.[5] Enormous efforts—sponsored by the international com-

---

activities including training aimed at a recipient country's internal capacity can be surely labeled as development cooperation.

[5] Yoon and Lim, eds., *The New Paradigm for Economic Reform*; Eulchul Lim and Changyong Choi, "Prospects and Strategies for Development Assistance for North Korea" (in Korean), *Unification Policy Studies*, vol. 14, No. 2 (2005), 70-

munity—were made to improve education in market economics in order to nurture a high-class workforce in the early stages (and beyond) of reform and openness. In the case of China, for instance, numerous people were sent annually to the West for training in market economics. These people have correspondingly taken a leading role in economic reform and the drafting of essential policies in China.[6]

Although North Korea has been dispatching trainees (estimated at over 100) to the West annually since 1998 with the aims of learning and reviewing the market economy, systems, and industry, the number is too small to expect that these trainees could realistically lead the country's reform and opening. To make substantial progress, significantly higher numbers of people need to partake in such training. This, of course, will require the support of the international community.

Under North Korea's Kim Jong Il regime, one notable change in relation to North Korea's attitude on the development of human resources has taken place. Since 2002, some North Korean bureaucrats have been allowed to take part in overseas training programs

---

71; David Zweig and Stanley Rosen, "How China Trained a New Generation Abroad," *Science and Development Network*, May 22, 2003, online at www.scidev.net.

[6] "Since the 1980s, the government has introduced sweeping economic reforms, and the IMF has played a substantial role in helping China design and implement them. The reform program has entailed far-reaching legal and other changes that have created a need for officials to be trained in a variety of fields. The major government agencies—the People's Bank of China, the State Administration of Taxation, the Ministry of Finance, and the National Statistical Bureau—have all been recipients of IMF technical assistance." See "IMF Technical Assistance: Transferring Knowledge and Best Practice," May 2003, online at http://www.imf.org/External/pubs/ft/exrp/techass/techass.htm (accessed March 31, 2009).

for economic research purposes. Indeed, Pyongyang had only been engaged with the states that it considered as useful to strengthen its administration and leadership system. Training and education in finance and management also has been limited to such countries that are considered "politically friendly."[7]

However, Kim later emphasized the gravity of investigating the condition of the world economy and capitalistic market, and utilizing it in a way to profit North Korea. Investigation in the world economy and capitalistic market were then pursued as a means to maintain current structures and policies and utilized in a "pragmatic" manner. As a part of these efforts, three institutions— the North Korean University of International Relations, University of People's Economy, and Kim Il Sung University—have operated a special education program on capitalism, international trade, and market economy, with a very limited number of personnel participating. However, being of such a small scale, not many bureaucrats of the party or government have benefited from these education programs. Also, the contents of this special education consist of programs that seek growth with a pragmatic purpose while preserving the current structure of North Korea. Outcomes of such special education did not directly lead to North Korea's policy, and thereby transform Pyongyang. Instead, such educa- tion has proceeded mainly in an effort to deal with international exchange. As a result, various publications related to capitalism were underutilized. Unsurprisingly, such a passive approach did not contribute to inducing students and participants involved to engage in in-depth study on capitalism.[8]

---

[7] Kyung-Ae Park, "North Korea's Non-Governmental Foreign Contacts," *The Korean Journal of Defense Analysis*, vol. 12, No. 2 (Winter 2000).

[8] Based on author's interview with a North Korean refugee (who will remain

As a means of complementing these limits, Pyongyang has encouraged bureaucrats as well as scientists and technicians to participate actively in human resource development programs organized by Western countries and international organizations in the hope of understanding Western capitalism and taking an active part in the international society. Specifically, North Korea has participated in various domestic and external human resource development programs;[9] yet it also has been reluctant to participate in such programs that explicitly call for reform and opening of North Korea, since leaders in Pyongyang consider both reform and opening as political threats to the regime. At the same time, Pyongyang has sent people to participate in various educational and training programs related to market economics and the development of human resources. In particular, it has been known that training programs on capitalism, initially aimed at officials of the Ministry of Foreign Affairs and Ministry of Trade, have developed into a program in which officials of the Economy Inspection Division of the Labor Party, National Planning Committee, Department of National Security Defense, as well as key personnel, professors, and doctors of the University of People's Economy and Kim Il Sung University have participated.[10] With the financial support of advanced countries and international organizations, North Korea is currently and actively participating in courses, lectures, seminars, and training related to capitalism, market economics,

---

anonymous), Seoul, April 15, 2008.

[9] Park, "North Korea's Non-Governmental Foreign Contacts"; Jin Park and Seung-Ho Jung, "Ten Years of Economic Knowledge Cooperation with North Korea," *Asian Perspective*, vol. 31, No. 2 (2007), 75-93.

[10] Based on interview with a North Korean refugee (anonymous) who participated in a human resources development program; interview by author, Seoul, June 27, 2008.

human rights, disarmament, environment, diplomacy, and advanced scientific technology—all of which are basic concepts, provisions, and regulations of international relations.

Nevertheless, one can hardly accept that the main purpose of such training programs and associated activities of North Korea lives up to the expectations of the international society, which anticipates Pyongyang's progress toward reform and opening. North Korea has promoted certain economic reformative measures such as market openness—though to a restricted degree—and financial management improvement in an attempt to escape from the country's financial difficulties. All the same, the regime still focuses on reinforcing political education in order to maintain its control over the people. Given this, it is not surprising to see North Korea's passive (to some extent, negative) attitude on participation in human resource development programs offered by the international community. For example, it is not uncommon that North Korea inspects all data in the name of national security, and that officials are reluctant to present basic financial and social statistics about the country. Also, trainees often lack sufficient willingness and clarity such that they are rarely able to maximize the training and learning opportunities given to them. Furthermore, there are external stumbling blocks to education derived from cultural differences, excessive wariness, and the accompaniment of surveillants at training sessions.

Yet, in the long term, it is obvious that these human resource development programs will play a crucial role in inducing, expediting, and preparing for reform and opening of the country. If the human resource development programs are to be medium and long term, they will ultimately assist North Korea in overcoming its financial difficulties and contribute to laying a foundation for economic development. Canada, France, Germany, Italy, Sweden,

Switzerland, the United Kingdom, and the United States, as well as international organizations including UNDP and UNIDO have organized or financially sponsored projects to assist in the development of North Korea's human resources.[11] Especially, due to the expansion of humanitarian aid to North Korea from European countries and frequent exchanges of economic missions since 2000, cooperation between North Korea and Europe has increased, with Pyongyang focusing on "economic diplomacy" with the aim of maintaining relations with European countries in order to avoid being isolated from the international community.

Beyond the direct food aid that European countries previously provided to North Korea as emergency relief when it suffered a severe famine in the late 1990s, European countries have recently focused on supporting agricultural resource development and technical support for reconstructing the North's agricultural basis and facilities, which leads to improving North Korea's food production capabilities. In addition, in-field commission education in Europe and on-site inspection activities on advanced technology aimed at government officials of major ministries and experts of scientific technology and economics in order to improve management capabilities of North Korea in areas such as trade, finance, science, and technology have been activated.

---

[11] L. Gordon Flake and Scott Snyder, *Paved with Good Intentions: The NGO Experience in North Korea* (Westport, Conn.: Praeger, 2003); Erich Weingartner, "NGO Contributions to DPRK Development: Issues for Canada and the International Community," *North Pacific Policy Papers 7*, Institute of Asian Research, University of British Columbia, 2001; Hazel Smith, "Overcoming Humanitarian Dilemmas in the DPRK (North Korea)," United States Institute of Peace, Special Report No. 90, (July 2002); Park and Jung, "Ten Years of Economic Knowledge Cooperation"; and Park, "North Korea's Non-governmental Foreign Contacts."

The main subjects of the European Commission's technological support toward North Korea had been cultivating capabilities of North Korean governmental organizations capable of leading efficient economic development; sustainable development and management of natural resources including energy; and improving efficiency and modernization of transportation systems and progressing management capabilities in regional development.[12] Currently, European countries are supporting in-field commission education (market economy study, language training, etc.) and on-site inspection activities for government officials and financial experts. The projects of a handful of Canadian nongovernmental organizations, and the human resource development cooperation project held between Syracuse University (USA) and Kim Chaek University of Technology (DPRK), also provide relevant examples.

III. Development of North Korea's Human Resources: Contributions of Switzerland and Canada

1. Switzerland

1) Background

Compared to most Western nations, Switzerland has had a rel-

---

[12] European Commission, "The EU-Democratic People's Republic of Korea (DPRK): Country Strategy Paper 2001-2004," online at http://ec.europa.eu/external_relations/korea_north/docs/01_04_en.pdf. However, the European Commission's implementation of its strategy paper expired in 2004, with the EU having no plans to draft a new one or engage in cooperation assistance—although it claims to remain open to such prospects in the future. See EC Web site at http://ec.europa.eu/external_relations/korea_north/index_en.htm.

atively unique relationship with the DPRK, as they have shared diplomatic relations since 1974, and have been conducting a political dialogue since 2003.[13] Shortly after drought and famine struck North Korea in the mid-1990s, and the DPRK put out an SOS for international assistance, the Swiss began providing humanitarian aid to the country. In 1997, the Swiss Humanitarian Aid Unit—a branch of the Swiss Agency for Development and Cooperation (SDC),[14] which sits under the direction of the Swiss Ministry of Foreign Affairs—responded by becoming active in the country, setting up the first liaison coordination office in the DPRK capital of Pyongyang to organize the humanitarian and development aid efforts. It was formally expanded in 2001 and renamed the Swiss Cooperation Office (SCO), steering and developing projects

---

[13] Swiss Agency for Development and Cooperation, "Le dialogue est plus fort que l'isolement," December 1, 2003. It is important to note that the Swiss have not ignored North Korea's provocative behavior, either. In 2003, North Korea withdrew from the Nuclear Nonproliferation Treaty (NPT), and Switzerland appealed to the DPRK to rejoin the treaty. Following the North Korean nuclear test of October 2006, the Swiss government condemned the test, saying that it "represented a threat to regional security," that it could launch an arms race in the region, and that such a test was essentially counter to international efforts to prevent the proliferation of nuclear weapons in the world. Switzerland later supported the United Nations Security Council (UNSC) response, that is, UNSC Resolution 1718. In general, the Swiss government holds the position that the North Korea nuclear issue should be resolved by peaceful means within the framework of the Six Party Talks. See Federal Authorities of the Swiss Federation, "La Suisse condamne l'essai nucleaire effectue par la Republique populaire démocratique de Coree (Corée du Nord)," October 10, 2006.

[14] At the bilateral level, SDC's development cooperation focuses on seventeen priority countries and seven special programs in Africa, Asia, and Latin America, with approximately 750 projects in operation at the present time. At the multilateral level, the agency collaborates with UN organizations, the World Bank, and regional development banks.

in collaboration with partners; developing new project ideas with local partners[15]; monitoring Swiss-financed projects; executing management and follow-up reports on a regular basis; staying involved in domestically ongoing discussions regarding development cooperation—as the SDC is the sole bilateral donor working toward such in the DPRK; maintaining exchange of information with Swiss and other international donors; and working closely with donors, especially on agricultural-related projects.[16] The office also maintains close contact with the UNDP and World Food Program.[17]

The Swiss commitment to providing aid and pursuing engagement despite the challenges and limitations placed on donors (and despite the concerns over North Korea's nuclear programs and human rights practices) has in one sense allowed them to transform their humanitarian aid efforts in North Korea into sustainable development assistance projects. Over the last seven years, the Swiss contribution has involved government and NGOs in various activities, in particular training and knowledge-sharing projects both in the DPRK and in Europe. In terms of Swiss humanitarian

---

[15] The North Korean partners are from the public sector, mainly the Ministry of Foreign Affairs (MFA), the Flood Damage Rehabilitation Committee (FDRC), the Ministry of Agriculture, and the Academy of Agricultural Sciences. Other partners are the Ministry of Light Industry, the Ministry of Land and Environment Protection, and other bodies such as universities and friendship associations.

[16] See "Who is Who in SDC Pyongyang?" at http://www.sdc-dprk.ch/en/Home/SDC_s_Staff_in_DPR_of_Korea.

[17] With the issues of food availability and food utilization and access to food main concerns, in 2007 alone, the Swiss government provided 400 tons of milk powder, valued at CHF 2.13 million, through the UN World Food Program (WFP). This was said to be highly appreciated by the North Korean recipients.

assistance to and development cooperation involving the DPRK, the Swiss liaison office in Pyongyang has been most important.[18]

The SDC assistance to the DPRK falls in line with Swiss government policy, which is to contribute to overcome important development constraints; to support internal reform; and to alleviate access to international organizations. The SDC works to realize these aims in the DPRK by actively supporting efforts to improve food security in the country, promoting economic units to raise both efficiency and autonomy, and supporting capacity-building in aid coordination. This also includes the understanding that humanitarian aid is not just the provision of food, but the ability to address basic needs in sectors such as clean water, health care, education, and energy, among others. Of itself, through Swiss NGOs and through UN agencies, the government has provided humanitarian assistance (supply of food, winter clothing, and meat from Switzerland) to the people of North Korea over a period of several years. Presently, the main focus is now on development cooperation in agriculture, with the aim of improving food production in a sustainable way, transfer know-how, support the indigenous reform process, and assist the country in opening up to and integrating into the global community.

According to the Swiss government, the collaboration between Switzerland and the DPRK is appreciated at all levels. "North Korea is not an easy partner," yet the Swiss are making a contribution, "one that is greatly appreciated on the spot and is recognized

---

18 Including in 2004, following the explosion at the Ryongchon railway station in Ryongchon, North Korea. The Swiss government responded by allocating CHF 100,000 in aid for the victims of the disaster, mainly to support reconstruction efforts in Ryongchon. SDC, "Explosion in North Korea: CHF 100,000 for Victims," April 29, 2004, at www.sdc.admin.ch/en/Home/News/Close_up?itemID=20583.

by the international community."[19] The government believes that its role (i.e., of the SDC) is of a pioneering nature due to the fact that concepts of development cooperation are new for the North Koreans, and thus the Swiss are committed to continue the mutual learning process. This is important, as fewer actors have been around in the development assistance area since the end of 2005.[20]

2) Projects

More specifically, SDC funds a capacity-development program (CDP) designed to ensure training, knowledge sharing, and field experience for participants. The program focuses on international cooperation and institution building, economics and global trade, vocational training, and agricultural methods and techniques. According to SDC, over the years, nearly 200 of North Korea's officials (including women) from various ministries, institutions, counties, and farm cooperatives have benefited from the program's

---

[19] Adrian Schlapfer, "North Korea: SDC Programme on Track," April 27, 2007, online at www.sdc.admin.ch/en/Home/News/Close_up?itemID=154944.

[20] In fall 2005, the North Korean authorities determined that international humanitarian aid was not offering long-term solutions to their problems, thus requested that all international donors change to development assistance. While other international donors were not prepared to make such a shift, Switzerland had already begun back in 2001 to shift their programs in that direction. In May 2008, the European Community Humanitarian Office (ECHO) closed its programs in North Korea, primarily because Pyongyang requested its donors to end humanitarian aid and enforced its demand in 2005. The European Aid Cooperation Office (AidCo) is to assume the lead on the EU assistance program, with a plan to allocate a total of €35 million between 2007 and 2010, largely concentrating on food security. See "ECHO: Operational Strategy 2008," at http://europa.eu/scadplus/leg/en/lvb/r13020.htm; See also http://www.parliament.the-stationery-office.com/pa/cm200607/cmhansrd/cm071008/text/71008w0002.htm.

short- and long-term training—with long-term training being a new option since 2007. Its formal partners are the Ministry of Foreign Affairs (MFA) and its Korean-European Coordination and Cooperation Agency (KECCA), with the SDC team being its natural partner and ancillary component-specific partners on board as well.

All partners are actively engaged in exchanges regarding policy and strategies to ensure that training is appropriate and contributes to modernization of the DPRK. Explicitly, the program's goals are to build the skills and knowledge of DPRK company managers so that their companies can compete internationally; to increase the skills and knowledge of officials that deal with the international community so as to foster better understanding and promote access to international networks; to ensure that DPRK counterparts understand international organizations and development cooperation so that they may better work with the SDC; and to provide young and mid-career Koreans with comprehensive knowledge and training regarding the program's themes.[21]

Six components make up the CDP: Pyongyang Business School (PBS) (which was launched in 2004, running twelve three-day seminars per year sanctioned by examinations; courses covering a broad range of themes relevant to business management and administration; students composed of senior professionals from DPRK companies, ministries, and institutions; and top managers from leading European corporations and prominent academics from European and Asian universities brought in to lecture, with materials published in English and Korean);[22] international training

---

[21] See Swiss Agency for Development and Cooperation Web site at www.sdc -dprk.ch.

[22] Note that although SDC finances this venture, in the first two years, Felix

for diplomats and other government officials (with more extensive two- to four-month training in areas like international law, diplomacy, crisis management, negotiation skills, finance, and foreign trade); study tours, short-term training, and international conference attendance; long-term training (from six months to one year in areas such as agro-forestry, sloping land management, economics, and business); familiarization with international organization and team building (with training provided locally to Korean partners); and support of UNFPA for 2008 Census of Population.[23] However, despite the benefits of these capacity-building projects, the amount of knowledge transfer to other personnel and sectors in the DRPK are hard to assess.[24]

In the area of agriculture, the SDC operates three projects in the DPRK focused on improving agriculture and food sustainability. The Agricultural Support Program (ASP)—whose DPRK partners are the Ministry of Agriculture, the Academy of Agriculture Science, and the Ministry of Land and Environment Protection—contributes to improvement in agricultural production and intro-

---

Abt, a representative of foreign companies and investors and based in the DPRK, was a cosponsor. The school later took the form of a public private partnership (PPP) between sponsor SDC and Abt. See Web site at www .business-school-pyongyang.org.

[23] See SDC Web site at www.sdc-dprk.ch.

[24] Jurg Krauer, a senior research scientist at Bern University's Centre for Development and Environment, lectured at the Academy of Agricultural Science under the program. Although his specialty is geoprocessing, an "essential aspect was to get the various departments of the academy used to the idea of passing the information among themselves and to help them to network with the international community. 'They have a completely different attitude to disseminating knowledge . ... They need to change their communications culture.'" "North Koreans Seek Inspiration in Switzerland," Swissinfo.ch, March 9, 2009, online at www.swissinfo.ch/ eng/swissinfo.html?siteSect=105&sid=10430335&ty=st.

duces new approaches in sloping land management and mixed farming. The ASP emphasizes food security, encourages increasing the efficiency of institutional units by means of training and enhanced cooperation, and facilitates access to international development institutions and networks. The SDC has worked at eight cooperative farms, two seed farms, and two agricultural research stations in seven counties in the provinces of North Hwanghae, South Hamgyong, and Yanggang, and also in the capital, Pyongyang. According to the SDC, the projects with the highest potential to improve agriculture and livelihoods—integrated pest management for maize and cabbage,[25] integrated crop management, and sloping land management[26]—are to be streamlined, with the aim of replicating these projects in other rural areas.

The second is the Agro-Processing and Marketing Support Program, which contributes to improved food supply and income generation. It supports agro-processing and marketing with financial, managerial, and technical tools. Ten cooperative farms have been supported with primary processing units and four potato starch and noodle factories have so far been established, with conceptual differences and limited access to data and information noted as stumbling blocks in smooth implementation.

The third is the Pilot Agricultural Credit Scheme (a micro-credit project), which supports sub-work teams of nine cooperative farms with small loans (so far over one thousand loans have been provided) of up to approximately US$1,000, mainly for the

---

[25] For specific details of the project on integrated pest management, see SDC, "Cabbage for All in DPR Korea—Partnership Results," *Asia Brief* (October 2007).

[26] For more details, see Green Table, ed. "International Cooperation in the Democratic People's Republic of Korea: Sloping Land Management (SLM)—Proceedings on International Experiences and Opinions," November 2005.

purpose of diversifying agricultural production. This project is a novel one for North Korean farmers, thus it poses some difficulties, and problems need to be worked out. It was said, however, that the learning opportunities provided are positive, not only for farmers but also for staff at the Central Bank and its county branches.[27]

Another major Swiss contributor is the Centre for Applied Studies in International Negotiations (CASIN), which is an independent, nonprofit foundation. CASIN concentrates on a variety of issues that are related to national and international governance and which address problems confronting modern societies and the international system. Governed by a board of trustees and supervised by the Swiss Federal Department of the Interior, the foundation attempts to help crisis-ridden and conflict-prone governments find ways to apply instruments of governance such as negotiation, mediation, and dialogue, and allow them to find mutually acceptable solutions to the complex global problems that they face (in trade, finance, energy, natural resources, population, agriculture, science and technology, and human rights, to name a few).

Although CASIN is an independent foundation that derives its revenues from its activities, it is important to note that SDC is one of CASIN's chief partners, in particular in the provision of scholarships to program participants, including those from the DPRK. In addition, many of CASIN's projects, including those on

---

[27] According to Adrian Schlapfer, SDC's assistant director-general, North Korea is showing "many promising signs of changes," such as the emergence of consumer markets that are now established as part of the country's economic system. Farmland is now providing scope for activities. "The SDC, together with North Korea's Central Bank, is therefore in the process of testing a micro-credit program to encourage farmers to base their investment decisions on economic feasibility considerations—an innovation for North Korea." "N. Korea, Switzerland Try New Bank Program to Help N.K.'s Farmers," *Yonhap News*, April 30, 2007.

multidimensional diplomacy organized for officials of North Korea, are initiated and developed jointly with SDC.

At the request of, and in participation with, governments and international organizations, CASIN organizes "diplomatic professional training programs" (DPTPs) for the DPRK. These programs are custom-made; their contents designed in close cooperation with the interested ministries. They are initiated at the request of governments and international organizations, and these partnerships come under the banner of CASIN's "21st Century Multidimensional Diplomacy: Building Partnerships for Development." In general, the objectives of these programs are to enhance the participants' capacity to execute their country's foreign policy as well as to promote a better understanding of global decision-making processes to foster development amid globalization.

More specifically, these programs seek to accomplish a number of objectives. For instance, they attempt to present the participants with some of the latest trends in international relations and to acquaint participants with the functioning of the international system. They also introduce participants to the making and functioning of commercial diplomacy, and develop participants' negotiation and communication skills and enhance their operational capacities and expertise. Furthermore, they try to provide participants with the necessary knowledge and tools to understand trends and practices relating to the functioning and the management of the international system through multidimensional diplomacy, commercial negotiations, and effective management systems. It is these DPTP programs that diplomats and civil servants from the DPRK have taken part in.

The capacity-building programs for North Korean officials have largely been short term (i.e., six-week programs), with the central objective being to expose participants from the DPRK to the latest trends in international relations, as well as to strengthen their skills in negotiation, communication, leadership, and decision making. The programs have also given participants the opportunity to interact with international civil servants, diplomats, and experts whose work or interests relate to the DPRK. Overall, over the last decade (1997-2007), CASIN has trained over 125 participants from the different ministries and institutions of North Korea.[28]

In October 2007, to celebrate the 10th anniversary of CASIN's projects with the North, a two-day refresher training program for former North Korean participants of CASIN's programs was held

---

[28] An illustration of these programs includes the 7th Annual Professional Training for Officials and Diplomats from the DPRK, where fourteen mid-career and senior diplomats and officials from several government ministries attended a six-week program in 2004 aimed at enhancing the participants understanding of the international economy and the functioning of the global trading system. Key topic areas included modern diplomacy and international relations, international law, the European Union, international relations and the functioning of the United Nations system, market economics, international trade and commercial diplomacy, and economic reform processes. Over the course of the six weeks, participants were also taken on various study tours, which included a three-day visit to Bern, including discussions with Swiss government officials from the Ministry of Foreign Affairs (DFAE), the SDC, and the Secretariat for Economic Affairs (SECO), Federal Department of Economy, and a visit to the Parliament; four half-day visits to the major international organizations based in Geneva; visits to production chains, distribution centers, and successful Swiss small and medium-size enterprises; and a three-day study tour to the European Union. The 2004 program embraced a more economics-oriented agenda, something that was believed to demonstrate the "valuable progress on the ground in terms of acknowledging the value of market economy principles in today's world." See CASIN, Presentation, 7th Annual Professional Training for Officials and Diplomats from the DPRK, September 2004, at www .casin.ch/web/news/cds/presentationc2.pdf; CASIN, "DPRK: Challenging Expectations," Press Release, October 18, 2004.

in the North Korean capital by CASIN, SDC, and authorities of the DPRK. The objective of the October 2007 session was to conclude the cycle of capacity-building programs. At the conclusion of this refresher program, one of CASIN's staff had this to say: "After many years of tensions, there is a new window of opportunity [in North Korea] that should not be underestimated. From CASIN's perspective, we will continue to strengthen our engagement to provide DPRK officials and scholars with exposure and knowledge of the international system and to support SDC's capacity-building activities in the DPRK."[29]

Another Swiss organization that has done significant capacity-building work with the DPRK is the Adventist Development and Relief Agency (ADRA). ADRA is an independent international humanitarian agency operated by the Seventh-day Adventist Church for the specific purpose of providing individual and community development and disaster relief.[30] ADRA has been involved in the DPRK with the particular aim of improving the energy supply for nurseries, kindergartens, orphanages, and hospitals in the North Hwanghae Province, and since 1999 has installed solar mirrors and solar kitchens for these institutions. It also distributes food, clothes, and other non-food items.[31]

ADRA established its resident office in the DPRK in June 1999, following a number of years of food aid support. Through a variety of development projects, ADRA strived to improve the quality of life for the North Korean people, especially children. ADRA was working in five provinces and undertook a diverse range of activi-

---

[29] Oscar Solera, "Capacity Building Seminar in Pyongyang: 10 Years of Training DPRK Officials," *Dimensions* (CASIN Newsletter) (October 2007).

[30] "A Guide to Humanitarian and Development Efforts of InterAction Member Agencies in North Korea," September 2005, at www.interaction.org.

[31] See ADRA Web site at www.adra.org.

ties under their five primary focal points:[32] health care (i.e., the support of hospital rehabilitation and equipment provision),[33] nutrition (i.e., operation of a bakery in Pyongyang),[34] economic development (i.e., operation of a cafe in Pyongyang with a capacity-building component),[35] rural energy (i.e., biogas applications to improve household living conditions and cooperative farm productivity; solar technologies for water heating), and development research. As of this writing, ADRA has no future projects in the works; however, if the conditions were right, they would be willing to reestablish themselves in the DPRK.

Another religious-based organization of relevance is Campus for Christ Switzerland (CfC), an interdenominational Christian non-governmental organization. In 1995, the North Korean government gave permission to CfC to start an agricultural development project as an outlet for humanitarian aid. Thus CfC's largest ministry, Agape International Switzerland, became involved in a variety of agricultural projects in the DPRK including fodder production, goat husbandry and milk processing,[36] and agricultural training of North

---

[32] "A Guide to Humanitarian and Development."

[33] In partnership with the World Health Organization (WHO).

[34] In collaboration with the WFP. The bakery is still in operation without ADRA monitoring.

[35] ADRA initiated a cafe in central Pyongyang to gauge the degree to which the environment is suitable for high-quality service-oriented businesses and any obstacles to profitability and potential investment. ADRA used its experience in the food manufacturing sector to determine the viability of business models for light industry within the existing context. Profits from the cafe and the annexed shop were used to make the industrial bakery financially sustainable, thus providing the basis for further food production. "ADRA Opens Cafe in North Korea," *ADRA News*, August 15, 2005, at www.adra.org/site/News2?page=NewsArticle&id=5789.

[36] Six goat dairies were set up and installed by 2002. Another six were planned in 2006. AGAPE is responsible for the production of the first cheese in

Korean government officials and farmers. Over the past ten years it has set up, monitored, and supported twelve facilities in seven provinces, as well as having been responsible for various agriculture training projects both in the DPRK and Switzerland. According to statements by the DPRK government, CfC was the first resident NGO to do long-term development aid work in North Korea. CfC had a resident staff in Pyongyang until they closed their office in February 2006 due to the request of DPRK authorities for all resident NGOs to complete their projects by the end of December 2005 and leave the country by the end of March 2006.[37]

In terms of knowledge sharing, since 1997 Agape's Swiss project partners have trained ten to fifteen North Korean farmers on a regular basis. The visiting North Koreans live and work for about four months with Swiss mountain farming families and learn and practice Swiss farming techniques and culture. They are also provided an additional intensive two-week training course at one of the agricultural schools in Salez, Switzerland. Agape hopes that the knowledge will be passed on, as the trained local Koreans will in turn, train others. It is estimated that over 25,000 people are directly supported through these partnership projects. The projects

---

North Korea, as well as the training of local staff in yogurt cheese and tofu production. They have also constructed a laboratory for bacteria strain cultivation for yogurt and milk production. In 2002, AGAPE increased goat milk production, installing two new milk processing units on two cooperative farms. At that time, both of the units had a capacity of up to 2000 lt fresh milk per day. In addition, technicians on the two cooperative farms in North Hwanghae and North Pyongan Province received training for several weeks in milk processing. United Nations Office for the Co-ordination of Humanitarian Affairs, DPR Korea: Situation Bulletin, No. 06/02 (June-July, 2002), 6.

[37] Daniel Gerster, *Yeomso News*, Nr. 40, April 2006, www.vuw.ac.nz/~caplabtb/dprk/ReviewKorea05.pdf.

in Sinhung and Unguri have been successful and are now operating on their own, with local staff. In cooperation with SDC, the established knowledge is spread to the locations and farms that are supported by the Swiss government.

In the future, CfC will place its focus on the area of milk production. They plan to provide continuing education for local leaders who have been successful in the production of yogurt and cheese over the past five years, and who are now ready for more advanced training in order to diversify their activities. From 2007-2011, Agape plans to emphasize the existing production and training centers (domestic and overseas), as well as launching new projects such as fruit and berry production, leather production, slaughtering, and butchering processes. They are also looking into alternative energy projects such as biogas, wind, and solar power to support and power the facilities at the sites of their current and future projects.[38]

However, when asked if the NGO had any plans (of returning as a resident NGO) if the situation improves between the DPRK and European nations, and a settlement of the nuclear issue is reached, one source responded, "There is no plan, but certain programs that we had are not reasonable to continue if you don't have cooperation with the Koreans ... We would then first of all, do what was done before, [but] there's no big plan or big change. ... Maybe because we didn't really interrupt the situation with the Korean government, so there is no interruption there, [the projects are] ongoing, but certain things are postponed, they would continue again, if there was the possibility to be at least seasonal or on site."[39]

---

[38] See Agape Web site at www.agape.ch/nordkorea/en/aktuell/newsjuni 2007.htlm#1.

[39] Interview with NGO personnel, Seoul, March 29, 2008.

In general, in terms of humanitarian aid and assistance, the Swiss seem to be targeting some of the major persisting problems hampering international development cooperation, including the issues of insufficient water supplies, climate change, and the destruction of biological diversity. They also expressed a need to improve staff in the area of disaster preparedness.[40] Although this is the general view for Swiss humanitarian aid and assistance worldwide, it goes along with the problems of water contamination, deforestation, and food scarcity that we see in the DPRK, and is in synch with what other NGOs operating in the DPRK have expressed as major concerns and are targeting as problems to address in their future projects in the DPRK.[41]

Others have emphasized the importance of "knowledge sharing" with the DPRK.[42] Looking at what CASIN and PBS have and are doing, and NGOs like ADRA and Agape are planning with their training centers, this type of engagement is likely to continue to be the focus of projects and the target of expansion of engagement with North Korea, considering the current nature of the regime in Pyongyang, and the political impasse at the geopolitical level (i.e., Six-Party Talks). In the words of one Swiss national working with an NGO involved in development cooperation in the

---

40 SDC Director-General Walter Fust commenting at the SDC annual conference held in Zurich: "Humanitarian Aid: 'Yesterday–Today–Tomorrow'"; SDC, "Swiss Humanitarian Aid Ready to Meet Future Challenges," Press Release, March 28, 2008.

41 International Federation of the Red Cross and Red Crescent Societies, "Programme Update 2007: Democratic People's Republic of Korea," Appeal no. MAA54001, Programme Update No. 7 (2008).

42 Stanley Foundation, "Prospects for International Cooperation in Economic Development Knowledge Sharing with the DPRK," Conference Report, March 2008; Bradley O. Babson, "Knowledge Sharing with the DPRK," CanKor Report No. 297 (November 2007).

DPRK, "Right now you can do things, but it ends always at a certain level because the whole structure of course doesn't allow you to go beyond."[43]

2. Canada

1) Background

Although Canada did not share diplomatic relations with North Korea until 2001, Canadian NGOs had been active in the DPRK since the mid-1990s, providing much in the way of humanitarian aid to deal with the severe food crisis in the North during the 1990s. In fact, the Canadian International Development Agency (CIDA)—the funding arm of Canada's Department of Foreign Affairs and International Trade (DFAIT)—began in 1997 a program of humanitarian food aid to the DPRK.[44] There were also a variety of academic contacts and exchanges, which were often initiated by Canadian NGOs and universities.[45]

After constructive progress on a number of fronts, including the vast improvement in inter-Korean relations, Ottawa endorsed more active engagement with Pyongyang beginning in 1998 with the intent of formalizing diplomatic relations with the DPRK. "While not underestimating the difficulties or risks," delegations from Canada reported that "the only sensible strategy for promoting stability on the peninsula, meeting basic human needs, and opening up the future is a judicious balance of deterrence and

---

[43] Interview with Swiss NGO personnel (anonymous), March 29, 2008.

[44] CIDA food aid was primarily channeled through the World Food Program and Canadian NGOs. Hartmuth Kroll, "Canada-DPRK Relations," CAN-CAPS Bulletin, No. 42 (August 2004).

[45] Ibid.; see also Weingartner, "NGO Contributions to DPRK Development," 12-17.

engagement. It is on the engagement side of the equation that Canada has the skill set and opportunity to play an important role."[46] Additional negotiations culminated in the establishment of formal diplomatic relations on February 6, 2001.[47] Ambassadors were accredited on a non-resident basis, with Canada's Ambassador to China presenting his credentials in Pyongyang, and North Korea's Permanent Representative to the UN presenting his credentials in Ottawa. After this, Canada followed a moderate path in expanding contacts with the DPRK.[48]

However, bilateral relations were strained following North Korea's alleged admission to U.S. envoys in October 2002 that the DPRK possessed a uranium-enrichment program. Canada's opening to the DPRK was based on the understanding that the North was in compliance, and would continue to comply, with its obligations and undertakings in the IAEA and under the NPT, and that the DPRK would observe the norms of international behavior, in particular in regard to its nuclear obligations. Canada's foreign minister soon after announced a "no business as usual" policy in Canada's relations with the DPRK. This stance remains in place.[49]

---

[46] See statement by Lois Wilson, Senate of Canada, "Canadian Parliamentary Delegation Reports on DPRK Visit," CanKor, October 11, 2000.

[47] Canadian foreign minister John Manley announced that "The establishment of diplomatic relations will create formal channels through which Canada and the DPRK can further enhance communications and cooperation, and develop a deeper understanding of each other. At this juncture, Canada believes that closer relations with Pyongyang are the best way to contribute to security, non-proliferation and address the humanitarian challenges in the region." See CanKor Newsletter, No. 169, January 9, 2004.

[48] Kroll, "Canada-DPRK Relations."

[49] Bilateral relations between the two counties took another hit in July 2006 when North Korea test-fired several ballistic missiles—which Canada condemned—and then took a substantial turn for the worst when the North conducted a nuclear test in October 2006. Canadian Prime Minister Stephen

Canada's view has been that long-term engagement offers the best prospect for integrating the DPRK into the community of nations. The government of Canada has often said that once the DPRK takes steps to meet its denuclearization commitments, Canada will review the scope and scale of its engagement with the DPRK.[50] A revitalization of exchanges at higher levels is con-

---

Harper condemned the nuclear test carried out by North Korea in early October 2006, saying that "This irresponsible and dangerous act seriously undermines both regional peace and stability, and global efforts to halt the spread of nuclear weapons." See "Canada Condemns North Korean Nuclear Test," Press Release, Office of the Prime Minister of Canada, October 9, 2006. Then Foreign Minister Peter MacKay later announced Canada's strong support of United Nations Security Council resolution 1718 in response to the North's test: "Canada is pleased that the UN Security Council has responded to the provocative action of the nuclear test by North Korea on October 9 and approved Resolution 1718, which we strongly support." See "Statement by Minister MacKay on U.N. Resolution on North Korea," Press Release, Department of Foreign Affairs, October 14, 2006. Though Canada is not at the table in the six-party negotiations and does not have a leading role in the issue, it does consult with the six parties to the talks regularly, and actively supports efforts to find a peaceful, multilateral solution to the nuclear crisis. Furthermore, Canada has repeatedly urged Pyongyang to continue with the six-party process, and has—through its ambassadors—called on the DPRK to resume membership in the IAEA and the NPT, and to respect the international norms of behavior in nuclear matters. Interview with Canadian embassy staff in Seoul, January 2008.

50 Canadian Foreign Minister Peter MacKay indicated during a tour of Panmunjom in May 2007 that Canada would "re-examine all our future aid in conjunction with the successful completion" of the six-party negotiations to end North Korea's nuclear weapons programs. See "Improvement in Canada-DPRK Relations Possible," CanKor Newsletter, September 4, 2007. A similar statement was repeated after North Korea shut down its 5 MWe reactor at Yongbyon in July 2007 and after North Korea's presentation of its declaration of nuclear programs to China (the head of the Six-Party Talks) in June 2008. "Canada Welcomes Presentation of Nuclear Declaration by North Korea," DFAIT, June 26, 2008, see online at http://w01.international

stantly requested by North Korea, in particular for Canada to establish an embassy in Pyongyang; but due to the nuclear impasse, this
is unlikely to happen anytime soon[51]—although the "not business as usual" position has been adjusted somewhat to allow for
political contacts, and relations are improving given the progress
at the Six Party Talks to resolve the nuclear issue.[52] In addition,
until Pyongyang's intransigence in dealing with international
donor agencies' concerns over issues such as monitoring of food
aid is mitigated, it is safe to assume that the Canadian government
will most likely proceed under an "engagement without illusions"
approach to bring North Korea into the community of nations.[53]

2) Projects

Canada's Department of Foreign Affairs and International
Trade, through the Canadian International Development Agency,[54]

.gc.ca/MinPub/Publication.aspx?isRedirect=True&Language=E&publica
tion_id=386335&docnumber=149. See also Canadian Statement at 51st
General Conference of the International Atomic Energy Agency (IAEA),
and "Bilateral Relations: Canada-Democratic People's Republic of Korea,"
http://geo.international.gc.ca/cip-pic/geo/dprc-bb-en.aspx.

[51] Canada still does not have an embassy in Pyongyang, but covers North
Korea from the Canadian embassy in Seoul. Canada changed its ambassador to the DPRK in the fall of 2007, giving its resident representative in
the ROK dual responsibilities.

[52] Interview with an official from the Embassy of Canada in Seoul, February
2008. With progress at the Six-Party Talks, Canada approved an adjustment in Canadian policy to allow for greater engagement with North
Korea which would permit Canada to promote full denuclearization and
advance long-term goals such as political reform, improved human rights,
and regional security. However, the scope of Canada's engagement remains
contingent on the continuing progress in resolving the North Korea nuclear
issue.

[53] Kroll, "Canada-DPRK Relations," 5.

[54] As Canada's lead agency for development assistance, CIDA programming

funds various development assistance projects around the world. However, as it stands, CIDA sponsors only humanitarian aid to the DPRK,[55] as development assistance funding is tied to the nuclear issue: "In principle, the DPRK, like all countries and territories eligible for Canadian development assistance, could benefit from various programs, should the situation change. However, under the current circumstances, CIDA continues to limit assistance to humanitarian programs only."[56]

CIDA's position, however, has not prevented a handful of Canadian-based NGOs from engaging in capacity-building projects meant to improve the human resources of North Korea. One such organization is the International Institute for Sustainable Development (IISD), an international nonprofit organization that promotes change worldwide toward sustainable development. Based on its understanding of North Korea and the country's years of international isolation and decades of inadequate environmental management practices, and the institute's ability to gain the trust of North Korean officials,[57] in 2004 IISD developed a pro-

---

is concentrated in governance, health, basic education, private sector development, and environmental sustainability. These five priority sectors are directly related to achieving the United Nations' Millennium Development Goals, and are crosscut by the theme of gender equality.

[55] In 2004-2005, Canadian official development assistance to the DPRK totaled $7.33 million in humanitarian assistance through multilateral channels. See CIDA Web site at http://www.acdi-cida.gc.ca.

[56] See CIDA Web site at www.acdi-cida.gc.ca.

[57] "The next morning, [our minder] set up the second meeting with the Ministry of Land and Environment people that I had been requesting for two days. This seemed to confirm my feeling that access came with trust, and that he wasn't going to put his neck out arranging senior meetings unless he felt certain that only good could come from it." Comments by IISD associate Graham Ashford, "DPRK: One Canadian's Observations and Impressions," CanKor Newsletter, No. 189, September 30, 2004.

ject to help the DPRK build government capacity for sustainable development. The project involved strategic planning at the national and sub-national levels; building capacity to monitor and assess environmental pressures, impacts, and responses; improving DPRK ability to analyze policies and emerging issues in the context of sustainable development planning; and strengthening knowledge transfer and environmental cooperation between organizations in China, Canada, and North Korea.[58] IISD staff collaborated with Chinese experts to organize an intensive ten-day workshop in November 2005 in Beijing,[59] which brought five officials from the DPRK Department of Environmental Protection to the city to visit institutions involved in China's sustainable development efforts. The workshop focused on monitoring and reporting on environmental conditions; establishing sustainable development strategies; and strengthening knowledge transfer among the three countries.[60]

Another Canadian nonprofit that has been active in capacity-building is Global Aid Network (GAiN). While providing humanitarian aid to orphanages in the North for some time, GAiN also established training programs in both graphic design and English language education. The latter program, the Canada-Korea Science and Technology English Education Center (CKSTEEC), was set up in the Korea Computer Center (KCC) of Pyongyang in July 2004 with the mission to provide English language training for the

---

[58] See www.iisd.org. Interestingly, this project was not funded by CIDA. Rather, the project received support in the form of a grant from the International Development Research Centre (IDRC), a Canadian Crown corporation created by the Parliament of Canada (1970) and that is guided by a 21-member international Board of Governors, who report to the Canadian Parliament through the Minister of Foreign Affairs.

[59] This workshop was carried out in partnership with the Chinese Society for Environmental Sciences.

[60] Correspondence with IISD associate, December 2007.

country's scientists and technicians. The project ran two classes (Information Technology English Education and Basic Science English Education), which coincided with the graphics design project's schedule.

Students attended classes five days per week over a ten-week semester. A total of forty students went through the English language program. Two English language courses were also offered to Korea Computer Center staff. The other project, the Canada-Korea Computer Graphics Design Institute (CKCGDI), was established in October 2002. Classes for this project were also held in the KCC, with fifteen graphic design students completing their first semester of coursework by December 2002. However, due to the SARS epidemic, the operation of the school was put on hold for a year and a half. The school finally re-opened in July 2004 as two instructors from Canada resumed classes. The students worked toward their one-year diploma in Computer Graphic Design, which was completed in June 2005. Despite the apparent need for the programs, both were shut down abruptly in December 2005 in response to Pyongyang's demand that all resident NGOs leave the country.[61]

A third noteworthy organization is Canadian Foodgrains Bank (CFGB),[62] which was one of the first NGOs to respond to the food crisis in the DPRK in 1996. CFGB is a Christian non-resident NGO which has taken a four-pronged approach to its programming in

---

[61] Despite the closures, GAiN is actively negotiating to restart the English language training program with a different partner, minus the IT (graphic design) component. Authors' discussions with GAiN personnel and a former teacher of one of the programs, January 2008.

[62] Foodgrains Bank serves as a fund-raiser for its member church agencies, collecting grain, cash donations, and other resources from members and donors.

North Korea: food aid, food security, capacity-building, and public engagement. While its core contributions (i.e., donations of food, seeds, fertilizers, and other agricultural inputs) have been in the first dimension,[63] in terms of capacity-building and public engagement, CFGB has hosted North Korean officials and agricultural specialists for study tours in Canada since 1999.[64] Primarily, these have promoted knowledge sharing to support North Korea's agricultural development. Subsequently, these tours have provided CFGB's members and North Koreans the opportunity to increase their mutual understanding.

A final organization worth mentioning is Trinity Western University, a Christian university based in Vancouver that hosted three North Korean officials in the spring of 2007 for six weeks of language training.[65] The university also invited five leaders from the DPRK Ministry of Education to Vancouver to tour universities in the area in order to see if North Korea could send students to them.[66]

Under the current political circumstances, many experts and

---

[63] Since 1996, CFGB has delivered over 100,000 tonnes of food and seed to the DPRK, including 10,000 tonnes worth an approximate 4.5 million in 2005/2006. Canadian Foodgrains Bank, Annual Report 2006. However, according to the CFGB Annual Report 2008, the DPRK was not a recipient of CFGB-member donations in the 2007/2008 period.

[64] These sought to bring specialists selected by the DPRK Ministry of Agriculture to Canada for short-term training to learn about various agricultural production methods, as well as visit farms, university research centers, and breeding programs. As of March 2008, however, no food study tours have been scheduled involving participants from the DPRK. See CFGB Web site at www.foodgrainsbank.ca; Weingartner, "NGO Contributions to DPRK Development," 37.

[65] The project was funded by the Canadian branch of English Language Institute China (ELIC).

[66] Personal interview with project coordinator, January 2008.

Canadian NGO personnel believe educational exchanges and knowledge sharing are relevant and the best way to proceed with engagement: "My preference for Canadian involvement at this stage is in the field of 'knowledge sharing' ... it is precisely the direction that I would take."[67] Other recent studies corroborate this view.[68] Yet despite the goodwill efforts to date, the projects have been quite small-scale, sporadic, and too few to address the immense deficiencies in North Korea's human resource capacity. And even though a few Canadian NGOs are weighing the possibility of new projects, they most likely will have to await decisions by CIDA regarding funding, which will no doubt depend on substantial progress being made by Pyongyang on the nuclear issue. Without substantial funding assistance from Ottawa, Canadian NGOs can do little to help North Korea address its internal needs, or to understand the outside world. The linking of government

---

[67] Correspondence with Erich Weingartner, a Canadian expert who has had longtime and extensive experience in carrying out international humanitarian and other projects in the DPRK, December 14, 2007.

[68] See Bradley O. Babson, "Knowledge Sharing with the DPRK," CanKor Report No. 297, November 2007; Stanley Foundation, "Prospects for International Cooperation in Economic Development Knowledge Sharing with the DPRK," Conference Report, March 2008; Weingartner, "NGO Contributions to DPRK Development," 28-29. That said, if history is any indication of what is possible, then funding for such projects may be limited at this time. Several years ago CIDA contributed funds (approximately CDN$500,000) to the United Nations University for Peace specifically for knowledge sharing with the North, and also researched options to provide English-language training for DPRK students in Canada. In the end, however, the latter failed to materialize, and the former funds were channeled by the university to Sweden for DPRK training programs. Correspondence with CanKor editor Erich Weingartner, December 14, 2007; Erich Weingartner, "Current Status of Canadian Knowledge Sharing with the DPRK," comments from a presentation in Seoul, November 1, 2007.

development assistance funding ties the development community to the ups and downs and peculiarities of the political processes, making it almost impossible to plan activities with certainty and expectations, build and maintain effective communication with the DPRK partners, or even test the willingness of Pyongyang to engage the outside world—for even if the government purse strings do open in the near future, without a genuine commitment from the regime in Pyongyang to dispatch the right people in sufficient numbers, the potential projects will have little immediate effect in developing the human resources that North Korea will require to carry out meaningful reform.

IV. Conclusion

North Korea's involvement in human resources development programs supported by the international community is bounded within its own notion of "independence is the way of prosperity and foreign assistance is opium," which put high importance on establishment of an independent national economy. Thus the involvement and participation of North Korea in economic development programs by the outside world do not indicate a fundamental change in North Korea. Although North Korea emphasizes an independent national economy, it has not refused (and to be sure cannot avoid) international exchange activities. Former DPRK leader Kim Il Sung himself stated that "independent national economy" does not refer to an economy run with only domestically laden materials without any exchange with other counties. In other words, what he meant by independent national economy is a kind of economic development strategy through which an economy can flourish based on domestic resources and technologies, while buttressed by international exchange activities for supplementing domestically lacking goods and techniques.

Yet, as one can readily notice, the international exchange is limited and regarded as a supplementary means in North Korea. Simply put, North Korea's international exchange rests not on a principle of "comparative advantage," but on a notion of "inter-supplementation between existence and nonexistence" (in Korean, *yumoosangtong*). In this vein, it cannot be said that North Korea's cooperation with the international community for the development of human resources has derailed the notion of *yumoosangtong*, which renders the international cooperation inconsistent with global standards. Put another way, North Korea's involvement and participation in economic development programs in conjunction with the international community can be interpreted as a pragmatic effort to enhance the foundation of the independent national economy of North Korea through a better understanding of capitalism, market economics, and advanced science technologies.

Yet it is not difficult to aver that Pyongyang's limited and sporadic human resources development programs do not produce enough human resources. Stated differently, it is necessary for North Korea to nurture experts and bureaucrats who understand these programs so as to fully utilize the received and invested foreign capital into its economic development.

Nonetheless, the current cooperation for development of human resources with the West—though insufficient and with its own limitations—deserves certain attention, since such cooperation has paved a way for North Korea to learn capitalism, market economics, finance, management, and advanced technologies, as well as acknowledge the necessity of their introduction. To prepare for and expedite North Korea's modernization and reform and openness, it is necessary to improve the internal capacity-building of

North Korea, establish institutional infrastructure, and nurture human power, all of which require us to have a long-term perspective. More crucially, leaders of Pyongyang should realize the importance and necessity of the development of capacity-building through the cooperation for human resources development with the international community. Participation in a variety of human resources development education/training programs would help not only to learn capitalist economic policy and governance, but to transform negative and inflexible perceptions held by North Korean officials as well.[69] Education on international law, finance and trade, and foreign investment is absolutely important in a process of opening the domestic market to and participating in the global market. It is, indeed, a good example that government officials and economy experts dispatched to the West in the late 1990s influenced the changes in North Korea's economic policy, resulting in the economic improvement measures of July 2002 (7/1 Measures).[70] This implies that human resources development programs can influence economic policy and management strategy in North Korea.

As discussed in the case study, Switzerland has focused on small-scale development assistance programs through which

---

[69] Such change in North Korean perceptions is not always immediately noticeable, but North Korea has shown glimpses of change and openness over the last fifteen years. As Richard Corsino, former country director of the World Food Program in the DPRK, noted, you can see it when "'There's less reticence to talk. You see it in the sorts of questions you're able to ask and the information you get on hunger and employment.' It's probably that an easing signal has come down from on high ... 'In a country like (North Korea), people don't suddenly wake up one day and decide to be more open'." Mark Magnier, "Aid Workers See More Openness in North Korea," *Korea Herald* (Seoul), November 22, 2003.

[70] Based on author's interview with a North Korean refugee (who will remain anonymous), Seoul, May 28, 2008.

North Korean officials, diplomats, and farmers may learn and share knowledge on relevant areas. Instead of requesting the North make a radical transformation, Swiss human resources development cooperation has proceeded from a long-term perspective based on an incremental process in which Pyongyang itself gradually takes a leading role such that it can handle the divergent situations at hand, and therefore the cooperation has been well received by the North. Similarly, Canadian NGOs took a long-term view initially to support North Korea. In the short-term, the sharing of knowledge can be the most appropriate starting point for stimulating positive interaction between the international community and the DPRK, and this can lead to a brighter future for North Korea's economy, and more importantly, for its people.

Bibliography

Babson, Bradley O. "Designing Public Capital Mobilization Strategies for DPRK." Paper presented at the conference "Peaceful Resolution with North Korea: Towards a New International Engagement Framework," Washington, D.C., February 12-13, 2004.

_____. "The International Financial Institutions and the DPRK: Prospects and Constraints," *North Pacific Policy Papers*, No. 9, Institute of Asian Research, University of British Columbia, 2002.

_____. "Knowledge Sharing with the DPRK," CanKor Report No. 297 (November 2007).

Canada-DPR Korea Association. Newsletter, various issues from 2004-2006.

Canadian Centre for Foreign Policy Development, "Report from the North Korea Roundtable," University of Victoria Conference Centre, January 22, 2001.

CanKor Newsletter, various issues (2001-2007).

CASIN. *Dimensions* (newsletter), (various issues 2003-2007).

_____. "DPRK: Challenging Expectations," Press Release, October 18, 2004.

CFGB Update Newsletter, various issues (2003~2007).

Federal Authorities of the Swiss Federation. "La Suisse condamne l'essai nucléaire effectué par la République populaire démocratique de Corée (Corée du Nord)," October 10, 2006.

Feffer, John. "Time to Lift North Korea's Quarantine," *YaleGlobal*, June 8, 2006, at http://yaleglobal.yale.edu/display.article?id=7535.

Flake, L. Gordon and Scott Snyder. *Paved with Good Intentions: The NGO Experience in North Korea*. Westport, Conn.: Praeger, 2003.

Gerster, Daniel. "Project Korea (DPRK)," *Yeomso News* Nr. 40 (April 2006).

Green Table, ed. "International Cooperation in the Democratic People's Republic of Korea: Sloping Land Management (SLM)—Proceedings on International Experiences and Opinions," November 2005.

International Federation of the Red Cross and Red Crescent Societies. "Programme Update 2007: Democratic People's Republic of Korea," Appeal no. MAA54001, Programme Update No. 7 (2008).

Kroll, Hark. "The Current Status of Canada-DPRK Relations," Foreign Affairs Canada, Ottawa, May 2004.

Kroll, Hartmuth. "Canada-DPRK Relations," CANCAPS Bulletin, No. 42 (August 2004), 3-5.

_____. "Scope and Nature of Economic Change in the DPRK: Motivations and Directions." Paper presented at the 12th Annual CANCAPS Conference, Quebec City, December 3-5, 2004.

Lim Eulchul and Choi Changyong. "Prospects and Strategies for Development Assistance for North Korea" (in Korean), *Unification Policy Studies*, vol. 14, No. 2 (2005), 49-76.

McCarthy, Thomas F. "The Management of Economic Development Assistance in the Democratic People's Republic of Korea," *Asian Perspective*, vol. 26, No. 1 (2002), 141-150.

Morrow, Daniel. "Possible World Bank Assistance to North Korea: Issues and Challenges," *Asian Perspective*, vol. 30, No. 3 (2006), 37-67.

Park, Jin and Seung-Ho Jung. "Ten Years of Economic Knowledge Cooperation with North Korea," *Asian Perspective*, vol. 31, No. 2 (2007), 75-93.

Park, Kyung-Ae. "North Korea's Non-governmental Foreign Contacts," *The Korean Journal of Defense Analysis*, vol. 12, No. 2 (Winter 2000).

Rickerd, Donald. "Experiences in Track Two Diplomacy: Canada and the DPRK." Presentation at the 2004 Roundtable for Knowledge Sharing with the DPRK," Seoul, Korea, February 13-14, 2004.

"Report of Canadian Research Delegation to the DPRK," CanKor Report No. 12 (October 2000).

Robinson, Sherman. "Foreign Aid and Development: Summary and Synthesis," in Finn Trap, ed., *Foreign Aid and Development*. London: Routledge, 2000.

Schlapfer, Adrian. "North Korea: SDC Programme on Track," Swiss Agency for Development and Cooperation, April 27, 2007.

Smith, Hazel. "Overcoming Humanitarian Dilemmas in the DPRK (North Korea)," United States Institute of Peace, Special Report No. 90, (July 2002).

Stanley Foundation. "Prospects for International Cooperation in Economic Development Knowledge Sharing with the DPRK," Conference Report, March 2008.

Swiss Agency for Development and Cooperation. "Cabbage for All in DPR Korea-Partnership Results," *Asia Brief* (October 2007).

_____. "Humanitarian Aid in North Korea," News, February 28, 2003.

_____. "Le dialogue est plus fort que l'isolement," News, December 1, 2003.

_____. "Swiss Humanitarian Aid Ready to Meet Future Challenges," Press Release, March 28, 2008.

"Swiss Folk Handicraft Exhibition in Pyongyang," Korea Is One! (Web site), December 21, 2004, at www.korea-is-one.org/spip.php?article1263.

Weingartner, Erich. "Equipping Potential Reformers: Knowledge Sharing and Capacity-Building as Interim Steps toward DPR Korea Development." Paper presented at the International Symposium on International Cooperation for North Korean Development, Seoul, Korea, July 6, 2006.

_____. "NGO Contributions to DPRK Development: Issues for Canada and the International Community," *North Pacific Policy Papers 7*, Institute of Asian Research, University of British Columbia, 2001.

_____. "Recent Developments in DPRK," Canada-DPR Korea Association, Annual General Meeting 2006.

_____. "Initiating Non-governmental Contacts for Peace in Korea," unpublished manuscript.

Yoon, Dae-Kyu and Eul Chul Lim, eds. *The New Paradigm for Economic Reform: Theory and Practice of Development Cooperation for North Korea* (in Korean). Paju: Hanul, 2006.

Zellweger, Kathi. "The North Korean Crisis: Concern for People in Need," *The Korea Society Quarterly*, vol. 4, No. 1 (2004), 20-22.

Web sites

Adventist Development and Relief Agency (ADRA), www.adra.org.

AGAPE International (Campus fur Christus), Switzerland, www.agape.ch.

Canada DPR Korea Association, www.canada-dprk.org.

Canadian Foodgrains Bank (CFGB), www.foodgrainsbank.ca.

Canadian International Development Agency (CIDA), www.acdi-cida.gc.ca.

CANCAPS (Canadian Consortium for Asia-Pacific Security), www.cancaps.ca.

Centre for Applied Studies in International Negotiations, www.casin.ch.

Department of Foreign Affairs and International Trade (DFAIT), www.international.gc.ca.

European Business Association (EBA), www.eba-pyongyang.org.

Federal Department of Foreign Affairs, Government of Switzerland, www.eda.admin.ch.

GAiN (Global Aid Network), www.globalaid.net.

International Development Research Centre (IDRC), www.idrc.ca.

International Institute for Sustainable Development (IISD), www.iisd.org.

Pyongyang Business School, www.business-school-pyongyang.org

Swiss Agency for Development and Cooperation, www.sdc.admin.ch.

Swiss Cooperation Office in DPR Korea, www.sdc-dprk.ch.

The Contributors

Bong Dae Choi is research professor at the Institute for Far Eastern Studies, Kyungnam University.

Kap Woo Koo is associate professor of North Korea Studies, University of North Korea Studies.

Jung Chul Lee is assistant professor of political science, Soongsil University.

Dean J. Ouellette is research fellow at the Institute for Far Eastern Studies, Kyungnam University.

Phillip H. Park is associate professor of political science and diplomacy, Kyungnam University.

Kevin Shepard is research fellow at the Institute for Far Eastern Studies, Kyungnam University.

Jong Dae Shin is assistant professor of North Korea Studies, University of North Korea Studies.

Moon Soo Yang is associate professor of North Korea Studies, University of North Korea Studies.

Dae Kyu Yoon is professor of law, Kyungnam University

Index

About the Book

North Korean society is undergoing economic and legal transformation. One of the last bastions of socialism in the post-Cold War era, North Korea struggles to cope with a failing economy and a weakening central authority.

This volume examines the origins, impacts, and implications of this transformation. By analyzing the experiences of North Korean defectors, the expansion of markets and transitions in corporate governance are explored, and the North Korean government's role in, and response to, these changes is examined by looking at the transformation of the North's legal code, and the expansion of economic and corporate training, both within the country and abroad. Finally, clues to the implication of these North Korean transitions are sought in the market transformation experiences in other countries.

By understanding the real changes that affect the daily lives of North Koreans and examining the impact these economic shifts have, both on the government's control and their view of authority, this volume sheds new light on the inner workings of North Korean society, and offers insight into how these domestic changes will impact the direction of future North Korean transformation as the government struggles to survive and find its place in the region and in the international community.

Phillip H. Park is an associate professor of Mass Media and Politics and Diplomacy at Kyungnam University, Korea since March 2008, and was an associate professor at the School of International Liberal Studies at Waseda University, Japan. He is the author of, among others, *Self-Reliance or Self-Destruction?: Success and Failure of the Development Strategy of Self-Reliance (Juche) in the Democratic People's Republic of Korea* (2002); *The Neutrality of Korea: A Strategy for Political Stability and Economic Prosperity* (2007, in Korean); *Monolithic Leadership: Leadership Secrets of Jack Welch (GE), Kun Hee Lee (Samsung) and Kim Jong Il (DPRK)* (2008, in Korean)